MW01519159

WILLS LAW AND CONTESTS

WILLS LAW AND CONTESTS

WRITING A VALID WILL, TRUST ADMINISTRATION, AND TRUST FIDUCIARY DUTY

ADEYEMI OSHUNRINADE

authorHOUSE®

AuthorHouse™
1663 Liberty Drive
Bloomington, IN 47403
www.authorhouse.com
Phone: 1-800-839-8640

© 2011 by Adeyemi Oshunrinade. All rights reserved.

No part of this book may be reproduced, stored in a retrieval system, or transmitted by any means without the written permission of the author.

First published by AuthorHouse   05/18/2011

ISBN: 978-1-4634-0327-0 (sc)
ISBN: 978-1-4634-0326-3 (dj)
ISBN: 978-1-4634-0325-6 (ebk)

Library of Congress Control Number: 2011907285

Printed in the United States of America

Any people depicted in stock imagery provided by Thinkstock are models, and such images are being used for illustrative purposes only.

Certain stock imagery © Thinkstock.

This book is printed on acid-free paper.

Because of the dynamic nature of the Internet, any web addresses or links contained in this book may have changed since publication and may no longer be valid. The views expressed in this work are solely those of the author and do not necessarily reflect the views of the publisher, and the publisher hereby disclaims any responsibility for them.

CONTENTS

Chapter 10. Trusts Fiduciary Duty 185

This book is designed to provide accurate information regarding the law of Wills. While this book contains facts of law, it is not an attempt to give legal advice; for all your legal needs, consult a licensed attorney.

All cases are for educational purposes, no copyright is claimed in the text of statutes, regulations, and court opinion quoted within this book. Permission to copy material exceeding fair use, 17 U.S.C. § 107, may be obtained by contacting a copyright clearance center.

DEDICATION

Dedicated to my wife Maria Dolores Fernandez Perez, for her love and support. Words alone cannot express my gratitude. Also to my children: Carmen MaryAnn, Nicolas Luke, and Sofia Brooke.

SPECIAL THANKS

Very special thanks to the following people for their support: Mrs. Agnes Osuntogun; Adi Zekcher (*United Nations*); Olabisi Ogunlayi (*Attorney*); Folu Ogunlayi; Olufemi Oshunrinade (*Attorney*, London and Wales); Dr. Voonchin Phua (PHD); James Osuhon, Dr. Ojo Babatunde (PHD, LLB, *Barrister*—London and Wales) and Dr. Bayo Olowe (DDS) and Nana Yaw Deisakyi.

AUTHOR'S NOTE

Wills and testament, rights of inheritance, and successions are all designs of civil or municipal laws, and accordingly are in all respects regulated by them. Every distinct nation having different requirements, rules, and regulations to make a testament completely valid; during life, a person may use his wealth to influence his acquaintances and family however, to what extent may one use his wealth to influence behavior after he is deceased? In the United States, the law does not grant courts any general authority to question the reasons for the testator's decisions to dispose of his property the way he chooses. The law forbids the courts from questioning the wisdom, fairness, and reasonableness of the testator's decision about how to devise his or her belongings.

The law however, serves its purpose in making a reliable determination on the content of the donor's intention; the law prohibits freedom of disposition only, to the extent where the donor attempts to make illegal dispositions that are against the rule of law.

Wills and Contests deals with the subject of inheritance and the administration of trusts; no matter how long you live, there comes a day when you shall take the voyage to the land of no return and then what happens to your loved ones, spouse, and children? Your will is the only voice that speaks for you when you are gone, it is that which shows your intentions, and the only instrument that determines how you want your belongings distributed among your survivors; however, for your will to speak from the grave it must be valid or else it is worth nothing but just a piece of paper that has no effect of the law and therefore, not suitable for probate. Without a valid will, your estate falls under intestacy and is subject to the default rule, meaning your belongings must be distributed according to the law of the jurisdiction not according to your intention. Wills and Contests is about: how to write a valid will, what is probate and nonprobate property, what happens if one dies intestate without a will, what is the right of the adopted child, what rights does a posthumously conceived child has to a deceased donor's estate, who is the parent of a child born by a surrogate mom for inheritance purposes, what rights do same sex couples and homosexuals have under the law of wills, intestacy and more. Wills and Contests provides answers to these questions and many more, using major Supreme Court and State Court cases dealing with the subject of wills, wills contests, and trusts.

ABOUT THE AUTHOR

Dr. Adeyemi Oshunrinade (EJD) is the author of MURDER OF DIPLOMACY '*Disarmament of Iraq and the Sanction regimes*' his first publication. Adeyemi completed his BA at Brooklyn College New York and his MS at Long Island University New York. He went on to take PHD classes in conflict analysis and resolution at NOVA Southeastern University in Florida and completed his E.JD degree at Concord law school in California. He resides in Brooklyn where he is hard at work on his next publication; Constitutional Law 'The First Amendment'.

Chapter One

INTRODUCTION

Williams Blackstone, commentaries

The right of inheritance, or descent to the children and relations of the deceased seems to have been allowed more earlier than, the right of devising by testament; we are apt to conceive, at first view, that it has nature on its side; yet we often mistake for nature what we find established by long and inveterate custom. It is certainly a wise and effectual, but clearly a political, establishment; since the permanent right of property, vested in the ancestor himself, was no natural but clearly a civil right . . . . It is probable that the right of inheritance arose from a plainer and more simple principle; A man's children or nearest relations are usually about him on his death bed, and are the earliest witnesses of his decease. They become therefore the next immediate occupants, till at length, in process of time, this frequent usage ripened into general law. And therefore, also, in the earliest ages, on failure of children, a man's servants, born under his roof, were allowed to be his heirs; being immediately on the spot when he died.

While property continued only for life, testaments were useless and unknown: and, when it became inheritable, the inheritance was long indefeasible, and the children or heirs at law were incapable of exclusion by will; till at length, it was found, that so strict a rule of inheritance made heirs disobedient and headstrong, defrauded creditors of their just debts, and prevented many provident fathers from dividing or charging their estates as the exigencies of their families required. This introduced the right of disposing of one's property, or a part of it, by *testament*; meaning, by written or oral instructions properly *witnessed* and *authenticated,* according to the wish of the deceased, which we, therefore, emphatically call his *will.*

Wills, therefore, and testaments, rights of inheritance and successions, are all creatures of the civil or municipal laws, and accordingly are in all respects regulated by them; every distinct country having different requirements, rules, and regulations to make a testament completely *valid*; neither does anything vary more than the right of inheritance under different national establishments.[1]

During life, an individual can use his wealth to influence the behavior of his acquaintances, friends, and family. However, the question is, to what extent should a person be able to use his wealth to influence behavior after death? Considering the fact that, there are events obvious to the individual during his life that he can see and make proper judgment on, according to his wish. Likewise, there are other events, which the individual cannot see after he is deceased; must external law then step in to make judgment for the deceased? And if so must the judgment be based on his wish and intention?

Restatement (third) of Property: Wills and Other Donative Transfers (2003)

§ 10.1 DONOR'S INTENTION DETERMINES THE MEANING OF A DONATIVE INSTRUMENT AND IS GIVEN EFFECT TO THE MAXIMUM EXTENT ALLOWED BY LAW

According to the Restatement, the controlling issue in determining the meaning of a donative instrument is the *intention* of the donor. It is what matters, and that which is given effect to the maximum extent allowed by law.

> a. *Rationale. The controlling principle of the American law of donative transfers is to allow the transferor every right and freedom to dispose of his property according to his intention and as he see fit.*
>
> c. *Effect of a donative instrument. Unless where the law says otherwise, the donor's intention determines both the meaning and the effect of a donative instrument.*

---

[1] William Blackstone, commentaries: Dukeminier; Wills, Trusts, and Estates; 7th edition p. 1-2

In the United States, the law does not grant courts any general authority to question the reasons for the donor's decision to dispose of his belonging in whatever way he chooses to. The law forbids the courts from questioning the wisdom, fairness, and reasonableness of the donor's decision about how to dispose of his or her property. The law however, serves its purpose in making a reliable determination on the content of the donor's intention. The law prohibits freedom of disposition only, to the extent where the donor attempts to make illegal transfers that are restricted by the rule of law.

Among the transfers which the law prohibits, are those involving spousal rights; creditors' rights; unreasonable restraint on alienation or marriage; any transfer that promote separation or divorce; transfers involving impermissible racial or other similar restrictions; those involving or promoting illegal activity; and the rules against perpetuities and accumulations.[2]

As discussed earlier, there is a limitation on the extent, to which the law may intervene or prohibit the intention of the donor, in the way he chooses to dispose of his belongings at death; however, in many situations, heirs of the deceased or family members may take steps to challenge the intention of the deceased as provided for in his will whenever they feel the disposition violates the law or whenever they feel dissatisfied with one or more condition to be satisfied by would be beneficiary before the disposition or transfer may occur. The case below is an example of such situation in which *the dead hand* is challenged and the question is raised as to whether it is constitutional for the transferor to condition disposition of his belongings to his children upon marriage to only *Jewish women.*

Shapira v. Union National Bank
Ohio Court of Common Pleas, Mahoning County, 1974
39 Ohio Misc. 28, 315 N.E. 2d 825

HENDERSON, J. This is an action for a declaratory judgment and the construction of the will of David Shapira, M.D. who died April 13, 1973. He was a resident of Mahoning County and by agreement of the parties the case has been submitted upon the pleadings and the exhibit.

---

[2]   Dukeminier: Wills, Trusts, and Estates; 7th edition p. 21

Will in question:

Item VIII. *All the rest, residue and remainder of my estate, real and personal of every kind and description and wheresoever situated, which I may own or have the right to dispose of at the time of my disease, I give, devise and bequeath to my three (3) beloved children, to wit:* Ruth Shapira Aharoni, *of Tel Aviv, Israel, or wherever she may reside at the time of my death; to my son* Daniel Jacob Shapira, *and to my son* Mark Benjamin Simon Shapira *in equal shares, with the following qualifications:* . . .

(b) *My son* Jacob Shapira *should receive his share of the bequest only, if he is married at the time of my death to a Jewish girl whose both parents were Jewish. In the event that at the time of my death he is not married to a Jewish girl whose both parents were Jewish, then his share of the bequest should be kept by my executor for a period of no longer than seven (7) years and if my said son* Daniel Jacob *gets married within the seven year period to a Jewish girl whose both parents were Jewish, my executor is hereby instructed to turn over his share of my bequest to him. In the event however, that my said son* Daniel Jacob *is unmarried within the (7) years after my death to a Jewish girl whose both parents were Jewish or if he is married to a non Jewish girl, then his share of my estate, as provided in item 8 above should go to the state of Israel absolutely.*

The provision of the will for the testator's other son Mark, is worded similarly. Daniel Jacob Shapira, the plaintiff in this case alleges that the condition placed upon his inheritance by his father is *unconstitutional, against public policy, and unenforceable because of its unreasonableness,* and that he should be given his bequest without the conditions.

CONSTITUTIONALITY

Under the Fourteenth Amendment to the Constitution of the United States, the right to marry is protected. *Meyer v. Nebraska (1923), 262 U.S. 390; Skinner v. Oklahoma (1942), 316 U.S. 535; Loving v. Virginia (1967), 388 U.S. 1* plaintiff argues that the condition placed upon his inheritance by his father violates the constitution based on the premise that right to marriage is protected by the Fourteenth Amendment. In *Meyer v. Nebraska,* holding unconstitutional a state statute prohibiting the teaching of languages other than English, the court stated that the Fourteenth Amendment denotes the right to marry among other basic rights. In *Skinner v. Oklahoma,*

4

holding unconstitutional a state statute providing for the sterilization of certain habitual criminals, the court stated that marriage and procreation are fundamental to the very existence and survival of the race. In *Loving v. Virginia*, the court held unconstitutional as violative of the Equal Protection and Due Process Clauses of the Fourteenth Amendment an anti-miscegenation statute under which a black person and a white person were convicted for marrying. In its opinion, the Supreme Court of the United States delivered the following statements, *388 U.S. at page 12.*

It is without doubt that restricting the right to marry solely because of racial classification violates the central meaning of the Equal Protection Clause. The freedom to marry has long been recognized as one of the vital personal rights essential to the orderly pursuit of happiness by free men. Marriage is one of the basic civil rights of man, fundamental to our very existence and survival . . . The fourteenth Amendment requires that the freedom of choice to marry not be restricted by invidious racial discriminations. Under our constitution, the right to marry, or not marry, a person of another race resides with the individual and cannot be infringed by the state.[3]

From the Supreme Court opinion in *Loving v. Virginia*, it appears as plaintiff contends that, the right to marry is constitutionally protected from restrictive State legislative action. Plaintiff argues that under the doctrine of *Shelley v. Kraemer (1948), 334 U.S. 1,* the constitutional protection of the Fourteenth Amendment is extended from direct state legislative action to the enforcement by state judicial proceedings of private provisions restricting the right to marry. {*In a nutshell plaintiff is asking the court to extend the same constitutional protection that prohibits the state from legislative actions on the right to marry to the enforcement by state judicial proceedings of private provisions restricting the right to marry}.* Plaintiff contends that a judgment of this court upholding the condition restricting marriage would, under *Shelley v. Kraemer*, constitute State action prohibited by the Fourteenth Amendment as much as a State Statute.

In *Shelley v. Kraemer*, the U.S. Supreme Court held that the action of the State to which the Fourteenth Amendment has reference includes action of State Courts and State judicial officials. Before this decision, the Court had invalidated city ordinances which denied blacks the right to live in white

---

[3]   Supreme Court Opinion: Loving v. Virginia, Ibid Dukeminier p. 22

neighborhoods. In the action, owners of neighboring properties sought to enjoin blacks from occupying properties which they had bought, but which were subjected to privately executed restrictions against use or occupation by any persons except those of the Caucasian race. Chief Justice Vinson noted, in the course of his opinion at page 13: 'These are cases in which the purpose of the agreements were secured only by judicial enforcement by State Courts of the restrictive terms of the agreement"[4]

In the case at bar, this court is not being asked to enforce any restriction upon Daniel Jacob Shapira's constitutional right to marry. Rather, this court is being asked to enforce the testator's restriction upon his son's inheritance. If the facts and circumstances of this case were such that the aid of this court, were sought to enjoin Daniel marrying a non Jewish girl, then the doctrine of *Shelley v. Kraemer* would be applicable, but not, it is believed, upon the facts as they are . . .

The right to receive property by will is a creature of the law, and is not a natural right or one guaranteed or protected by either the Ohio or the United States Constitution . . . It is a fundamental rule of law in Ohio that a testator may legally entirely disinherit his children . . . that is from a constitutional standpoint, a testator may restrict a child's inheritance. The court concludes, therefore, that the upholding and enforcement of the provisions of David Shapira's will conditioning the bequests to his sons upon their marrying Jewish girls does not offend the constitution of neither Ohio nor of the United States.

Note: Based on the ruling of the court, it is clear that for the ruling in *Shelley v. Kraemer* to be applicable to the case at bar, it must be found that David Shapira, placed a restriction on his sons right to marry in violation of the U.S constitution; however, in this case the court found that the testator only placed a restriction on his sons inheritance and since the principle of law is that, a testator may devise his belonging as he sees fit as long as the transfer does not violate the law, the testator's action restricting his sons inheritance is not unconstitutional.

Counsel for the plaintiff asserts, however that his position with respect to the applicability of *Shelley v. Kraemer* to this case is fortified by two later decisions of the United States Supreme Court: *Evans v. Newton (1966),*

---

[4]   Justice Vinson Ibid: Dukeminier P. 22-23

382 U.S. 296, 86 S.Ct.486 and *Pennsylvania v. Board of Directors of City Trusts of the City of Philadelphia (1957), 353 U.S. 230, 77 S.Ct.806. Evans* involved land willed in trust to the mayor and the city council of Macon, Georgia, as a park for white people only, and to be controlled by a white board of managers. To avoid the city having to enforce racial segregation in the park, the city officials resigned as trustees and private individuals were installed. The court held that such successor trustees, even though, private individuals, became agencies or instrumentalities of the state and subject to the Fourteenth Amendment by reason of their exercising powers or carrying on functions governmental in nature. On the other hand *Pennsylvania v. Board of Directors* is a case in which money was left by will to the city of Pennsylvania in trust for a college to admit poor white male orphans. The court held that the board which operated the college was an agency of the state of Pennsylvania, and that, therefore, its refusal to admit the plaintiffs because they were Negroes was discrimination by the state forbidden by the Fourteenth Amendment.

So, in neither *Evans v. Newton* nor *Pennsylvania v. Board Directors* was the doctrine of *Shelley v. Kraemer* applied or extended. Both of them involved restrictive actions by state governing agencies, in one case with respect to a park, in the other with respect to a college. Although both the park and college were founded upon testamentary gifts, the state action struck down by the court was not the judicial completion of the gifts, but rather the subsequent enforcement of the racial restrictions by the public management.

Basically, the right to receive property by will is a creature of the law, and is not a natural right or one guaranteed or protected by either the Ohio or the United States Constitution. Therefore, Dr. Shapira's will, conditioning the bequests to his sons upon their marrying Jewish girls does not offend the *33 constitution of Ohio or of the United States.

PUBLIC POLICY & REASONABLENESS

The condition that Daniel's inheritance be turned to him only if he should marry a Jewish girl whose both parents were Jewish, would constitute a partial restraint upon marriage; only, if the condition were that Daniel not marry anyone, this would violate constitutional dictates of the Fourteenth Amendment, the restraint would be general or total, and in the case of a first marriage, would be held contrary to public policy and as a result void. A partial restraint on marriage which imposes only reasonable restriction is valid, and not contrary to public policy. The principle of law and the authority in the United States, is that gifts conditioned upon the beneficiary marrying within a particular religious sect or faith are reasonable.

Plaintiff argues however, that in Ohio a condition such as the one in this case is void as against the public policy of this state. Plaintiff's position that the free choice of religious practice cannot be circumscribed or controlled by contract is substantiated by *Hackett v. Hackett 150 N.E. 2d 431.* This case held that a covenant in a separation agreement, incorporated in a divorce decree, that the mother would rear a daughter in the Roman Catholic faith was unenforceable. However, the controversy in *Shapira* is a partial restraint upon marriage and not a restraint upon the freedom of religious practice; and the court is not being asked to hold the plaintiff in contempt for failing to marry a Jewish girl of Jewish parentage.

Counsel contends that if Dr. David Shapira, during his life, had tried to impose upon his son those restrictions set out in his will he would have violated the public policy of Ohio as shown in *Hackett v. Hackett.* The public policy is equally violated by the restrictions Dr. Shapira has placed on his son by his will. This would be true, by analogy, if Dr. Shapira, in his lifetime, had tried to force his son to marry a Jewish girl as the condition of a completed gift. But it is not true that if Dr. Shapira had agreed to make his son an inter-vivos gift if he married a Jewish girl within seven years, that his son could have forced him to make the gift free of the condition.

It is noted, furthermore, in this connection, that the courts in Pennsylvania distinguish between testamentary gifts conditioned upon the religious faith of the beneficiary and those conditioned upon marriage to persons of a particular religious faith. In re Clayton's Estate (1930) 13 Pa. D. & C. 413, the court upheld a gift of a life estate conditioned upon the beneficiary's not marrying a woman of the catholic faith. In its opinion the court distinguishes the earlier case in *Drace v.Klinedinst (Pa. 1922), 118 A. 907,* in which a life estate willed to grandchildren, provided they remained faithful to a particular religion, was held to violate the public policy of Pennsylvania. In *Clayton's Estate,* the court said that the condition concerning marriage did not affect the faith of the beneficiary, and that the condition, operating only on the choice of a wife, was too remote to be regarded as a coercive of religious faith.

Counsel relies upon an Ohio case much nearly in point, that of *Moses v. Zook (C.A. Wayne 1934). Ohio Law Abs. 373.*[5]

The only case cited by plaintiff's counsel in accord with the holding in *Moses v. Zook,* are some English cases and one American decision. In England the courts have held that partial restrictions upon marriage to persons not of Jewish faith, or of Jewish parentage, were not contrary to public policy or invalid. *Hodgson v. Halford (1879 Eng.) L.R.11Ch. Div 959.* Other cases in England, however, have invalidated forfeitures of similarly conditioned provisions for children upon the basis of uncertainty or indefiniteness . . . . Since the foregoing decisions, a later English case has upheld a condition precedent that a granddaughter—beneficiary marry a person of Jewish faith and the child of Jewish parents . . . . The court found no difficulty with indefiniteness where the legatee married unquestionably outside the Jewish faith.

The American case cited by plaintiff is that of *Maddox v. Maddox* (1854), 52 Va. (11 Grattain's) 804. The testator in this case, willed a remainder to his niece if she remains a member of the Society of Friends. When the niece arrived at a marriageable age there were but five or six unmarried men of the society in the neighborhood in which she lived. She married a non-member and thus lost her own membership. The court held the condition to be an unreasonable restraint upon marriage and void, and that there being no gift

---

[5] *Moses v. Zook* involves a will in which the testatrix gave the income of her residual estate in trust to her niece and nephews for two years and then the remainder to them. Item twelve of the will provides that 'if any of my nieces or nephews should marry outside of the protestant faith, then they shall not receive any part of my estate devised or bequeathed to them' the will contained no gift over upon violation of the marriage condition. The holding of the trial court was that item twelve was null and void as being against public policy and the seven other items of the will should be administered as specified in detail by the court. There is nothing in the reported opinion to show to what extent, if at all, the question of public policy was in issue or contested in the trial court; and although the court of appeal adopted the unexcepted—to holdings of the trial court, there is no citation of authority or discussion concerning the public policy question itself. Moreover, *Moses v. Zook* differs in its facts in not containing a gift over upon breach of the condition, and appears not to have been a sufficiently litigated or reasoned establishment of the public policy of Ohio which the court should be obliged to follow.

over upon breach of the condition, the condition was in terrorem, and did not avoid the bequest. It can be seen that while the court considered the testamentary condition to be a restraint upon marriage, it was primarily one in restraint of religious faith. The court said that with the small number of eligible bachelors in the area, the condition would have operated as a virtual prohibition of the niece's marrying, and that she could not be expected to 'go abroad' in search of a helpmate or to be subjected to the chance of being sought after by a stranger . . . . The other ground upon which the Virginia court rested its decision, that the condition was in terrorem because of the absence of a gift over, is clearly not applicable to the case at bar, even if it were in accord with Ohio law, because of the gift over to the state of Israel contained in the Shapira will.

In arguing for the applicability of the *Maddox v. Maddox* test of reasonableness to the case at bar, counsel for the plaintiff asserts that the number of eligible Jewish females in this county would be an extremely small minority of the total population especially as compared with the comparatively much greater number in New York, whence has come many of the cases comprising the weight of authority upholding the validity of such clauses. There are no census figures in evidence. While this court could probably take judicial notice of the fact that the Jewish community is a minor, though important segment of our total local population, nevertheless the court is by no means justified in judicial knowledge that there is an insufficient number of eligible young ladies of Jewish parentage in this area from which Daniel would have a reasonable latitude of choice. And of course, Daniel is not at all confined in his choice to residents of this county, which is a very different circumstance in this day of travel by plane and freeway and communication by telephone, from horse and buggy days of the 1854 *Maddox v. Maddox* decision. Consequently, the decision does not appear to be an appropriate yardstick of reasonableness under modern living conditions.

Plaintiffs counsel contends that the Shapira will falls within the principle of *Fineman v. Central National Bank (1961 Ohio Com. Pleas), 175 N.E.2d 837,* holding that the public policy of Ohio does not countenance a bequest or device conditioned on the beneficiary's obtaining a separation or divorce from his wife. Counsel argues that the Shapira condition would encourage the beneficiary to marry a qualified girl just to receive the bequest, and then to divorce her afterwards. This possibility seems too remote to be a pertinent application of the policy against bequests conditioned upon divorce. Most other authorities agree with *Fineman v. Bank* that as a general proposition, a testamentary gift effective only on condition that the recipient divorce or separate from his or her spouse is against public policy and invalid. *14 A.L.R.3d 1222* . . . Indeed in measuring the reasonableness of the condition in question, both the father and the court should be able to assume that the son's motive would be proper. And surely the son should not gain the advantage of the avoidance of the condition by the possibility of his own impropriety.

Finally, counsel urges that the Shapira condition tends to pressure Daniel, by the reward of money, to marry within seven years without opportunity for mature reflection, and jeopardizes his college education. It seems to the court on the contrary, that the seven year time limit would be a most reasonable grace period, and one which would give the son ample opportunity for exhaustive reflection and fulfillment of the condition without constraint or oppression. Daniel is no more being 'blackmailed into a marriage by immediate financial gain,' as suggested by counsel, than would be beneficiary of a living gift or conveyance upon consideration of a future marriage—an arrangement which has long been sanctioned by the courts of this state. *Thompson v. Thompson (1967), 17 Ohio St. 649.*

In the opinion of this court, the provision made by the testator for the benefit of the state of Israel upon breach or failure or failure of the condition is most significant for two reasons. First, it distinguishes this case from the bare forfeiture in *Moses v. Zook* and in *Maddox v. Maddox* (including the technical in terrorem objection), and, in a way, from the vagueness and indefiniteness doctrine of some of the English cases. Second, and of greater importance, it demonstrates the depth of the testator's conviction. His purpose was not merely a negative one designed to punish his son for not carrying out his wishes. His unmistakable testamentary plan was that his possessions be used to encourage the preservation of the Jewish faith and blood, hopefully through his sons, but if not, then through the state of Israel. Whether this judgment was wise is not for this court to determine. But it is the duty of this court to honor the testator's intention within the limitations of law and of public policy. The prerogative granted to a testator by the law of this state to dispose of his estate according to his conscience is entitled to as much judicial protection and enforcement as the prerogative of a beneficiary to receive an inheritance.

*It is the conclusion of this court that public policy should not, and does not preclude the fulfillment of Dr. Shapira's purpose, and that in accordance with the weight of authority in this county, the conditions

contained in his will are reasonable restriction upon marriage, and valid.[6]

NOTE: QUESTIONS

(a) What does the society achieve by allowing the deceased to control behavior of the beneficiary of his or her estate after death, is it proper and reasonable for the court to honor such dictates knowing that situations may change over time?

(b) Do you think it would have been reasonable for the beneficiary in the Shapira case to honor his father's wishes even if it creates unreasonable burden on his life?

(c) Consider yourself the attorney for the beneficiary, would you advise him to marry a Jewish girl and later file for divorce? Remember what the court said that this possibility seems too remote to be a pertinent application of the policy against bequests conditioned upon divorce; do you think so and what about the ethical issue? Before you answer this question consider the ruling in *Fineman v. Bank* that as a general proposition, a testamentary gift effective only on condition that the recipient divorce or separate from his or her spouse is against public policy and invalid.

Note: **Restatement (second) of Property: Donative Transfers §6.2 (1983)** Provide that a restraint to induce a person to marry within a *religious faith* is valid, if and only if, under the circumstances, the restraint does not unreasonably limit the transferee's opportunity to marry.

COMMENT (a) Provides that, the restraint, unreasonably limits the transferee's opportunity to marry if a marriage permitted by the restraint is not likely to occur. The likelihood of marriage is a factual question, to be answered from the circumstances of the particular case. The motive or purpose of the testator is irrelevant. Based on this set of rules, what should happen if Daniel Shapira is in a situation where marriage is impossible; for example what happens if Daniel were gay could he have been forced to marry in order to get the inheritance?

---

[6] West Reporter: Ohio Com.Pl. 1974. *Shapira v. Union Bank, 39 Ohio Misc.28, N.E.2d 825.*

Chapter Two

PROBATE & NONPROBATE PROPERTY

In the United States and many other industrialized countries, there is a process for dealing with the estate of the deceased. It is a legal process by which the belongings of the deceased person, is distributed according to his or her wishes. Think of the chaos that would result if someone dies and the law allows anyone to take his belongings on a 'first come' basis. Instead, there is a system in place that protects and directs the distribution of property on a person's death. Our laws recognize that some order must be maintained and so, they provide, among other things, the 'freedom of testation' and a legal process to deal with those estates that have exercised that right and those that have not.

Freedom of testation simply means the right to transfer your property on your death in almost any manner you choose. Few people realize that this is not a natural right for it is not impossible for instance, for the government to rule that on a person's death, all of his property would belong to the government. Such an approach, however, would, among, other things, discourage the acquisition of property and would soon undermine our capitalistic system.[7] To avoid such problems, we are allowed to freely acquire property during our life time, to keep it, and to transfer it the way we see fit, and on our death, we are allowed to decide subject to certain

---

[7]   The Complete Book of Wills and Trusts 3rd edition P.5

obligations to keep our spouse and children in mind, who will get what is left. However, for those decisions to be carried out, they must be reflected in a *valid* will.

Probate Property: Is the property that passes under the decedent's will or by intestacy. People often have the idea that probate under a will or intestacy is the usual way to pass property at death, however, this is not so. Most property is transferred at death outside of probate, through a nonprobate means which we shall discuss later. Probate property is any type of property that stands in your name *alone* at the time of death or that would require action on the part of your executor or administrator to transfer. It would not include for example, property or assets that are jointly held or that are payable to a named beneficiary at death. It includes property over which you *alone* have control and own. Probate is the system that determines and governs the distribution of the probate estate to the heirs and beneficiaries, the payment of estate debts after death, the resolution of disputes which may arise from sharing of estate's property, the resolution of creditor's claims against the estate, and contests against the will.

Nonprobate Property: Is property passing under an instrument other than a will. Nonprobate property includes the followings:

(a) *Joint tenancy property both real and personal*: Under the doctrine of joint tenancy, interests of the decedent, vanishes at death and the survivor attains the right of survivorship. The survivor has the entire property and the decedent is relieved of any participation, However, the interests does not pass automatically to the survivor, he still needs to perfect title by filing a death certificate of the decedent. Bank accounts, mutual funds, and mortgages are often held in joint tenancy most especially by husband and wife. This is different from a *tenancy in common* in which there is no right of survivorship. Under a tenancy in common, there is no right of survivorship and the death of a party does not give the other right to inherit the entire estate, the survivor can only take his share of the estate and the other share reverts to the estate of the decedent. Note: *The instrument creating a joint tenancy speaks the whole truth. In order to go behind the terms of the agreement, the one claiming adversely has the burden of proof.*

(b) Life Insurance: Life insurance proceeds of a policy on a decedent's life are paid by the insurance company to the beneficiary named in the policy contract and are not considered probate property. The insurance company will pay upon receipt of a death certificate of the insured. If the deceased was the insured under a policy and if the proceeds were payable to the deceased *estate* (usually a bad idea) and not a particular beneficiary, then the proceeds would be probate property to be shared among the heirs according to the will. If the deceased was the owner of a policy on someone else's life, then the policy itself *(not the proceeds since the insured person would still be alive)* would be a part of the probate estate.

(c) Payable-on-death provisions(P.O.D.): A decedent may enter into a contract with a bank, an employer, or some other person or corporation to distribute the property held under the contract at the decedent's death to a specified beneficiary. IRAs, Keoghs, and the like are examples. To collect property held under a payable-on-death contract, a filing of the decedent's death certificate suffices. Under the traditional rule, a P.O.D designation in many contracts other than life insurance, are invalid. Under the new rule, a partnership agreement which provides that, upon death of one partner, his interest shall pass to the surviving partner or partners, resting as it does in contracts is unquestionably valid and may not be defeated by labeling it a testamentary disposition. Unlike the traditional rule, the Uniform Probate Code in 1969 authorized P.O.D. designation in all contracts, and all but a few states have followed suit. U.P.C. § 6-101 (a) states: A provision for a nonprobate transfer on death in an insurance policy, contract of employment, bond, mortgage, promissory note, certificated or un-certificated security, account agreement, custodial agreement, deposit agreement, compensation plan, pension plan, individual retirement plan, employee benefit plan, trusts, conveyance, deed of gift, marital property agreement or other written instrument of a similar nature is non-testamentary. U.P.C § 6-101 (1) states: Money or other benefits due to, controlled by, or owned by a decedent before death must be paid after the decedent's death to a person whom the decedent designates, either

in the instrument or in a separate writing including a will, executed either before or at the same time as the instrument or later. (Meaning *such monies is non-probate if a specific beneficiary is named in the instrument of creation.*) U.P.C. § 6-101 (2) states: Money due or to become due under the instrument ceases to be payable in the event of death of the promisee or the promisor before payment or demand or; U.P.C. § 6-101 (3) :Any property controlled by or owned by the decedent before death which is the subject of the instrument passes to a person the decedent designates either in the instrument or in a separate writing including a will, executed either before or at the same time as the instrument or later.

(d) Annuities: Is a payment every year for the rest of the beneficiary's life. Its main purpose is to shift the financial risk of living too long to a pension fund or insurance company. By buying into a pool with other people worried about the same risk, those who die younger pay those who die older. Note: 29 U.S.C. § 1144 (a) states: ERISA (Employee Retirement Income Security Act) shall supersede any and all state laws insofar as they may now or hereafter relate to any employee benefit plan covered by ERISA. ERISA commands that a plan shall specify the basis on which payments are made to and from the plan. § 1102(b)(4) and that the fiduciary shall administer the plan in accordance with the documents and instruments governing the plan. § 1104(a)(1)(d). Making payments to a beneficiary who is designated by a participant or by the terms of the plan § 1002(8).

(e) Interest in trust: Whenever property is transferred in trust, the trustee has a fiduciary duty to hold the property for the benefit of the designated beneficiary, who may have life estate or remainder on the property. The trustee must distribute the property to the beneficiaries according to the terms of the instrument of creation. If the trust is created by the decedent, it may be *revocable* or *non-revocable*. If the decedent has a testamentary power of appointment over the trust *(power to devise the trust property as he wants rather than give the power to the trustee)*, then, the decedent's will must be admitted to probate, but the trust assets are distributed to the beneficiaries according to the will and do not go through probate. If however, the decedent does not retain a power of appointment, the trust assets are

considered non-probate and must be distributed to the beneficiaries according to terms of the trust. Note: *Distribution of non-probate assets does not involve a court proceeding but must be done according to the terms in the instrument of creation. Distribution of probate assets however, require a court proceeding involving probate of a will or a finding of intestacy followed by appointment of a personal representative to settle the probate estate.*

Estates Administration

One of the important parts of administering an estate is the choosing of the estate *administrator or executor.* When a person dies and probate is necessary, the first step is the appointment of the executor a personal representative who oversees the administration of the estate. In your will, you may not only name one or more executors but, as with guardianship, you may name successors if for any reason the principal executor cannot serve. Duties of the executor are (1) to make the necessary inventories and collect assets of the estate (2) to manage the assets during administration (3) to pay creditors and tax collectors (4) to distribute assets of the decedent according to his will designates (5) to clear title to cars, other assets, and real estate (6) if the deceased had started a lawsuit against someone before his death and the action survives his death, the estate executor or administrator may continue the lawsuit and proceeds from the action become part of the probate estate. You may wonder what the terms *administrator and executor* means, if the testator dies living a will *(testate)* and names someone to distribute the assets, that person is called the *executor.* On the other hand, when no executor is named in the will, a personal representative known as the *administrator* is appointed by, under the control of, and accountable to a court. In selecting an administrator for the estate, a statutory list of persons, are to be given preference; surviving spouse, children, parents, siblings, and creditor are selected according to order.

In most jurisdictions, the administrator must give bond before assuming the position. If the will names an individual rather than a corporate fiduciary, the executor must also give bond except where the will waives this requirement. In the United States, one court in each county has jurisdiction over estate administration, it may be called the surrogate court, the orphan's court, the probate court, or the chancery court.

The Probate Process

Simplified

Locating the will

At the death of the testator, the first step that must be taken concerning the distribution of his estate is to determine whether he left a will. In most cases relatives will know or have an idea that there was or was not a will. In some European countries for example, in Spain, it is not uncommon for parents to inform their children about the location of their will, some even go as far as telling their children about the contents of their will. In many states in the United States it is a crime for someone aware of the location of a will to conceal it. If the location of the will is unknown, a search of the deceased's papers and safe-deposit box may yield some lead. If the deceased had a lawyer, the lawyer should be asked if he has knowledge of a will.

Opening Probate

The procedure of opening probate is governed by a collection of statutes which vary from state to state. The will should first be probated or letter of administration is sought in the jurisdiction where the decedent lived at the time of death. Each state has a detailed statutory procedure for issuance of *testamentary letters or letters of administration;* when issued, the letter authorizes the administrator to act on behalf of the estate. In an *ex parte* proceeding, no notice is issued to any person, due execution of the will was done by the oath of the executor or other witnesses as might be required; the will was admitted to probate at once, letters of testamentary were granted, and the executor began administration of the estate. If no objection or question is raised the procedure is certified. On the other hand, under probate *in solemn form,* notice of the administration is forwarded to interested parties by citation and due execution was proved by testimony of the attesting witnesses and administration of the estate involved greater court participation. Petitions for the probate of a will are relatively simple forms available at the probate court for the district or county of the decedent's domicile. The petition simply asks the court, to allow the submitted will as the last and valid will of the deceased.

NOTE: Most jurisdictions in the United States do not allow *ex parte* proceedings but require given notice to the interested parties before appointment of a representative or probate of a will.

Choosing the Executor/Administrator

If there is no opposition to the petition to allow the will for probate, then the court will appoint the executor named in the will to be the sole legal representative of the estate. At this stage, the executor takes legal title to all the properties of the estate and he is now responsible legally to the beneficiaries to settle the estate of the deceased. If on the other hand, no executor is named or there is no will (*in the case of intestacy*), the court will appoint a representative or administrator who takes legal title to the properties of the estate, manage the estate, and settle it for the beneficiaries. The executor or administrator is responsible for paying debts of the estate, paying taxes, dealing with pending lawsuits or claims against the estate, and finally distributing estate properties to the beneficiaries.

Inventory of Estate Property

After assuming legal title to the estate property, the executor or administrator, must now make inventories of estate properties; he must document all the belongings and assets of the deceased however, this will include only probate assets since non-probate assets in most cases, already have named beneficiaries and are not subject to probate. The inventory is delivered to the probate court and thus become part of public record for interested parties who may want to look at it. Filing inventories is essential because, it allows for proper and accurate accounting of the estate assets and it enables the beneficiaries, creditors, and other interested parties to know the contents of the estate for recovery and contest purposes.

Payment of Claims

After making inventories, the executor/administrator, must now begin to settle claims against the estate. Depending on the jurisdiction, there are special requirements for the time period within which claims against the estate must be filed; once the time period passes, the claims become invalid and are no longer collectible however, in special cases the court may allow an extension if determined necessary. The period usually begins say three months after the appointment of the executor and ends from six to twelve months after that. The executor is required to give notice to interested parties and in some cases constructive notice may be enough.

Payment of Debts, Fees, Expenses and Estate Taxes

The executor is responsible after settling the claims, for making sure all debts owed creditors which are properly filed are paid. He must also pay all fees and expenses associated with probating the estate; these include all court fees, filing fees, doctors' bills, utility bills, and legal fees. Part of the executor' job is to file the estate tax; this is usually due within nine month after death is recorded unless an extension is granted by the court.

Sharing Estate' Property among Beneficiaries

After paying all necessary taxes, the executor may now begin to distribute the remainder among the beneficiaries according to the deceased' will if the deceased died living a will. In the case of intestacy *(when there is no will)* the belongings are distributed according to the default rule of the jurisdiction involved; each state in the United States has its *statute of will* that serves as the default rule if the deceased left no will.

Before making payments or transferring property to the beneficiaries, the executor, will prepare a release for each beneficiary to sign, in the release, the beneficiary accepts the proposed distribution in full settlement of any claims or legacies he may possess in the estate and releases the executor from further claims or future liability. Although, the executor must still make account to the court on how the estate is distributed, beneficiaries are encourage not to sign a release of the executor until the beneficiary has seen the account and satisfied with the executor' account.

Closing the Estate

When the executor has paid all fees, settled all debts, distributed the estate and has prepared all accounts and obtained release from the beneficiaries, the executor now petitions the court to allow his account that is, to seek approval of the court that his report is complete and accurate settlement of the estate; when this happens, the estate may be closed and the executor discharged of his duties.

Note: *(The executor or administrator is paid a fee for his service to the estate; the payment comes from estate assets.)*

Is an Attorney Necessary?

Many have asked the question; do you really need a lawyer or is probate necessary? The answer is that probate can be avoided if, the property owner during life transfer his or her property into a joint tenancy or a revocable or irrevocable trust. Also if the property owner executes a contract providing for distribution of his or her property to named beneficiaries at death, then probate may not be necessary. However, it is always a good idea to consult a lawyer when the estate is large to avoid estate tax problems that may arise incase of improper filing. Even, when it is a small estate, there are formalities that are essential to all wills and if not properly followed may render a will invalid at the testator' death that is, even when there is a will, the deceased' estate may fall under the default rule and distributed according to the law of the state where the deceased is domiciled at death, rather than according to his intention in the will. Having a professional do your will, helps you overcome the complications of estate settlement, and if a mistake is made, the professional is responsible and in most cases may be found liable to you in a court of law however, if you do your will yourself without the help of a professional, you assume all responsibilities and consequences including subjecting your estate to the default provision incase your will is invalid.

It is difficult for a wealthy person with a big and variety of assets in different places, to dispose of all property by non-probate means. Some property is not suitable for joint tenancy or trust or is not subject to transfer by contract. Even though, a large portion of a person's assets can be arranged so as to avoid probate, probate may be necessary especially for assets that pass by will or intestacy.

Chapter Three

INTESTACY
THE DEFAULT RULE

While it is not uncommon for people to leave a will, many die living no will or means by which their property may be distributed at their death. In a 1950 poll, only 19% of American adults reported having made a will.[8] While many die leaving no will, those that claim to leave one did not consult a lawyer before doing so; they die intestate, forsaking wills and legal advice.

Intestacy is the blank page upon which the law of wills is written; it represents the default model for distributing property at death. Imagine what would happen if you die leaving no will and everyone including your remote relatives just come from no where and take a share of your estate, leaving little or nothing for your young children; without doubt if the dead could talk you must be turning in your grave feeling unhappy for not leaving a will. In any given year, approximately two-thirds of all deceased Americans die *intestate.*[9] Intestate succession is the default plan for distributing the deceased' estate at death, it is the rule of law that governs how a deceased person's assets are distributed when there is no will or if the person does not have a valid will, then the law will transfer his property, in accordance with the appropriate law of intestacy in effect at his state of domicile at

---

[8]   Ibid, Dukeminier 7th edition p.59
[9]   Robert Mennell, Will and Trust p.6

death. The distribution of the probate property of a person who dies without a will or whose will does not make a complete disposition of the estate is governed by the appropriate statute of descent. If a will is poorly drafted that it transfers only part of the probate estate, then the result is *partial intestacy*. The principle is that, the law of the state where the decedent is domiciled at death governs the disposition of personal property, and the law of the state where the decedent's real property is located determines the disposition of his real property.

The default rule in each state differs, it is therefore, important for you to be familiar with the intestacy law of your state or domicile if you are a lawyer and you intend on helping your clients with their will. To know who succeeds to a particular property, it is essential to know the intestacy statute of the state. To have an idea of what the intestacy rule represent, you must look at the Uniform Probate Code for guidance.

Uniform Probate Code {UPC 1990}

§ 2-101. INTESTATE ESTATE

(a) Any part of a decedent's estate not effectively disposed of by will passes by intestate succession to the decedent's heirs as prescribed in this code, except as modified by the decedent's will.

(b) A decedent by will may expressly exclude or limit the right of an individual or class to succeed to property of decedent passing by intestate succession. If that individual or a member of that class survives the decedent, the share of the decedent's intestate estate to which that individual or class would have succeeded passes as if that individual or each member of that class had disclaimed his (or her) intestate share.

COMMENT: New subsection (b) authorizes the decedent, by will, to exclude or limit the right of an individual or class to share in the decedent's intestate estate, in effect disinheriting that individual or class. By specifically authorizing so-called negative wills, subsection (b) reverses the usually accepted common law rule, which defeats a testator's intent for no sufficient reason; whether or not in an individual case the decedent's will has excluded or limited right of an individual or class to take a share of the estate.

§ 2-102. SHARE OF SPOUSE

The intestate share of a decedent's surviving spouse is:

(1) The entire intestate estate if:
  (A) no descendant or parent of the decedent survives the decedent; or
  (B) all of the decedent's surviving descendants are also descendants of the surviving spouse and there is no other descendant of the surviving spouse who survives the decedent;

(2) the first {$300,000}, plus three-fourth of any balance of the interstate estate, if no descendant of the decedent survives the decedent, but a parent of the decedent survives the decedent;

(3) the first {225,000}, plus one-half of any balance of the interstate estate, if all of the decedent's surviving descendants are also descendants of the surviving spouse and the surviving spouse has one or more surviving descendants who are not descendant of the decedent;

(4) the first {150,000}, plus one-half of any balance of the intestate estate, if one or more of the decedent's surviving descendants are not descendants of the surviving spouse.

NOTE: This section was revised in 1990 to give the surviving spouse a larger share than the pre-1990 UPC.[10] If the decedent leaves no surviving descendant and no surviving parent or if the decedent does leave surviving descendants but neither the decedent nor the surviving spouse has other descendants, the surviving spouse is entitled to all of the decedent's intestate estate.

§ 2-102 SHARE OF HEIRS OTHER THAN SURVIVING SPOUSE

Any part of the intestate estate not passing to the decedent's surviving spouse under § 2-102, or the entire intestate estate if there is no surviving

---

[10] As revised in 1990, the dollar amount in paragraph (2) was $200,000, in paragraph (3) was $150,000, and in paragraph (4) was $100,000. To adjust for inflation, these amounts were increased in 2008 to $300,000, $225,000, and $150,000 respectively. The dollar amounts in these paragraphs are subject to annual cost-of-living adjustments under section 1-109.

spouse, passes in the following order to the individuals who survive the decedent:

(1) to the decedent's descendants by representation;
(2) if there is no surviving descendants, to the decedent's parents equally if both survive, or to the surviving parent if only one survives;
(3) if there is no surviving descendant or parent, to the descendants of the decedent's parents or either of them by representation;
(4) if there is no surviving descendant, parent, or descendant of a parent, but the decedent is survived on both the paternal and maternal sides by one or more grandparents or descendants of grandparents:

   (A) half to the decedent's paternal grandparents equally if both survive, to the surviving paternal grandparent if only one survives, or to the descendants of the decedent's paternal grandparents or either of them if both are deceased, the descendants taking by representation; and
   (B) half to the decedent's maternal grandparents equally if both survive, to the surviving maternal grandparent if only one survives, or to the descendants of the decedent's maternal grandparents or either of them if both are deceased, the descendants taking by representation.

§ 2-105.

If there is no taker under the provision of this Article, the intestate estate passes to the {state}.

Share of the Surviving Spouse

When there are no children from a prior marriage, most persons want everything to go to the surviving spouse, and not to parents, brothers, and sisters. A surviving spouse always receives an intestate share and under the current law, the surviving spouse usually receives at least one-half share of the decedent's estate. There are two situations under which the Uniform Probate Code gives the entire estate to the surviving spouse: (1) the surviving spouse gets everything if no descendant or parents survives the decedent and (2) if all of the descendants of the decedent are also descendants of the spouse. This happens in most cases in a marriage where children are involved, the decedent may prefer to leave his entire estate for his wife with the hope that his wife will make provision for the children in her will however; in such a situation it is always a good idea to make sure there are no other children outside marriage.

If no descendant or parent of the decedent survives the decedent, and all of the decedent's surviving descendants are also descendants of the spouse, the spouse gets the entire estate; if no descendant of the decedent survives the decedent, but a parent of the decedent survives the decedent, in 2008, the UPC was revised and the revised 1990 UPC gives the spouse the first $300,000 plus three-fourth of any balance of the intestate estate; the spouse gets the first $225,000 plus one-half of any balance of the intestate estate, if all of the decedent's surviving descendants are also descendants of the surviving spouse and the surviving spouse has one or more surviving descendants who are not descendants of the decedent; and gets the first $150,000 plus one-half of the intestate estate, if one or more of the decedent's descendants are not descendants of the surviving spouse. For example, where there is a step child who is a descendant of the decedent but not of the surviving spouse.

Share of Descendants

The descendants such as the parents always share the balance of the estate, after the surviving spouse receives his or her share. Surviving children usually take equal share and others such as grandchildren or great-grandchildren always receive their share of the intestate estate by representation (*representing their parents*). If there is only one descendant, he or she takes the entire portion. If there are no descendants living, then parents are favored to inherit the balance of the decedent's estate after the spouse received his or her portion.

Parents

In the case where there is no spouse or the decedent dies without a descendent then, parents are favored to inherit the estate and in some cases the parent's issue will receive the entire estate. If both parents are alive, they take equal share of the estate; but if one is alive he or she takes the entire estate. If the decedent leaves a surviving spouse but no descendants, then the parents take one-fourth of whatever is left after the spouse has received her entire share of the estate.

Grandparents

If there is no surviving spouse, children, or parents then, grandparents and their descendants are considered. One-half goes to the paternal grandparent and his descendants and the other half goes to the maternal grandparent and her descendants.

Relatives

Collateral relatives, most especially of the first generation are considered when there are no grandparents or surviving descendants to take the estate. The search may go on and on to the second and third generation relatives until finally no one is left to take the estate.

State

In a situation where there is no descendant or relative to take the estate, under the Uniform Probate Code § 2-105, the entire estate *escheat* to the state; the state takes over the estate and becomes the ultimate heir of the decedent. Before this happens, the state will make sure there are no remote relatives or (*laughing heirs*) who may take the estate; when the state certifies there are none, it then assumes the responsibility to take over the estate.

UNREASONABLE DISPOSITION

Rights of the Surviving Spouse

Of the fifty states in the United States, about forty one are separate property states where, the spouse own property in their individual capacity. There are two basic marital property systems: First, the system of *private or separate property* originating in the common law of England and second, the system of *community property*, which has its origin from Europe and later brought to the United States by French and Spanish settlers. Under the common law doctrine of *private property*, husband and wife own separately all property each acquires during their lifetime except for properties they both agreed to subject to joint ownership. In a *community property* jurisdiction, both spouses own an undivided half interest in each other's income and property acquired during marriage. Under this system, all acquisitions after marriage, is owned by both husband and wife in equal share. Some states in the United State are considered community property states; among such states are: Arizona, California, Idaho, Louisiana, Nevada, New Mexico, Texas, and Washington. These states treat marriage as a partnership and whatever the husband and wife own during their marriage is considered jointly owned by both.

Under the *private property* system, whatever a husband or wife earns is his or hers. There is no sharing so, if only the husband works, he is the owner of the entire income and if only the wife works she owns the income as well. If one spouse is the wage earner while the other stays at home, the wage earner will own all the property acquired during marriage except for inheritances, gifts, and other items that are considered personal belongings of the non-working spouse.

Dower and Curtesy

Almost every jurisdiction has some provision allowing the surviving spouse to claim a portion of the decedent's estate despite, a valid will attempting to dispose of it to others. *Dower* is the common-law right of the widow to a life estate in one-third of the realty of which the husband was seized or in possession of at any time during their marriage. The right to *dower* attaches the moment the husband acquires title to land or upon marriage, whichever is later. *Dower* remains inchoate until the husband's death, when it becomes possessory; once inchoate, *dower* has attached the husband cannot sell the property free and clear of the wife's consent or *dower* interest.

Curtesy, was the corresponding right of the husband to one-half interest in fee simple to the wife's lands when children had been born of the marriage. At common-law, a husband acquired a support interest in his wife's lands called *curtesy* however, the husband did not acquire *curtesy* unless children were born of the marriage and the husband was given a life estate in the entire parcel. Few states in the United States today recognize *curtesy* and *dower* has been abolished in majority of states.

Elective Share

In a private property state, an issue that has been a problem, is how to protect the surviving spouse from unreasonable disinheritance; to provide solution, the law gives the surviving spouse what is known as an *elective share (forced share)* in the estate of the deceased spouse. The elective share not only covers the earnings, but also enforceable against all property owned by the decedent's spouse at death. The fundamental principle behind this is that, all earnings and acquired property are community property; each spouse is the owner of an undivided one-half-share in the community property. The death of a spouse dissolves the community giving the deceased spouse testamentary power over just one-half of the community property and the other half to the surviving spouse. By cutting the deceased spouse testamentary power in half, the law protects the surviving spouse from unreasonable disinheritance by will, giving the surviving spouse a *forced share* of the estate.

The community property system, is based on the notion that, husband and wife are marital partners who put all their time, money, and effort together to acquire the community property; based on this principle, they must share the happiness of the marriage and fruits of their labor equally however, all earnings and property acquired before marriage are not considered part of the community property.

When a spouse dies, the law gives the surviving spouse the right to support and benefits from the deceased's earnings acquired during his or her lifetime and those due to the deceased spouse after death. All but one of the separate property states gives the surviving spouse, in addition to any other support rights an *elective share* of the decedent's property. Traditional statutes provide the surviving spouse with an *election* that is: (a) the spouse can take under the decedent's will, or (b) the spouse can renounce the will and take a fractional share of the decedent's estate. Under typical American *elective share* doctrine {UPC 1990,} a surviving spouse may claim a one-third share of the decedent's estate. The surviving spouse gets a sliding-scale percentage of the *elective share* amount based upon the duration of the marriage {3 percent after one year, growing to 50 percent after 15 years of marriage.} UPC § 2-202 (a) {1990, as amended 1993}

Social Security

We are all familiar with social security, part of our income earnings goes into social security every time we get paid and sometimes we may wonder where the money goes. If a worker dies, his or her surviving spouse receives the worker's whole monthly social security benefit. The worker has no testamentary power to transfer the spousal right to benefit to any other person. A divorced ex-spouse of the worker, has a right to benefit if the marriage lasted for 10 years or longer; the ex-spouse is considered to have contributed part of the community property during his or her marriage to the deceased and even though they might not be married at the time of death, the ex-spouse is still entitled to a forced share.

There are also situations where a spouse who is not a legal spouse may have rights on the death of a partner, this happens in a common-law marriage. In a number of states, if a couple lives together as husband and wife for a number of years seven years and more, then by the law of that state, they can be considered married. In that case, the surviving common-law spouse has the same rights as a legally married spouse, including the right to waive the will and take a forced share.

It is always good for married couples to know what law operates in their jurisdiction and whether their state is a private or a community property state. The attorney, drafting a will must also be aware of the state law as to spousal benefits and other related non-probate matters.

Pension Plans

ERISA (Employee Retirement Income Security Act of 1974,) requires that the spouse of an employee must have survivorship rights if the employee predeceases the spouse. If the employee spouse survives to retirement age, the pension must be paid as a joint and survivor annuity to the employee and his or her spouse, unless the non-employee spouse consents to some other form of payment of the retirement benefit, such as a lump sum. If the employee dies before retirement and the pension is vested, the surviving spouse is entitled to a pre-retirement survivor annuity. All these means that, a deceased spouse may not intentionally choose by will or other means to prevent the surviving spouse from taking his or her share of the benefit; ERISA discourages such thinking and gives a surviving spouse survivorship rights if the employee pre-deceases the surviving spouse.

A spouse may choose to waive his or her rights to benefits under the employee pension plan however, ERISA discourages waivers by rules regarding their validity; all waivers requires the written consent of the spouse. Workers under the age of 35 cannot effectuate a waiver of spousal rights to benefits.

Homestead

The homestead, represent the principal dwelling and adjoining land occupied by a family; special statutory provisions prevents the homestead from probate and allows it to be set aside for the use of a surviving spouse. Under the *homestead doctrine*, the surviving spouse has the right to occupy the family home for his or her lifetime. Some states require that the homestead be established by the decedent during life, usually by filing a declaration of homestead in some public office designated for the purpose; in other states, the probate court has the ultimate right to set aside real estate as homestead. The decedent, may not dispose of the homestead by probate in an attempt to deprive the surviving spouse of his or her right to it.

Personal Property

Some personal items such as furniture, clothing, and other tangible personal property of the decedent, may be set aside for the use of the surviving spouse and the children. In most cases such items are also exempt from creditor's claim; such items are considered necessities of life and a decedent may not deprive the surviving spouse from taking possession. It is important to say however, that there is a limit to the amount that may be set aside from personal property, for use of the surviving spouse; UPC § 2-403 {1990} sets the limit at $10,000.

Allowances

Every state has laws that offer some protection for the welfare of a surviving spouse and, to a lesser extent, minor children of the decedent in situations where the decedent failed to provide for them in his or her will or where the family requires some financial assistance while the estate is being settled. The allowance may be limited by state law to a fixed period {usually one year} and it may continue further while the will is still undergoing settlement. In Massachusetts, for example, while a widow's allowance is only limited by need and by the proportion the allowance bears to the entire estate, allowance for minor children may not exceed $100 per child however, a minor child has the right to sue the estate of a Massachusetts' parent for support, since the parent had the pre-existing legal obligation to support the child while the parent was alive.[11] UPC § 2-404 allows a reasonable allowance which cannot continue for more than one year, if the estate is inadequate to pay creditors. Maintenance of decedent's spouse and dependent children is not allowed after the estate is closed.

Marital Tax Deduction

The estate tax marital deduction, gives a spouse a deduction of up to 50 percent of the value of his or her estate, for property left to the surviving spouse in a form comparable to the outright ownership the community property spouse had. Under the 1982 Federal Estate Tax Marital Deduction Act, inter-spousal transfers will not be taxed at all, provided the donor spouse gives the beneficiary spouse at least a life estate in the property. A gift of a fee simple couple with a power of appointment is no longer required for marital deductions and the marital deduction is unlimited in amount {IRS Code 1986.}

It is always important for the attorney, to be aware of the necessary tax law in drafting the will of their client to avoid overpayment or reduction in the value of estate assets which may be due to poor drafting and tax oversight.

NOTE: *Disability and Abandonment*

Where a surviving spouse is under a disability, the probate court is given the authority under RC.*2106.08* to appoint a suitable person to ascertain the surviving spouse's adequate support needs and to compare the value of the surviving spouse's rights under the will with the value of his or her rights under the statute of descent and distribution. The court may elect for the surviving spouse to take against the will only if it finds that election

---

[11]   Ibid, Wills, Estates, and Trusts 3rd edition p.110

to take is necessary to provide support based on the circumstances. In some states, *elective share* is denied to a spouse who has abandoned or failed to support the deceased spouse during his or her lifetime however, in most states a spouse who abandons the other spouse is still entitled to an *elective share*. In most community property states if the couple separate, the earnings of both spouses continue to be community property until divorce. In California, earnings acquired after separation are not considered part of community property.

It is always a good idea for the lawyer to warn the client of the possibility of an elective share in estate planning, failure to do so may dismantle the estate and be ground for malpractice and recovery. The next case illustrates how a court, may elect for a surviving spouse to take against the will, when such is ascertained to be necessary for the support of the surviving spouse.

Estate of Cross
Supreme Court of Ohio, 1996
75 Ohio St. 3d 530, 664 N.E.2d 905

On August 23, 1992, Carroll R. Cross died testate (*leaving a will*) leaving his entire estate to his son, Ray G. Cross, who was not a child of the surviving spouse. At the time of his death, Beulah Cross, the surviving spouse, was apparently close to eighty years old, was suffering from Alzheimer's disease, and was living in a nursing home paid by Medicaid.[12] Due to Mrs. Cross's incompetency, she was unable to make an election under R.C. 2106.01 as to whether she should take against her husband's will. Therefore, pursuant to R.C. 2106.08, the probate court appointed a commissioner, who investigated the matter and determined that the court elect for Mrs. Cross to take her intestate share under R.C. 2106.06 and against the will. As a result of this election, Mrs. Cross would receive twenty five thousand dollars in spousal allowance and one-half of the net estate, which was approximately nine thousand dollars. Following a hearing before

---

[12] Medicaid is a government sponsored health insurance for the poor; in most cases eligibility is determined according to the income of the recipient and to be qualified, the recipient must meet the requirement of minimum income which varies from state to state.

a referee, Judge John E. Corrigan of the probate court elected for Mrs. Cross to take against decedent's will.

Decedent's son appealed the probate court's decision. While the appeal was pending, Mrs. Cross died the court of appeal with one judge dissenting, reversed, finding that the election to take against the will was against Mrs. Cross's best interest and was not necessary to provide her adequate support, since the cost of her nursing home care was already covered by Medicaid. Rosemary D. Durkin, administrator of the estate of Beulah Cross, filed a notice of appeal to this court (case No. 95-782,) as did intervenor, Cuyahoga County Board of Commissioners (Case No. 95-784).

FRANCIS E. SWEENEY. At issue in this case is whether judge Corrigan abused his discretion in electing for decedent Carroll Cross's surviving spouse, who depended solely upon Medicaid benefits for her support and care, to take against the will and under R.C. 2105.06. For the following reasons, we uphold the election made by Judge Corrigan for Mrs. Cross, and reverse the decision of the court of appeal.

REASONING & STATUTE

Where a surviving spouse is under a legal disability, the probate court is given the authority under R.C. 2106.08 to appoint a suitable person to ascertain the surviving spouse's adequate support needs and to compare the value of the surviving spouse's rights under the will with the value of her rights under the statute of descent and distribution. R.C. 2106.08 further provides that the court may elect for the surviving spouse to take against the will and under R.C. 2105.06 only if it finds, after taking into consideration the other available resources and the age, probable life expectancy, physical and mental condition, and present and reasonably anticipated future needs of the surviving spouse, that the election to take under 2106.06 of the Revised Code is necessary to provide adequate support for the surviving spouse during his life expectancy.

Prior to the amendment of former R.C. 2107.45 (now numbered R.C. 2106.08), effective December 17, 1986 the probate court made its determination of whether to elect to take under the will or against the will based upon which provision was better for such spouse . . . [13]

---

[13]   In essence the court based its decision on which provision was mathematically advantageous to the surviving spouse. However in passing R.C. 2106.08, the

In this case, the court of appeals determined that had Mrs. Cross been competent, she would have elected to take under the will, since her nursing home expenses were covered by Medicaid. However, in reaching this conclusion and in striking down the election made by Judge Corrigan for Mrs. Cross to take against the will, we believe that the court of appeals ignored Medicaid eligibility requirements and mistakenly relied on Ohio Adm. Code 5101:1-39-361 . . . [14] Since Mrs. Cross's spouse was deceased, Ohio Adm. Code 5101:1-39-361 is inapplicable to the facts presented here.

. . . Eligibility for Medicaid benefits is dependent upon a recipient's income or available resources . . . The term resources include property owned separately by the person, his share of family property, and property deemed to him from a parent or spouse . . . This also encompasses those resources in which an applicant/recipient has a legal interest and the legal ability to use or dispose of . . .

Mrs. Cross clearly had a legal interest in and the ability to use or dispose of her intestate share under her right to take against the will. Thus, she had available to her a potential resource for Medicaid eligibility purposes . . . [15] A basic tenet of public assistance is that all income must be explored prior to approving Medicaid. An individual, who does not avail himself of a potential income, is presumed to do so in order to make himself eligible for public assistance. Such non-utilization of income available upon request constitutes ineligibility . . .

As applied to this case, in order to maintain Mrs. Cross's Medicaid eligibility and to continue to have her nursing home expenses provided for by public assistance, Judge Corrigan was required to elect for Mrs. Cross to take

---

General Assembly moved away from a simple mathematical calculation, taking into consideration such factors as other available resources, age, life expectancy, physical and mental condition, and the surviving spouse's present and future needs. In either case, the probate court must ascertain what the surviving spouse would have done for her financial benefit had she been competent to make the decision herself.

[14] The code provides a method for determining Medicaid eligibility where one spouse is institutionalized and the other spouse is not but is instead a community spouse

[15] This is critical to the facts presented, since the Medicaid rules specifically state that the non-utilization of available income renders a Medicaid applicant or recipient ineligible for benefits. Ohio Adm.Code

under the will. Mrs. Cross would receive no income and would be deemed for benefit for failing to avail herself of a potential income. Thus, the election to take against the will was necessary for Mrs. Cross's future support and met the requirements of R.C. 2106.08. We find that the probate court, by appointing a commissioner to investigate the matter, and by electing for Mrs. Cross to take against the will, was correct in its action. Through his decision, Judge Corrigan acted in the best interest of this surviving spouse and protected the interests of all litigants coming before him. Consequently, Judge Corrigan did not abuse his discretion in electing for Mrs. Cross to take against the will.

Accordingly, we reverse the judgment of the court of appeals and reinstate the judgment of the probate court.

QUESTIONS

(a) How rational is the decision of the probate court to elect for Mrs. Cross to take against the will, when there is a will that clearly express the intention of Carroll Cross? How does this decision conflict with the majority rule that the right to an elective share is a personal right that the surviving spouse should make without any form of cohesion?

(b) Is it reasonable to say the decision to elect against the will was made by the probate court to protect state asset (Medicaid resources) rather than serve the interest of the surviving spouse? Remember Mrs. Cross died while the appeal was pending so, why is the election still necessary? Is public policy served in electing for Mrs. Cross to take against the will?

(C) Assuming Carroll Cross and Beulah Cross were homosexuals, would the probate court have chosen to elect for Beulah Cross as it did in this case?

HOMOSEXUAL COUPLES

In re Estate of Cooper
New York Supreme Court
Appellate Division Second Department, 1993
187 A.D.2d 128, 592 N.Y.S.2d 797

MANGANO, P.J. The question to be resolved on this appeal is whether the survivor of a homosexual relationship, alleged to be a "spousal relationship", is entitled to a right of election against the decedent's will, pursuant to EPTL.5-1.1.[16] In our view, the question must be answered in the negative.

William Thomas Cooper died on February 19, 1988. The decedent died testate, leaving everything to the petitioner as a specific and residual legatee, with the exception of certain real estate, allegedly constituting over 80% of the value of the estate, which was left to a former homosexual lover of the decedent.

In support of the this proceeding to determine that he is entitled to exercise a right of election against the decedent's will, the petitioner alleged, *inter alia,* as follows:

I met William Cooper in 1984 from approximately the middle of 1984 until his sudden death from a congenital heart condition in February 1988 I lived with him in apartment 1, 183 Wyckoff street Brooklyn, New York in a spousal-type situation. Except for the fact that we were of the same sex, our lives were identical to that of a husband and wife. We kept a common home; we shared expenses; our friends recognized us as spouses; we had a physical relationship, of course, we could not obtain a marriage license because no marriage license clerk in New York will issue such a document to two people of the same sex . . .

"The only reason Mr. Cooper and I were not legally married is because marriage license clerks in New York State will not issue licenses to persons of the same sex . . .

However, unconstitutional the denial of the right to a marriage license to Mr. Cooper and Myself may have been, the court cannot undo that now that

---

[16]   The survivor of a homosexual relationship, allegedly to be a spousal relation-ship is not entitled to a right of election against the decedent's will pursuant to EPTL 5-1.1, since the legislature has expressly defined a surviving spouse as a husband and wife, and even in the absence of such express definition, an interpretation of the statute to the same effect would be warranted, given the fact that the language of a statute is to be construed according to its natural and most obvious sense and in accordance with its ordinary and accepted meaning. Although the court of appeals has held that same sex partners were family members for purposes of rent control regulations prohibiting certain evictions, that court subsequently held that a lesbian partner was not a parent under the Domestic Relations Law. Accordingly the term "surviving spouse" as used in EPTL 5-1.1 cannot be interpreted to include homosexual partners.

Mr. Cooper is deceased. Since the court, however, also is an instrument of the state . . . it cannot compound this unconstitutionality by saying that because we could not obtain a state issued marriage license, I cannot be recognized as a spouse by state court for the purpose of claiming spousal rights . . .

I ask this court simply to declare that if I can establish that Mr. Cooper and I, at the time of his death, were living in a spousal-type relationship, I am entitled to spousal rights, and the state-imposed unconstitutional impediment of making it impossible for two people of the same sex to obtain a marriage does not alter this.

Upon submission of opposing papers and an application to dismiss the petition by the executrix of Cooper's estate, Acting Surrogate Pizzuto held that a survivor of a homosexual relationship, alleged to be a "spousal relationship" was not entitled to a right of election against the decedent's will pursuant to EPTL. 5-1.1, stating *inter alia*: "This court holds that persons of the same sex have no constitutional rights to enter into a marriage with each other. Neither Due Process nor equal protection of law provisions are violated by prohibiting such marriages. Nor does Mr. Chin have any right or standing to elect against decedent's will.

II

The right of election by a "surviving spouse", insofar as is relevant to the facts at bar, is contained in EPTL 5-1.1 (C) (1) (B), as follows:

(C) Election by surviving spouse against wills executed and testamentary provisions made after August thirty-first, nineteen hundred sixty six . . .

(1) Where, after August thirty-first, nineteen hundred sixty six, a testator executes a will disposing of his entire estate, and is survived by a spouse, a personal right of election is given to the surviving spouse to take a share of the decedent's estate, subject to the following . . .

(B) The elective share is one-third of the net estate if the decedent is survived by one or more issue and, in all cases, one-half of such net estate.

We reject the petitioner's argument that he must be considered a "surviving spouse" within the meaning of the statute. "Generally, in the construction of the statutes, the intention of the legislature is first to be sought from a literal reading of the act itself or of all the statutes relating to the same general subject matter" . . . The legislature has expressly defined a "surviving spouse" in EPTL.5-1.2, as follows: "§ 5-1.2 Disqualifications as surviving spouse "(a) A husband and wife is a surviving spouse within the meaning, and for the purposes of . . . 5-1.1.

Indeed, even in the absence of any express definition of the term "surviving spouse", an interpretation of the statute to the same effect would be warranted. It well settled that "{t}he language of a statute is generally construed according to its natural and most obvious sense . . . in accordance with its ordinary and accepted meaning, unless the legislature by definition or from the rest of the context of the statute provides a special meaning" (McKinney's Cons Laws of NY, Book 1, Statutes § 94, at 191-194). An illustration of this latter approach may be ascertained from the reasoning of the Supreme Court of Minnesota in *Baker v. Nelson* (291 Minn 310, 191 NW2d 185).[17] . . .

We reject, as meritless the contention of both the petitioner and the *amicus curiae* that based on the court of appeals decision in *Brashi v Stahl Assocs Co. (74 NY2d 201),*[18] the traditional definition of the term "surviving spouse" must be rejected, and replaced with a broader definition which would include the petitioner . . . Specifically the court of appeals stated *(Brashi v. Stahl Assoc. Co., supra, at 211):* "the intended protection against sudden eviction should not rest on fictitious legal distinctions or genetic history, but instead should find its foundation in the reality of family life. In the context of eviction, a more realistic, and certainly equally valid, view of a family includes two adult lifetime partners whose relationship is long term and characterized by an emotional and financial commitment and independence. This view comport with both our society's traditional

---

[17] In that case, the court rejected an argument that the absence of an express statutory prohibition against same-sex marriages evinced a legislative intent to authorize such marriages. The Supreme Court of Minnesota held in this regard... "The statute which governs marriage employs that term as one of common usage, meaning the state of union between persons of the opposite sex. It is unrealistic to think that the original draftsmen of our marriage statutes, which date from territorial days, would have used the term in any different sense"...

[18] In *Brashi v. Stahl,* the court of appeals held that same-sex partners were "family members" for purposes of the rent control regulations at issue therein, prohibiting the eviction of family members upon the death of the tenant of record.

concept of family and with the expectations of individuals who live in such nuclear units".

However in matter of *Alison D. v. Virginia M. (155 AD2d 11, affd 77 NY2d 651)*, this court held, in an opinion and order subsequently affirmed by the court of appeals, that a lesbian partner was not a "parent" under *Domestic Relations Law § 70 (a)* and rejected, as totally misplaced (Matter of *Alison D. v. Virginia M., supra, at 15)* the argument that the holding in *Brashi v. Stahl Assocs. Co. (supra)*, compelled a different result.

Accordingly, the term "surviving spouse", as used, in EPTL 5-1.1 cannot be interpreted to include homosexual partners.

III

The petitioner and the *amicus curiae* argue that such a narrow definition of the term "surviving spouse" is unconstitutional as it violates the Equal Protection Clause of the state constitution. Specifically, they argue that this unconstitutional definition directly derives from and compounds, the state unconstitutional conduct in interpreting the relevant provisions of the Domestic Relations Law as prohibiting members of the same sex from obtaining marriage licenses (see, e.g., *Frances B. v Mark B., 78 Misc 2d 112: Anonymous v. Anonymous, 67 Misc 2d 982, supra)*.

It is well settled there are three standards that may be applied in reviewing equal protection challenges: strict scrutiny, heightened scrutiny, and rational basis review (*Cleburne v. Cleburne Living Ctr., 473 US 432, 440-441)*.

We note that Acting Surrogate Pizzuto correctly held that any equal protection analysis in the instant factual scenario is to be measured under rational basis standard, i.e., the legislation (or government action) is presumed to be valid and will be sustained if the classification drawn . . . is rationally related to a legitimate state interest (*Cleburne v. Cleburne Living Ctr., supra, at 440)*, and not by the more stringent standard of heightened scrutiny or strict scrutiny.

In *Baker v. Nelson (291 Minn 310, 191 NW2d 185, supra)*,[19] . . . These constitutional challenges have in common the assertion that the right to

---

[19]   In *Baker v. Nelson* the petitioners, both adult males, made application to the clerk of the County District Court for a marriage license pursuant to the relevant

marry without regard to the sex of the parties is a fundamental right of all persons and that restricting marriage to only couples of the opposite sex is irrational and invidiously discriminatory. We are not independently persuaded by these contentions and do not find support for them in any decision of the United States Supreme Court.

The institution of marriage as a union of man and woman, uniquely involving the procreation and, rearing of children within a family, is as old as the book of Genesis. *Skinner v. Oklahoma ex rel. Williamson, 316 U.S. 535, 541, (1942),* which invalidated Oklahoma's Habitual Criminal Sterilization Act on equal protection grounds, stated in part: Marriage and procreation are fundamental to the very existence and survival of the race. This historic institution manifestly is more deeply founded than the asserted contemporary concept of marriage and societal interests for which petitioners contend. The Due Process Clause of the Fourteenth Amendment is not a charter for restructuring it by judicial legislation.

The Equal Protection Clause of the Fourteenth Amendment, like the Due Process Clause, is not offended by the state's classification of persons authorized to marry. There is no irrational or invidious discrimination. Petitioners note that the state does not impose upon homosexual married couples a condition that they have a proved capacity or declared willingness to procreate, posing a rhetorical demand that this court must read such condition into the statute if same sex marriages are to be prohibited. Even assuming that such a condition would be neither unrealistic nor offensive under the *Griswold rationale*, the classification is no more than theoretically imperfect. We are reminded however, that "abstract symmetry" is not demanded by the Fourteenth Amendment.

The appeal from the Minnesota Supreme Court to the United States Supreme Court was dismissed for want of a substantial Federal question (*Baker v. Nelson, 409 US 810),* and as Acting Surrogate Pizzuto accurately

---

Minnesota statute. The clerk declined to issue the license on the sole ground that the petitioners were of the same sex, "it being undisputed that there were otherwise no statutory impediment to a heterosexual marriage by either petitioner. The Supreme Court of Minnesota rejected the petitioners' argument that a prohibition on same sex marriage denied them equal protection of the laws, holding (*Baker v. Nelson, 291 Minn, supra at 312-314, 191 NW2d, supra, at 186-187)*

noted (*Matter of Cooper, 149 Misc 2d 282, 284, supra)*: Such a dismissal is a holding that the constitutional challenge was considered and rejected. (*Hicks v. Miranda, 422 US 332.*)

The rational basis standard has also been applied in other similar instances where equal protection challenges have been raised to classifications based on sexual orientation (*High Tech Gays v. Defense Indus. Sec. Clearance Off.,895 F2d 563(9th Circuit 1990,)* in which the court, relying on the Supreme Court's ruling in (*Bowers v. Hardwick 478 US 186)* that homosexual activity is not a fundamental right, applied the rational basis standard, and rejected an equal protection challenge to a Defense Department policy of conducting expanded investigations into backgrounds of all gays and lesbian applicants for secret and top secret security clearance; see also, *Adams v. Howerton, 673 F2d 1036 (9th Cir. 1982.)* In which the court held that a citizen's "spouse" within the meaning of section 201 {b} of the Immigration and Nationality Act of 1952 {as amended}, *8 USC § 1151 {b}*, must be an individual of the opposite sex and that, in accordance with the rational basis standard, such a bar against an illegal homosexual "spouse" was not unconstitutional.

Based on these authorities, we agree with Acting Surrogate Pizzuto's conclusion that "purported {homosexual} marriages do not give rise to any rights . . . pursuant to . . . EPTL 5-1.1 {and that} n{o} constitutional rights have been abrogated or violated in so holding.

Accordingly, the order and decree is affirmed insofar as appealed from.

Ordered, that the order and decree is affirmed insofar as appealed from, with costs payable by the appellant personally.

NOTE: Some states have legislations granting same sex couples elective share rights: Hawaii for reciprocal beneficiaries; Vermont for civil union and California for domestic partners however, the situation in California is still facing opposition from activists against same sex marriage and it is still being debated in the legislature. There are also debates over granting same sex couples some rights in states like New York and New Jersey. Under the Defense of Marriage Act *1 U.S.C. § 7 (2004)* no state may be required under the *Full Faith and Credit Clause* of the constitution, to give effect to a same sex marriage, contracted in another state. § 3 provides that, for all purposes of Federal Law, the word "marriage" means only a legal union between one man and one woman as husband and wife, and the word "spouse" refers only to a person of the opposite sex who is a husband or a wife. The latter section thus deprives same-sex marriage couples (*assuming they are recognized by a state)* of the social security, tax, and welfare benefits of Federal Law.

NOTE: A third party has no obligation to support someone else's spouse, and property owned by a third party has never been part of someone else's spouse elective share estate. Thus when a third party, places that property in a trust, the property is not being removed artificially or otherwise from the elective share estate because, the property was never in the first place considered part of the estate.

NOTE: Once the amount of the elective share has been determined, when the surviving spouse elects against the will, she is usually credited or charged with the value of all interests given her by the will. If the amount of bequests to the surviving spouse does not satisfy the elective share, the difference must be made up either by pro-rata contributions from all the other beneficiaries who have taken from the estate or from the residuary estate.

The Doctrine of Waiver

Prenuptial Agreements: One question that comes up often is can the spouses agree to waive the elective share? The Uniform Premarital Agreement Act {UPAA} recognized the enforceability of premarital agreements. Under the Act, an agreement may be used to enforce waiver of the right to elective share. Meaning that, before marriage, a spouse may choose to waive his or her right to elective share of the other spouse's estate at death; this is known as the {*prenuptial agreement.}* Fundamentally, a properly executed prenuptial agreement is given the same effect of the law as in contracts, commercial or otherwise; such an agreement is presumed to be valid as long as no fraud or cohesion is involved. The spouse attacking the prenuptial agreement, has the burden of coming forward with evidence of fraud, which in the absence of facts indicating concealment, fraud will not be presumed.

Matter of Estate of Garbade
Supreme Court Appellate Division, New York, 1995
221 A.D. 2d 844, 633 N.Y.S. 2d 878

MERCURE, J.

Appeals (1) from an order of the Surrogate Court of Broome County (Mathews, S.), entered December 23, 1994, which *inter alia,* granted petitioners' motion for summary judgment, (2) from the judgment entered thereon.

Respondent and J. Robert Garbade (hereinafter decedent) were married on February 2, 1990. Each had been previously married and divorced. Decedent was a wealthy executive who owned his own construction company and had interest in other enterprises; respondent was unemployed and brought no assets to the marriage. Prior to the wedding, respondent and decedent executed a prenuptial agreement, under the terms of which each waived any right to, *inter alia,* maintenance, equitable distribution or community property rights with regard to assets titled in the name of the other, or of primary relevance here, an elective share of the other's estate. However, the agreement required decedent to maintain a $100,000 policy of insurance on his life for respondent's benefit.[20]

In July 1992, decedent died unexpectedly at the age of 52, survived by respondent and petitioners, his two sons. Petitioners thereafter qualified as personal representatives of decedent's estate. Notwithstanding her waiver and the fact that she received assets totaling approximately $340,000 by virtue of decedent's death, respondent filed notice of her election to take her share of decedent's estate pursuant to EPTL 5-1.1. Petitioners thereafter moved for summary judgment setting aside respondent's right of election as barred by the waiver contained in the parties' prenuptial agreement. In defense of the motion, respondent alleged that the waiver of her statutory right to elect against decedent's estate was procured by fraud, misrepresentation, duress, imposition or undue influence. Surrogate Court granted petitioners' motion and authorized the entry of judgment setting aside respondent's notice of election. Respondent now appeals.

We affirm. Fundamentally, "a duly executed antenuptial agreement is given the same presumption of legality as any other contract, commercial

---

[20] This is what may be called a life insurance policy meant to provide for the surviving spouse in the event the other spouse dies.

or otherwise.[21] It is presumed to be valid in the absence of fraud" (*Matter of Sunshine, 51 AD2d 326, 327, Affd 40 NY2d 875*) . . . Moreover, the party attacking the validity of the agreement has the burden of coming forward with evidence of fraud, which, in the absence of facts from which concealment may reasonably be inferred, will not be presumed (see, *Matter of Phillip, 293 NY 483, 490-491*) . . . In light of that standard, even crediting every factual allegation advanced by respondent and drawing the most favorable inferences therefrom, we agree with Surrogate Court that respondent has raised no legitimate triable issue as to whether the prenuptial agreement and, more to the point, respondent's waiver of her right to elect against decedent's estate was the product of fraud, misrepresentation, duress, imposition or undue influence.

Respondent presented evidence establishing at most that (1) it was decedent, and not she, who first raised the issue of a prenuptial agreement and requested that one be executed prior to the wedding, (2) the agreement was prepared by decedent's attorneys, at his request and in accordance with his direction, (3) the prenuptial agreement was executed only a few hours prior to the parties' wedding, (4) respondent did not seek or obtain independent legal counsel and the agreement was not read by her or to her before she signed it,[22] (5) respondent was not specifically advised that the agreement provided for a waiver of her right to elect against decedent's will, and (6) respondent was not furnished with a copy of the agreement.

At the same time, it is uncontroverted that (1) respondent readily acceded to decedent's request that they enter into a prenuptial agreement and willingly signed the instrument because she did not want any of decedent's money or property, she only wanted to be his wife, (2) respondent was advised to obtain the services of independent counsel, (3) respondent was given an adequate opportunity to read the instrument before she signed it, and (4) prior to executing the prenuptial agreement, respondent was provided with detailed disclosure of decedent's $2.5 million net worth.

In our view, respondent has established nothing more than her own dereliction in failing to acquaint herself with the provisions of the agreement

---

[21] Under the Uniform Prenuptial Agreement Act (UPAA) an agreement may be used to enforce waiver of the right of election (prenuptial agreement) the enforceability of such agreement is recognized by the Act.

[22] Note: The absence of independent counsel will not of itself warrant setting aside the agreement though one is required for each party.

and to obtain benefit of independent legal counsel. Although the dereliction may have caused her to be ignorant of the precise terms of the agreement, the fact remain that, absent fraud or other misconduct, parties are bound by their signatures (*Pommer v. Trustco Bank, 183 AD2d 976, 978*) . . . Further, the absence of independent counsel will not itself warrant setting aside the agreement . . . There being no competent evidence of fraud, respondent has merely resorted to reliance upon a number of innocuous circumstances (such as the fact that the wedding date was changed from February 14 to February 2, 1990 to accommodate a Florida trip, that decedent's attorney did not finish drafting the agreement until shortly prior to the wedding and, incredibly, that the parties went out to lunch before going to sign the agreement) to fuel speculation that fraud was practiced upon her . . . [23]

Respondent's remaining contentions have been considered and found lacking in merit.

Ordered, that the order and judgment are affirmed, with costs.

QUESTIONS: Under § 2-213 (a) of the Uniform Probate Code, the right of election of a surviving spouse and the rights of the surviving spouse to homestead allowance, exempt property, and family allowance, or any of them, may be waived, wholly or partially, before or after marriage, by a written contract, agreement, or waiver signed by the surviving spouse. Do you think a surviving spouse should be entitled to at least a one-third share of the estate based on marriage alone? Why do you think the contract theory is so strictly enforced? Could the respondent in the case of Garbade have qualified for a share of the estate despite the prenuptial agreement, if she had a child with the decedent? Assuming the surviving spouse was found to be pregnant with the child of the decedent immediately after the decedent's death, could this have given her right to a share of the estate despite the prenuptial agreement?

THE OMITTED SPOUSE: § 6561 of the Uniform Probate Code states that: If a testator fails to provide for his or her surviving spouse who married the testator after the execution of the will, the *omitted spouse* shall receive a share in the estate consisting of : (a) the one-half of the community property that belongs to the testator (b) the one half of the quasi community property

---

[23] See, *Matter of Zach, 144 AD2d 19, 21, supra.*

that belongs to the testator (c) a share of the separate property of the testator equal in value to that which the spouse would have received if the testator had died intestate, but in no event is the share to be more than one-half the value of the separate property in the estate.

NOTE: There are exceptions to § 6561 as stated above, for more on the exceptions please read § 6561 of the code and § 2-301 on premarital will entitlements of a surviving spouse.

The Widow's Share

One of the limitations on the power of a testator is the provision, found in the inheritance law of all states, forbidding the testator to disinherit his widow completely. The limitation is believed to have an economic justification. The husband's wealth at death is considered part of *the investment* and a product, in part, of the wife's work even though she had no income. By staying home she enables money that would have been spent on maids, nurses, and nannies to be saved thereby increasing the amount of money from the husband's income that can be saved. The husband's estate is simply the amount of savings in his name at his death; otherwise, it is part of the community property and belonged to the wife as well. The statutory provision forbidding the testator to disinherit his widow completely minimizes transaction costs. It demonstrates the economic basis for exempting from estate tax on the husband's estate a part-under current law the whole-of the wife's share of the estate. Some of the money she inherits from her husband represents an accumulation of her own earnings. Also she is likely to be an older person (based on the notion that women live longer than men), and should she die soon after her husband his estate would be subject to estate taxation twice in a short period.[24]

---

[24] See Posner: Economic Analysis of Law, 4th edition(1992) p.513-514

Chapter Four

DEVISES TO CHILDREN

The Adopted Child

Adopted child is entitled to all the rights and privileges of an actual child insofar as the adoptive parents are concerned, but adoption does not confer upon the adopted child more rights and privileges than those entrusted by natural child. Adopted child may not inherit from or through its natural parents.[25] Once a child is adopted, the rights of both the natural parents and relatives are terminated.[26]

Every state possesses the power to regulate the manner or terms by which property within its territory may be devise by will or by inheritance and to decide who shall or shall not be capable of receiving the property; the state may choose to deny the privileges altogether and may impose whatever restrictions it deemed fit and guidelines that must be followed for anyone to take by a will or inheritance. One of the major issues that arise is whether or not an adopted child can still take under the will of the natural parent. Who is the adopted child? How do we define children? And does the adopted child have the rights to claim under the will of the natural parents?

---

[25] *Code, Estates and Trusts, § 1-207 (a)*
[26] *Code, Family Law, §5-308*

Hall v. Vallandingham
Court of Special Appeals of Maryland
75 Md. App. 187, 540 A.2d 1162

GILBERT C.J. Adoption did not exist under the common law of England, although it was in use "{a} mong the ancient peoples of Greece, Rome, Egypt and Babylonia". M Leary and R. Weinberg, Law of Adoption (4th ed. 1979) 1; Lord Mackenzie, Studies in Roman Law, 130-34 (3rd ed. 1870); American and English Encyclopedia of Law (1887) 204, n. 9. The primary purpose of adoption was, and still is inheritance rights, particularly in "France, Greece, Spain and most of Latin America." . . . Since adoption was not a part of the common law, it owes it existence in this state, and indeed in this nation, to statutory enactments . . .

The first two general adoption statutes were passed in Texas and Vermont in 1850.[27] Maryland first enacted an Adoption Statute in Laws 1892, Ch. 244, and that law has continued in existence, in various forms, until the present time. The current statute, Maryland Code, Family Law Article Ann. § 5-308 provides, in part:

(b) {A}fter a decree of adoption is entered:
  (1) the individual adopted:
    (i) Is the child of the petitioner for all intents and purposes; and Notwithstanding Maryland law, a child who is eligible for social security survivor's benefits through a deceased natural parent under Federal Law does not lose eligibility for the continuation of those benefits because of a subsequent adoption. *42 U.S.C.,§402*
    (ii) Is entitled to all the rights and privileges and is subject to all the obligations of a child born to the petitioner in wedlock;

  (2) each living natural parent of the individual adopted is:
    (i) relieved of all parental duties and obligations to the individual adopted; and
    (ii) divested of all parental rights as to the individual adopted; and

---

[27] Leary and Weinberg, Law of Adoption, 1.

(3) *all rights of inheritance between the individual adopted and the natural relations shall be governed by the Estates and Trusts Article*

The applicable section of the Md Estates and Trusts Code Ann., § 1-207 (a), Provides:

> *"An adopted child shall be treated as a natural child of his adopted parent or parents. On adoption, a child no longer shall be considered a child of either natural parent, except that upon adoption by the spouse of a natural parent, the child shall be considered the child of that natural parent . . .* [28]

With the thumbnail of history of adoption and the current statute firmly in mind, we turn our attention to the matter *sub judice.*

Earl J. Vallandingham died in 1956, survived by his widow, Elizabeth, and their four children. Two years later, Elizabeth married Jim Walter Killgore, who adopted the children.

In 1983, twenty-five years after the adoption of Earl's children by Killgore, Earl's brother William Jr., died childless, unmarried, and intestate. His sole heirs were his surviving brothers and sisters and the children of brothers and sisters who predeceased him.

Joseph W. Vallandingham, the decedent's twin brother, was appointed personal Representative of the estate. After the Inventory and the First Accounting were filed, the four natural children of Earl J. Valladingham noted exceptions, alleging that they were entitled to the distributive share of their natural uncle's estate that their natural father would have received had he survived William . . . [29]

The orphan's court transmitted the issue to the Circuit Court for St Mary's County. That tribunal determined that the four natural children of Earl, because of their adoption by their adoptive father, Jim Walter Killgore, were not entitled to inherit from William M. Valladingham Jr.

---

[28]   Although the statute speaks in terms of the adopted child, the person adopted need not be a minor child

[29]   Est. & Trusts Art. § 3-104 (b)

Patently unwilling to accept that judgment which effectively disinherited, the children have journeyed here where they posit to us:

> *"Did the Trial Court err in construing Maryland's current law regarding natural inheritance by adopted persons so as to deny the appellants the right to inherit through their natural paternal uncle, when said Appellants were adopted as minors by their stepfather after the death of their natural father and the remarriage of their natural mother?"*

When the four natural children of Earl J. Valladingham were adopted in 1958 by Jim Killgore, then Md. Ann. Code art.16, § 78 (b) clearly provided that adopted children retain the right to inherit from their natural parents and relatives. That right of inheritance was removed by the legislature in 1963 when it declared: "Upon entry of a decree of adoption, the adopted child shall lose all rights of inheritance from its parents and from their natural collateral or lineal relatives" . . . [30] Subsequently, the legislature in 1969 enacted what is the current, above quoted language of . . . [31]

"{N}othing in this subtitle shall be construed to prevent the person adopted from inheriting from his natural parents and relatives . . .

The appellants contend that since the explicit language of the 1963 Act proscribing dual inheritance by adoptee was not retained in the present law, Est. & Trusts Art. § 1-207(a) implicitly permits adoptees to inherit from natural relatives as well as the adoptive parents.

It may be that the legislature may want to revisit this area of the law and determine explicitly whether adopted children may inherit via representation through a deceased natural parent.

The right to receive property by devise or descent is not a natural right but a privilege granted by the state . . . [32] Every state possesses the power to regulate the manner or term by which property within its dominion may be transmitted by will or inheritance and to prescribe who shall or shall not be capable of receiving that property. A state may deny the privilege

---

[30] Laws 1963, ch. 174.

[31] Est.&Trusts Art. § 1-207 (a). Laws 1969, Ch. 3, § 4(c)

[32] *Safe Deposit & Trust Co. v. Bouse, 181 Md. 351(1943)*

altogether or may impose whatever restrictions or conditions upon the grant it deems appropriate . . . [33]

Family Law Art. § 5-308 (b) (1) (ii) entitles an adopted person to all the rights and privileges of a natural child insofar as the adoptive parents are concerned, but adoption does not confer upon the adopted child more rights and privileges than those possessed by a natural child. To construe Est. & Trusts Art. § 1-207 (a) so as to allow dual inheritance would bestow upon an adopted child a superior status. That status was removed in Laws 1963, Ch. 174 which as we have said, expressly disallowed the dual inheritance capability of adopted children by providing that "the adopted child shall lose all rights of inheritance from its parents and from their natural collateral or lineal relatives." We think that the current statute, Est. & Trusts Art. § 1-207(a), did not alter the substance of the 1963 act which eliminated dual inheritance. Rather, § 1-207(a) merely "streamlined" the wording while retaining the meaning.

Family Law Art. § 5-308 plainly mandates that adoption be considered a "rebirth" into a completely different relationship. Once a child is adopted, the rights of both the natural parents and relatives are terminated . . . [34] Est. & Trusts Art. § 1-207(a) and Family Law Art. § 5-308 emphasize the clean cut severance from the natural bloodline. Because an adopted child has no right to inherit from the estate of a natural parent who dies intestate, it follows that the same child may not inherit through the natural parent by way of representation. What may not be done directly most assuredly may not be done indirectly. The elimination of dual inheritance in 1963 clearly established that policy, and the current language of § 1-207(a) simply reflect the continuation of that policy.

We hold that because § 1-207(a) eliminates the adopted child's right to inherit from the natural parent it concomitantly abrogated the right to inherit through the natural parent by way of representation.

"The legislative giveth, and the legislative taketh away"

Judgment affirmed

Costs to be paid by appellants.

NOTE: That most inheritance statutes draw no distinction between the adoption of a child and the adoption of an adult. Just as a child may be

---

[33] *Mager v. Grima, 49 U.S. 490, (1850)*

[34] *L.F.M. v. Department of Social Services, 67 Md. App. 379 (1986)*

adopted, so also an adult however, some distinctions may be drawn from state to state according to the statutes.

NOTE: That under 42 U.S.C § 402 a child, who is eligible for social security survivor's benefits through a deceased natural parent, does not lose eligibility for the continuation of those benefits because of a subsequent adoption. Why is this so? Is it proper to say this presents a conflict of law? What is the intent of the legislature in conferring such Federal rights; while under the state law, an individual adopted loses all inheritance rights from the natural parents?

NOTE: That because an adopted child has no rights to inherit from the estate of a natural parent who dies intestate, it follows that the same child may not inherit through the natural parent by way of representation. Also, an adopted individual is the child of his or her adopting parent or parents and not of his or her natural parents, but adoption of a child by the spouse of either natural parent has no effect on : (1) the relationship between the child and the natural parent or (2) the right of the child or a descendant of the child to inherit from or through the other natural parent and (3) inheritance from or through a child by either natural parent or his or her kindred is precluded unless the natural parent has treated the child as his and has provided support for the child.

NOTE: That the only persons who have standing to challenge the validity of a will, are those persons who would take if the will were denied probate. If the testator adopts a child, the testator's collateral relatives cannot contest the will on the ground that they would inherit by intestacy. However, the relatives, can attack an adoption decree on grounds of mental incapacity or undue influence which we shall discuss later.

NOTE: Uniform Adoption Act § 5-101 (a)(1) (1994) permits adult adoption, but bars the adoption of one's spouse and the intestacy of the foster parent.

NOTE: In the case of *Virtual Adoption*, the first essential of a contract for adoption is that it be made between persons competent to contract for the disposition of the child. {Some showing of an agreement between the natural and adoptive parents, performance by the natural parent in giving up custody, performance by the child in living in the home of the adoptive parents, partial performance by the foster parents in taking the child into their home and treating the child as their own} has been found enough to establish an adoption. Where one takes an infant into his home upon a promise to adopt such as his own child, and the child performs all the duties growing out of the substituted relationship, of parent and child, rendering years of service, companionship, and obedience to the foster parent, upon the faith that such foster parent stands in *loco* parent and that upon his death the child will sustain the legal relationship to his estate of a natural child, there is equitable reason that the child may appeal to a court of equity to consummate, so far as it may be possible the foster parent's omission of duty in the matter of formal adoption.

NOTE: Where a child has fully performed the alleged contract over the course of many years, or a lifetime and can sufficiently establish the existence of such contract to adopt, equity is required to enforce the contract over the objection, of the adopting parent's heirs that the contract is unenforceable because one person who consented to the adoption did not have legal authority to do so.

Posthumously Conceived Child

With the history of adoption currently in mind, what happens when a child is conceived after the death of one or both of the child's genetic parents? Does a child conceived posthumously have the right to inherit from the natural father even though the child was not conceived while the genetic parent was alive? Is a child conceived posthumously a marital child even though the child's parents might have been married when both alive? Remember that the devolution of real and personal property in intestacy is neither a natural nor a constitutional right, but a privilege which is conferred by state statute; may the state then confer such rights on a posthumously conceived child? You already know that under 42 U.S.C., § 402 a child who is eligible for social security survivor's benefits through a deceased natural parent does not lose eligibility for the continuation of those benefits because of a subsequent adoption; does this extend to posthumously conceived child? Does a posthumously conceived child enjoy the rights of natural children, under state law of intestate succession? These and many other questions are answered in the case of Woodward v. Commissioner of Social Security.

Woodward v. Commissioner of Social Security
Supreme Judicial Court of Massachusetts
435 Mass. 536, 760 N.E.2d 257 (2002)

Wife who was artificially impregnated by sperm of dead husband and gave birth to twin daughters applied for mother's and children's social security survivor's benefits. The Social Security Administration denied such benefits, and wife appealed. The United States District Court for the District of Massachusetts certified to the Supreme Judicial Court of Massachusetts the question of whether children enjoyed the inheritance rights of natural children under Massachusetts law of intestate succession. The Judicial Court, Marshall, C.J., held that children could inherit if wife established their genetic relationship with the decedent, and that the decedent consented both to reproduce posthumously and support any resulting child.

MARSHALL., C.J.

The United States District Court for the District of Massachusetts has certified the following question to this court . . .

If a married man and woman arrange for sperm to be withdrawn from the husband for the purpose of artificially impregnating the wife, and the woman is impregnated with that sperm after the man, her husband, has died, will children resulting from such pregnancy enjoy the inheritance rights of natural children under Massachusetts' law of intestate succession?"

We answer the certified question as follows: In certain limited circumstances, a child resulting from posthumous reproduction may enjoy the inheritance rights of "issue" under the Massachusetts intestacy statute. These limited circumstances exist where, as a threshold matter, the surviving parent or the child's other legal representative demonstrate a genetic relationship between the child and the decedent. The survivor or representative must then establish both that the decedent affirmatively consented to posthumous conception and to the support of any resulting child. Even where such circumstances exist, time limitations may preclude a claim for succession rights on behalf of a posthumously conceived child. Because the government has conceded that the timeliness of the wife's paternity action under our intestacy law is irrelevant to her Federal appeal, we do not address that question today.

The term "natural child" or "natural children" does not occur in any applicable Massachusetts statute. It is a term drawn from Federal legislation.[35] . . . defining the term" natural child" our inquiry is directed solely to the language of the applicable Massachusetts statutes . . .

The undisputed facts and relevant procedural history are as follows: In January, 1993, about three and one-half years after they were married, Lauren Woodward and Warren Woodward were informed that the husband had *leukemia*. At the time, the couple was childless. Advised that the husband's *leukemia* might have him sterile, the Woodwards arranged for a quantity of the husband's semen to be medically withdrawn and preserved, in a process commonly known as "sperm banking." The husband then underwent a bone marrow transplant. The treatment was not successful. The husband died in October, 1993, and the wife was appointed *administratrix* of his estate.

In October, 1995, the wife gave birth to twin girls. The children were conceived through *artificial insemination* using the husband's preserved semen. In January, 1996, the wife applied for two forms of Social Security survivor benefits: Child's benefits under 42 U.S.C. § 402(d)(1) . . . and mother's benefits under 42 U.S.C § 402(g)(1). At the time of his death, the husband was a fully insured individual under the United States Social Security Act.

The Social Security Administration (SSA) rejected the wife's claims on the ground that she had not established that the twins were the husband's "children" within the meaning of the Act {because} . . . they are not entitled to inherit from the husband under the Massachusetts intestacy and paternity laws . . . The administrative law judge reasoned that the children were not ascertainable heirs as defined by the intestacy laws of Massachusetts because they were neither born nor in utero at the date of the husband's death . . . He also found that the children could not inherit as the husband's children under Massachusetts intestacy law because the evidence failed to establish that the husband, before his death either acknowledged the children as his own or intended to contribute to their support . . .

The wife appealed to the United States District Court for the District of Massachusetts, seeking a declaratory judgment to reverse the commissioner's ruling.

The United States District judge certified the above question to this court because "{t}he parties agree that a determination of these children's

---

[35] See 42 U.S.C. § 416 (e) (1994)

rights under the law of Massachusetts is dispositive of the case and . . . no directly applicable Massachusetts precedent exists."

II

We have been asked to determine the inheritance rights under Massachusetts law of children conceived from the gametes of a deceased individual and his or her surviving spouse. We have not previously been asked to consider whether our intestacy statute accords inheritance rights to posthumously conceived genetic children. Nor has any American court of last resort considered, in a published opinion, the question of posthumously conceived genetic children's inheritance rights under other states' intestacy laws . . . Although the certified question asks us to consider an unsettled question of law concerning the paternity of children conceived from a deceased male's gametes, we see no principled reason that our conclusions should not apply equally to children posthumously conceived from a deceased female's gametes.

We are aware of only two cases that have addressed, in varying degrees, the question before us. *Hecht v. Superior Court, 16 Cal. App. 4th 836 (1993)*[36] . . . *In the matter of estate of Kolacy, 332 N.J. Super. 593, 753 A.2d 1257 (2000).*[37].

---

[36] In *Hecht v. Superior Court* the California Court of Appeals considered, among other things, whether a decedent's sperm was "property" that could be bequeathed to his girlfriend... In answering in the affirmative, the court noted, in dicta and without elaboration, that, under the provisions of California's probate code, "It is unlikely that the estate would be subject to claims with respect to any such children" resulting from insemination of the girlfriend with the decedent's sperm

[37] In the matter of estate of Kolacy, the plaintiff brought a declaratory judgment action to have her children, who were conceived after the death of her husband, declared the intestate heirs of her deceased husband in order to pursue the children's claims for survivor's benefits with the Social Security Administration. A New Jersey Superior Court judge held that in circumstances where the decedent left no estate and an adjudication of parentage did not unfairly intrude on the rights of others or cause "serious problems" with the orderly administration of estates, the children would be entitled to inherit under the state's intestacy law.

This case presents a narrow set of circumstances, yet the issues it raises are far reaching. Because the law regarding the rights of posthumously conceived children is unsettled, the certified question is understandably broad. Moreover, the parties have articulated extreme positions. The wife's principal argument is that, by virtue of their genetic connection with the decedent, posthumously conceived children must always be permitted to enjoy the inheritance rights of the deceased parent's children under our law of intestate succession. The government's principal argument is that, because posthumously conceived children are not "in being" as of the date of the parent's death, they are always barred from enjoying such inheritance rights.

Neither parties position is tenable. In this developing and relatively uncharted area of human relations, bright-line rules are not favored unless the applicable statute requires them. The Massachusetts intestacy statute does not. Neither the statute's "posthumous children" provision . . . nor any other provision of our intestacy law limits the class of posthumous children to those in utero at the time of decedent's death . . . On the other hand, with the act of procreation now separated from coitus, posthumous reproduction can occur under a variety of conditions that may conflict with the purposes of the intestacy law and implicate other firmly established state and individual interests. We look to our intestacy law to resolve these tensions.

Section 1 of the intestacy statutes directs that, if a decedent "leaves Issue," such "issue" will inherit a fixed portion of his real and personal property, subject to debts and expenses, the rights of the surviving spouse, and other statutory payments not relevant here. See G.L. c. 190, § 1. To answer the certified question, then, we must first determine whether the twins are the "issue" . . .

The intestacy statute does not define "issue". However, in the context of intestacy the term "issue" means all lineal (genetic) descendants, and now includes both marital and nonmarital descendants . . . The term "{d} escendant' has long been held to mean persons 'who by consanguinity trace their lineage to the designated ancestor.'" *Lockwood v. Adamson, 566 N.E. 2d 96 (Mass.1991)* . . .

The Massachusetts intestacy statute thus does not contain an express, affirmative requirement that posthumous children must "be in existence" as of the date of the decedent's death. The legislature could surely have enacted such a provision had it desired to do so. Cf. *La.Civ.Code Ann. Art. 939 (effective July 1, 1999)* ("A successor must exist at the death of the decedent") . . . We must therefore determine whether, under our intestacy law, there is any reason that children conceived after the decedent's death who are the decedent's direct genetic descendants-that is, children who "by consanguinity trace their lineage to the designated ancestor"—may not enjoy the same succession rights as children conceived before the decedent's death who are the decedent's direct genetic descendants.[38]

To answer that question we consider whether and to what extent such children may take as intestate heirs of the deceased genetic parent consistent with the purposes of the intestacy law, and not by any assumptions of the common law.[39]. In the absence of express legislative directives, we construe the legislature's purposes from statutory indicia and judicial decisions in a manner that advances the purposes of the intestacy law.[40]

The question whether posthumously conceived genetic children may enjoy inheritance rights under the intestacy statute implicates three powerful state interests: the best interests of children, the state's interest in the orderly administration of estates, and the reproductive rights of the genetic parent. Our task is to balance and harmonize these interests to effect the legislature's over-all purposes.

1.} First and foremost we consider the overriding legislative concern to promote the best interests of the children. "The protection of minor children, most especially those who may be stigmatized by their 'illegitimate status . . . has been a hallmark of legislative action and of the jurisprudence of this court . . . Repeatedly, forcefully, and unequivocally, the legislature has expressed its will that all children be "entitled to the same rights and protection of the law" regardless of the accidents of their birth . . . Among the many rights and protection vouchsafed to all children are rights to financial support from their parents and their parents' estates. {"It is the public policy of this commonwealth that dependent children shall be maintained, as completely as possible, from the resources of their parents, thereby relieving or avoiding, at least in part, the burden borne by the citizens of the commonwealth"); G.L. c.

---

[38] *Lockwood v. Adamson, supra.*

[39] See, *Cassidy v. Truscott, supra at 520-521, 192 N.E. 164.*

[40] *Haughton v. Dickinson, 196 Mass. 389, 391, 82 N.E. 481 (1907)*

191, § 20[41]; G.L. c. 196, § 1-3 (permitting allowances from estate to widow and minor children); G.L. c. 209C, § 14 (permitting paternity claims to be commenced prior to birth). See also G.L. c. 190, §§ 1-2, 5, 7-8 (intestacy rights).

We also consider that some of the assistive reproductive technologies that make posthumous reproduction possible have been widely known and practiced for several decades . . . In that time, the legislature has not acted to narrow the broad statutory class of posthumous children to restrict posthumously conceived children from taking in intestacy. Moreover, the legislature has in great measure affirmatively supported the assistive reproductive technologies that are the only means by which these children can come into being . . . . We do not impute to the legislature the inherently irrational conclusion that assistive reproductive technologies are to be encouraged while a class of children who are the fruit of that technology are to have fewer rights and protections than other children.

In short, we cannot, absent express legislative directive, accept the commissioner's position that the historical context of G.L. c. 190, § 8, dictates as a matter of law that all posthumously conceived are automatically barred from taking under their deceased donor parent's intestate estate. We have consistently construed statutes to effectuate the legislature's overriding purpose to promote the welfare of all children, notwithstanding restrictive common-law rules to the contrary . . . Posthumously conceived children may not come into the world the way the majority of children do. But they are children nonetheless. We may assume that the legislature intended that such children be "entitled," in so far as possible, "to the same rights and protection of the law" as children conceived before death.[42] . . .

{2} However, in the context of our intestacy law, the best interests of the posthumously conceived child, while of great importance, are not in themselves conclusive. They must be balanced against other important state interests, not the least of which is the protection of children who are alive or conceived before the intestate parent's death. In an era in which serial marriages, serial families, and blended families

---

[41] Establishing inheritance rights for pretermitted children
[42] See G.L. c. 209C, § 1.

are not uncommon, according succession rights under our intestacy laws to posthumously conceived children may, in a given case, have the potential to pit child against child and family against family. Any inheritance rights of posthumously conceived children will reduce the intestate share available to children born prior to the decedent's death. Such considerations, among others, lead us to examine a second important legislative purpose: To provide certainty to heirs and creditors by effecting orderly, prompt and accurate administration of intestate estate.

The intestacy statute furthers the legislature's administrative goals in two principal ways: (1) by requiring certainty of filiation between the decedent and his issue, and (2) by establishing limitation periods for the commencement of claims against the intestate estate. In answering the certified question, we must consider each of these requirements of the intestacy statute in turn.

First, as we have discussed, our intestacy law mandates that, absent the father's acknowledgment of paternity or marriage to the mother, a nonmarital child must obtain a judicial determination of paternity as a prerequisite to succeeding to a portion of the father's intestate estate. Both the United States Supreme Court and this court have long recognized that the state's strong interest in preventing fraudulent claims justifies certain disparate classification among nonmarital children based on the relative difficulty of accurately determining a child's direct lineal ancestor.

Because death ends a marriage, posthumously conceived children are always nonmarital children. And because the parentage of such children can be neither acknowledged nor adjudicated prior to the decedent's death, it follows that, under the intestacy statute, posthumously conceived children must obtain a judgment of paternity as a necessary prerequisite to enjoying inheritance rights in the estate of the deceased genetic father. Although modern reproductive technologies will increase the possibility of disputed paternity claims, sophisticated modern testing techniques now make the determination of genetic paternity accurate and reliable . . .

We now turn to the second way in which the legislature has met its administrative goals: the establishment of a limitations period for bringing paternity claims against the intestate estate. Our discussion of this important goal, however, is necessarily circumscribed by the procedural posture of this case and by the terms of the certified question.

However, in his brief to the court, the commissioner represented that he had informed the United States District Court Judge that the wife "had been advised that she need not address" the timeliness issue on appeal in light of a change in Federal regulations . . .

Nevertheless, the limitations question is inextricably tied to consideration of the intestacy statute's administrative goals. In the case of posthumously conceived children, the application of the one-year limitations is not clear; it may pose significant burdens on the surviving parent, and consequently on the child. It requires, in effect, that the survivor make a decision to bear children while in the freshness of grieving. It also requires that attempts at conception succeed quickly . . . [43] ("It takes an average of seven insemination attempts over 4.4 menstrual cycles to establish pregnancy"). Because the resolution of the time constraints is not required here, it must await the appropriate case, should one arise . . .

Finally, the question certified to us implicates a third important state interest: to honor the reproductive choice of individuals. We need not address the wife's argument that her reproductive rights would be infringed by denying succession rights to her children under our intestacy law. Nothing in the record even remotely suggests that she was prevented by the state from choosing to conceive children using her deceased husband's semen. The husband's reproductive rights are a more complicated matter.

In *A.Z. v. B.Z., 431 Mass. 150, 725 N.E. 2d 1051 (2000)* . . . [44] We recognized that individuals have a protected right to control the use of their gametes. Consonant with the principle identified in *A.Z v. B.Z., supra,* a decedent's silence, or his equivocal indication of a desire to parent

---

[43]   Cf. Commentary, *Modern Reproductive Technologies: Legal Issues Concerning Crypreservation and Posthumous Conception, 17 J. Legal Med. 547, 549 (1996)*

[44]   In *A.Z v. B.Z.,* the court considered certain issues surrounding the disposition of frozen preembryos. A woman sought to enforce written agreements between herself and her former husband. The wife argued that these agreements permitted her to implant frozen preembryos created with the couple's gametes during the marriage, even in the event of their divorce. We declined to enforce the agreements. Persuasive to us, among other factors, was the lack of credible evidence of the husband's "true intention" regarding the disposition of the frozen preembryos, and the changed family circumstance resulting from the couple's divorce.

posthumously, "ought not to be construed as consent"[45] . . . The prospective donor parent must clearly and unequivocally consent to not only posthumous reproduction but also to support of any resulting child . . . . ("The law places on men to consider carefully the permanent consequences that flow from an acknowledgment of paternity"). After the donor parent's death, the burden rests with the surviving parent, or the posthumously conceived child's other legal representative, to prove the deceased genetic parent's affirmative consent to both requirements for posthumous parentage: Posthumous reproduction and the support of any resulting child . . .

The two-fold consent requirements arise from the nature of affirmative reproduction itself. It will not always be the case that a person elects to have his or her gametes medically preserved to create "issue" posthumously. A man, for example may preserve his semen for myriad reasons, including among others: to reproduce after recovery from medical treatment, to reproduce after an event that leaves him sterile, or to reproduce when his spouse has a genetic disorder or otherwise cannot have or safely bear children. That a man has medically preserved his gametes for use by his spouse thus may indicate only that he wished to reproduce after some contingency while he was alive, and not that he consented to the different circumstance of creating after his death. Uncertainty as to consent may be compounded by the fact that medically preserved semen can remain viable for up to ten years after it was first extracted, long after the original decision to preserve the semen has passed and when such changed circumstances as divorce, remarriage, and a second family may have intervened . . . [46]

Such circumstances demonstrate the inadequacy of a rule that would make the mere genetic tie of the decedent to any posthumously conceived child, or the decedent's mere election to preserve gametes, sufficient to bind his intestate estate for the benefit of any posthumously conceived child. Without evidence that the deceased intestate parent affirmatively consented (1) to the posthumous reproduction and (2) to support any resulting child, a court cannot be assured that the intestacy statute's goal of fraud prevention is

---

[45] See Schiff, *Arising from the Dead: Challenges of Posthumous Procreation, 75 N.C. L.Rev. 901(1997)*

[46] See Banks, *Traditional Concepts and Nontraditional Conception: Social Security Survivor's Benefits for Posthumously Conceived Children, 32 Loy. L.A. L. Rev. 251 (1999).*

satisfied . . . Where conception results from a third-party medical procedure using a deceased person's gametes, it is entirely consistent with our laws on children, parentage, and reproductive freedom to place the burden on the surviving parent (or the posthumously conceived child's other legal representative) to demonstrate the genetic relationship of the child to the decedent and that the intestate consented both to reproduce posthumously and to support any resulting child.

The certified question does not require us to specify what proof would be sufficient to establish a successful claim under our intestacy law on behalf of a posthumously conceived child. Nor have we been asked to determine whether the wife has met her burden of proof. The record reveals that the administrative law judge repeatedly requested that the wife provide objective corroboration of her claim that the husband consented to father children after his death. The administrative law judge's opinion indicates that he was willing to consider "additional declaration or written statements from the decedent's family, {the wife's} family, financial records or records from the fertility institute that demonstrate any acknowledgment {of the children} made by{ the husband}." . . . In the wife's probate court action, however, the judge held the husband to be the "father" of the children, but did not make any specific finding to support that determination. Nor did he determine whether the husband intended to support the wife's children . . .

It is undisputed in this case that the husband is the genetic father of the wife's children. However, for the reasons stated above, the fact, in itself, cannot be sufficient to establish that the husband is the children's legal father for the purposes of devolution and distribution of intestate property. In the United States District Court, the wife may come forward with other evidence as to her husband's consent to posthumously conceive children. She may come forward with evidence of his consent to support such children. We do not speculate as to the sufficiency of evidence she may submit at trial . . .

III

As these technologies advance, the number of children they produce will continue to multiply. So, too, will the complex moral, legal, social, and ethical questions that surround their birth. The questions present in this case cry out for lengthy, careful examination outside the adversary process, which can only address the specific circumstances of each controversy that presents itself. They demand a comprehensive response reflecting the considered will of the people.

In the absence of statutory directives, we have answered the certified question by identifying and harmonizing the important state interests implicated therein in a manner that advances the legislature's over-all purposes. In so doing, we conclude that limited circumstances may exist, consistent with the mandates of our legislature, in which posthumously conceived children may enjoy the inheritance rights of "issue" under our intestacy law. These limited circumstances exist where, as a threshold matter, the surviving parent or the child's other legal representative demonstrates a genetic relationship between the child and the decedent. The survivor or representative must then establish both that the decedent affirmatively consented to posthumous conception and to the support of any resulting child. Even where such circumstances exist, time limitations may preclude commencing a claim for succession rights on behalf of a posthumously conceived child. In any action brought to establish such inheritance rights, notice must be given to all interested parties.

The Reporter of Decisions is to furnish attested copies of this opinion to the clerk of this court who will transmit one copy to the Clerk of the United States District Court for the District of Massachusetts.

NOTES AND QUESTIONS:

(1) In the decades since assisted reproductive technologies have become widely known and used, the law has not acted to narrow broad statutory class of posthumous children to restrict posthumously conceived children from taking in intestacy. The laws, however, has expressed its will that all children are entitled to equal rights and protection irrespective of accidents of birth. Can these statements be corroborated considering how the *Woodward* case is decided?

(2) The law requires the intent of the decedent donor of the gametes, to conceive posthumously and support the resulting child be established. Can one conclude that mere leaving of the sperm for preservation is enough to establish intent, to father a child posthumously and support the resulting child? Why do you think the court disagree without further evidence to establish decedent's intent?

(3) Note: That under the Uniform Parentage Act §707 (2002). If an individual who consented in a record to be a parent by assisted reproduction dies before placement of eggs, sperm, or embryos, the deceased individual is not a parent of the resulting child unless the deceased spouse consented in a record that if assisted reproduction were to occur after death, the deceased individual would be a parent of the child. Suppose a man gives his sperm to be preserved and agree in a statement on record to be the father of any child that may result but due to some medical circumstances, the wife could not give birth until 20 years later, should the child be barred from intestacy rights based on the time limitations expressed in the *Woodward* case? Must the state's interests always be allowed to outweigh that of the resulting child?

SURROGACY AND MOTHERHOOD

One of the problems the law has been called to resolve is that involving the question, who is the parent of a child born via *artificial insemination*[47] when both parent contracts to have an embryo, genetically unrelated to them implanted in a surrogate mom who, under the surrogate contract, carried and gave birth to a child? Normally, by consenting to procedure in which embryo, which consisted of egg and sperm that came from unidentified persons, was implanted in a surrogate, common law estoppel precluded intended parents from avoiding responsibility for support of the resulting child; and forms of artificial reproduction in which intended parents have no biological relationship with the child do not result in legal parentless. One, who consented, to such arrangement with the intent to be a parent, may not later come and deny responsibility for the child; such denial is considered against public policy which favors, wherever possible, the establishment of legal parenthood with the concomitant responsibility. Under the Artificial Insemination Statute, a husband is the lawful father of a child, when the child is unrelated to him genetically as long as the intent to be a parent is

---

[47] A process where a sperm is artificially inseminated in the ovum to create an embryo, for procreation: Technically, artificial insemination may be of two kinds: (a) It can be homologous, that is with the husband's *semen* or (2) without the husband's *semen* heterologous artificial insemination.

established. The same law applied to both intended parents, husband and wife, who contracted with surrogate who agreed to implantation of embryo. Surrogate motherhood can take many forms: there may be a genetic relation of both husband and wife to the child, or there may be no connection at all. In some cases there may be a genetic connection of one of the parents to the child however, there are conflicts where the law must step in and determine who is the legal parent or parents of the child.

Buzzanca v. Buzzanca
Court of Appeals, Fourth District, Division 3, California
72 Cal. Rptr. 2d 280 (1998)

INTRODUCTION

Jaycee was born because Luanne and John Buzzanca agreed to have an embryo genetically unrelated to either of them implanted in a woman-a-surrogate-who would carry and give birth to the child for them. After the fertilization, implantation and pregnancy, Luanne and John split up, and the question of who are Jaycee's parents came before the trial court.

Luanne claimed that she and her erstwhile husband were the lawful parents, but john disclaimed any responsibility, financial or otherwise. The woman who gave birth also appeared in the case to make it clear that she made no claim to the child.

The trial court then reached an extraordinary conclusion: Jaycee had no lawful parents. First, the woman who gave birth to Jaycee was not the mother; the court had-astonishingly-already accepted a stipulation that neither she nor her husband were the "biological" parents. Second, Luanne was not the mother. According to the trial court, she could not be the mother because she had neither contributed the egg nor give birth. And John could not be the father, because, not having contributed the sperm, he had no biological relationship with the child.

We disagree. Let us get right to the point: Jaycee never would have been born had not Luanne and John both agreed to have a fertilized egg implanted in a surrogate.

The trial judge erred because he assumed that legal motherhood, under the relevant California statutes, could only be established in one of two ways, either by giving birth or by contributing an egg. He failed to consider the substantial and well-settled body of law holding that there are times when fatherhood can be established by conduct apart from giving birth or being genetically related to a child. The typical example is when an infertile husband consents to allowing his wife to be artificially inseminated. As our Supreme Court noted in such a situation over 30 years ago, the husband is the "lawful father because he consented to the procreation of the child.[48]

The same rule which makes a husband the lawful father of a child born because of his consent to *artificial insemination* should be applied here-by . . . the same parity of reasoning that guided our Supreme Court in the first surrogacy case . . . [49] to both husband and wife. Just as a husband is deemed to be the lawful father of a child unrelated to him when his wife gives birth after *artificial insemination*, so should a husband and wife be deemed the lawful parents of a child after a surrogate, bears a biologically unrelated child on their behalf. In each instance, a child is procreated because a medical procedure was initiated and consented to by intended parents. The only difference is that in this case-unlike *artificial insemination*—there is no reason to distinguish between husband and wife. We therefore must reverse the trial court judgment and direct that a new judgment be entered, declaring that both Luanne and John are the lawful parents of Jaycee.

CASE HISTORY

John filed his petition for dissolution of marriage on March 30, 1995, alleging there were no children of the marriage. Luanne filed her response on April 20, alleging that the parties were expecting a child by way of surrogate contract. Jaycee was born six days later. In September 1996 Luanne filed a separate petition to establish herself as Jaycee's mother. Her action was consolidated into the dissolution case. In February 1997, the court accepted a stipulation that the woman, who agreed to carry the child, and her husband, were not the "biological parents" of the child. At a hearing held in March, based entirely on oral argument and offers of proof, the trial court determined that Luanne was not the lawful mother and therefore John could not be the lawful father or owe any support . . .

The trial judge said: "So I think what evidence there is, is stipulated to. And I don't think there would be any more. One, there is no genetic tie

---

[48]   See *People v. Sorenson 68 Cal. 2d 280 (1968)*

[49]   *Johnson v. Calvert 5 Cal. 4th 84 (1993)*

between Luanne and the child. Two, she is not the gestational mother. Three, she has not adopted the child. That, folks, to me, respectfully, is clear and convincing evidence that she is not the legal mother."

After another hearing on May 7, regarding attorney fees, a judgment on reserved issues in the dissolution was filed, terminating John's obligation to pay child support, declaring that Luanne was not the legal mother of Jaycee, and declining "to apply any estoppel proposition to the issue of John's responsibility for child support." Luanne then filed a petition for a writ of *supersedeas* to stay the judgment; she also filed an appeal from it. This court then granted a stay which had the effect of keeping the support order alive for Jaycee. We also consolidated the writ proceeding with the appeal.

In his respondent's brief in this appeal, John tries to intimate-though he stops short of actually saying it that Jaycee was not born as a result of a surrogacy agreement with his ex-wife. He points to the fact that the actual written surrogacy agreement was signed on August 25, 1994, but the implantation took place a little less than two weeks before, on August 13, 1994. The brief states: "At the time that the implantation took place; no surrogacy contract had been executed by the parties to this action."

Concerned with the implication made in John's respondent's brief, members of this court questioned John's attorney at oral argument about it. It turned out that the intimation in John's brief was a red herring, based merely on the fact that John did not sign a written contract until after implantation. Jaycee was nonetheless born as a result of a surrogacy agreement on the part of both Luanne and John; it was just that the agreement was an oral one prior to implantation. The written surrogacy agreement, John's attorney acknowledged in open court, was the written memorialization of that oral contract . . .

. . . John's signature on the written surrogacy agreement was not forged, or anything of the sort. His one trump card, finessed out only after repeated questioning and the importuning of one of our panel to articulate his "best facts," was this: John would offer testimony to the effect that Luanne told him that she would assume all responsibility for the care of any child born. Luanne alone would assume "the burdens of childrearing."

Therefore, even though there was no actual trial in front of the trial court on the matter, this appellate court will assume *arguendo* that if there had been a trial the judge would have believed John's evidence on the point and concluded that Luanne had indeed promised not to hold John responsible for the child contemplated by their oral surrogacy agreement

DISCUSSION

{1} Perhaps recognizing the inherent lack of appeal for any result which makes Jaycee a legal orphan, John now contends that the surrogate is Jaycee's legal mother; and further, by virtue of that fact, the surrogate's husband is the legal father. His reasoning goes like this: Under the Uniform Parentage Act (the Act), and particularly as set forth in § 7610 of California's Family Code, there are only two ways by which a woman can establish legal motherhood, i.e., giving birth or contributing genetically. Because the genetic contributors are not known to the court, the only candidate left is the surrogate who must therefore be deemed the lawful mother. And, as John's counsel commented at oral argument, if the surrogate and her husband cannot support Jaycee, the burden should fall on the taxpayers . . .

The law doesn't say what John say it says. It doesn't say: "The legal relationship between mother and child shall be established only by either proof of her giving birth or by genetics." The statute says "may," not "shall," and "under this part," not "by genetics." Here is the complete text of § 7610: "The parent and child relationship may be established as follows: (a) Between a child and the natural mother, it may be established by proof of her having giving birth to the child, or under this part (b) Between a child and the natural father, it may be established under this part. (c) Between a child and an adoptive parent, it may be established by proof of adoption."

The statute thus contains no direct reference to genetics (i.e., blood tests) at all. The *Johnson* decision teaches us that genetics is simply subsumed in the words "under this part . . ."[50]

. . . The point bears reiterating: It was only by a parity of reasoning from statutes which on their face, referred only to paternity that the court in *Johnson v. Calvert* reached the result it did on the question of maternity. Had the *Johnson* court reasoned as John now urges us to reason-by narrowly confining the means under the Uniform Parentage Act by which a woman

---

[50] In *Johnson v. Calvert, supra 5 Cal.4ʰ (1993)* the court held that genetics con-sanguinity was equally "acceptable" as "proof of maternity" as evidence of giving birth.

could establish that she was the lawful mother of a child to texts which on their face applied only to motherhood (as distinct from fatherhood)-the court would have reached the opposite result. In re *Marriage of Moschetta 25 Cal. App. 4th 1218 (1994)*[51] . . . Relying on *in re Zacharia D. 6 Cal. 4th 435 (1993)*. We observed that there may be times when the Act cannot be applied in a gender interchangeable manner . . .

. . . In addition to blood tests there are several other ways the Act allows paternity to be established. Those ways are not necessarily related at all to any biological tie. Thus, under the Act, paternity may be established by:

-   Marrying, remaining married to, or attempting to marry the child's mother when she gives birth;[52]
-   Marrying the child's mother after the child's birth or either consenting to being named as the father on the birth certificate (§ 7611, subd. (C) (1)) or making a written promise to support the child.[53]

A man may also be deemed a father under the Act in the case of artificial *insemination* of his wife, as provided by § 7613 of the Family Code. To track the words of the statute: "If under the supervision of a licensed physician and surgeon and with the consent of her husband, a wife is inseminated artificially with semen donated by a man not her husband, the husband is treated in law as if he were the natural father of a child thereby conceived." . . .

If a husband who consents to *artificial insemination* under Section 7613 is "treated in law" as the father of the child by virtue of his consent, there is no reason the result should be any different in the case of a married couple who consent to in *vitro fertilization* by unknown donors and subsequent implantation into a woman who is, as a surrogate, willing to carry the embryo in term for them. The statute is, after all, the clearest expression of past legislative intent when the legislature did contemplate a situation

---

[51]   *In re Marriage of Moschetta,* the court refused to apply certain presumptions regarding paternity found in the Act to overcome the claim of a woman who was both the genetic and birth mother.

[52]   See § 7611, subds. (a) and (b)

[53]   See § 7611, subd. (c) (2)

where a person who caused a child to come into being had no biological relationship to the child.

Indeed the establishment of fatherhood and the consequent duty to support when a husband consents to the *artificial insemination* is one of the well-established rules in family law . . .

In *Sorenson*[54], the high court emphasized the role of the husband in causing the birth, even though he had no biological connection to the child: "{A} reasonable man who . . . actively participates and consents to his wife's *artificial insemination* in the hope that a child will be produced whom they will treat as their own, knows that such behavior carries with it the legal responsibilities of fatherhood and criminal responsibility for nonsupport."[55] The court went on to say that the husband was "directly responsible" for the "existence" of the child and repeated the point that "without defendant's active participation and consent the child would not have been procreated." . . .

Indeed, in the one case we are aware of where the court did not hold that the husband had a support obligation, the reason was not the absence of a biological relationship as such, but because of actual lack of consent to the insemination procedure . . . {It would be "unjust" to impose support obligation on husband who never consented to the *artificial insemination*}.

It must also be noted that in applying the *artificial insemination* statute to a case where a party has caused a child to be brought into the world, the statutory policy is really echoing a more fundamental idea . . . That idea is summed up in the legal term "estoppel." Estoppel is an ungainly word from the Middle French . . . expressing the law's distaste for inconsistent actions and positions-like consenting to an act which brings a child into existence and then turning around and disclaiming any responsibility . . . .

{2} There is no need in the present case to predicate our decision on common law estoppel alone, though the doctrine certainly applies. The estoppel concept, after all, is already inherent in the *artificial insemination* statute. In essence, *Family Code section 7613* is nothing more than the codification of the common law rule articulated in *Sorensen*: By consenting to a medical procedure which results in the birth of a child—which the

---

[54] See *People v. Sorenson, supra, 68 Cal.2d 280*

[55] *Id. At p. 285, 66 Cal.Rptr.7, 437 P.2d 495, emphasis added.*

Sorensen court has held establishes parenthood by common law estoppel-a husband incurs the legal status and responsibility of fatherhood.[56]

John argues that the *artificial insemination* statute should not be applied because, after all, his wife did not give birth. But for purposes of the statute with its core idea of estoppel, the fact that Luanne did not give birth is irrelevant. The statute contemplates the establishment of lawful fatherhood in a situation where an intended father has no biological relationship to a child who is procreated as a result of the father's (as well as the mother's) consent to a medical procedure.

Luanne is the Lawful Mother of Jaycee, Not the Surrogate, and Not the Unknown Donor of the Egg

{3} In the present case Luanne is situated like a husband in an *artificial insemination* case whose consent triggers a medical procedure which results in a pregnancy and eventual birth of a child. Her motherhood may therefore be established "under this part," by virtue of that consent. In light of our conclusion, John's argument that the surrogate should be declared the lawful mother disintegrates. The case is now postured like the *Johnson v. Calvert* case, where motherhood could have been "established" in either of two women under the Act, and the tie broken by noting the intent to parent as noted in the surrogacy contract . . . . The only difference is that this case is not even close as between Luanne and the surrogate. Not only was Luanne the clearly intended mother, no bona fide attempt has been made to establish the surrogate as the lawful mother.

. . . John's attorney did not object when the trial court accepted a stipulation taking the surrogate and her husband out of this case. Accordingly, nothing in this opinion is intended to address the question of who might be responsible for a child when only the surrogate mother is available.

We should also add that neither could the woman whose egg was used in the fertilization or implantation make any claim to motherhood, even if she were to come forward at this late date. Again, as between two women who would both be able to establish motherhood under the Act, the *Johnson* decision would mandate that the tie be broken in favor of the intended parent, in this case, Luanne . . . .

---

[56] See *Sorensen, supra,* 68 Cal.2d at p. 285

There is a difference between a court's enforcing a surrogacy agreement and making a legal determination based on the intent expressed in a surrogacy agreement . . . By the same token, there is also an important distinction between enforcing a surrogacy contract and making a legal determination based on the fact that the contract itself sets in motion a medical procedure which results in the birth of a child.

In the case before us, we are not concerned, as John would have us believe, with the question of the enforceability of the oral and written surrogacy contracts into which he entered with Luanne. This case is not about "transferring" parenthood pursuant to those agreements. We are, rather, concerned with the consequences of those agreements as acts which caused the birth of a child.

{4} The legal paradigm adopted by the trial court, and now urged upon us by John, is one where all forms of artificial reproduction in which intended parents have no biological relationship with the child result in legal parentlessness. It means that, absent adoption, such children will be dependents of the state. One might describe this paradigm as the "adoption default" model: The idea is that by not specifically addressing some permutation of artificial reproduction, the Legislature has, in effect, set the default switch on adoption. The underlying theory seems to be that when intended parents result to artificial reproduction without biological tie the Legislature wanted them to be screened first through adoption system. (Thus John in his brief, argues that a surrogacy contract must be "subject to state oversight.")

The "adoption default" model is, inconsistent with both statutory law and the Supreme Court's *Johnson* decision. As to the statutory law, the Legislature has already made it perfectly clear that public policy (and, we might add, common sense) favors, whenever possible, the establishment of legal parenthood with the concomitant responsibility. *Family Code section 7570, subdivision (a),* states that "There is a compelling state interest in establishing paternity for all children." The statute then goes on to elaborate why establishing paternity is a good thing: It means someone besides the taxpayers will be responsible for the child: "Establishing paternity is the first step toward a child support award, which, in turn, provides children with equal rights and access to benefits . . .

In light of this strong public policy, the statutes which follow *section 7570, subdivision (a)* seek to provide a "simple system allowing for the establishment of voluntary paternity."

Section 7570 necessarily expresses a Legislative policy applicable to maternity as well. It would be lunatic for the Legislature to declare that establishing paternity is a compelling state interest, yet conclude that establishing maternity is not. The obvious reason the Legislature did not include an explicit parallel statement on "maternity" is that the issue almost never arises except for extraordinary cases involving artificial reproduction.

Very plainly, the Legislature has declared its preference for assigning individual responsibility for the care and maintenance of children; not leaving the task to taxpayers. That is why it has gone to considerable lengths to insure that parents will live up to their support obligations. (Cf. *Moses v. Superior Court 17 Cal.4ᵗʰ 396 (1998)* {noting Legislative priority put on child support obligations}. The adoption default theory flies in the face of that Legislative value judgment . . . .

John now argues that the Supreme Court's statement should be applied only in situations, such as that in the *Johnson* case, where the intended parents have a genetic tie to the child. The context of the *Johnson* language, however, reveals a broader purpose, namely, to emphasize the intelligence and utility of a rule that looks to intentions . . . .

This rule, incidentally, has the salutary effect of working both ways. Thus if an intended mother who could carry a baby to term but had no suitable eggs was implanted with an embryo in which the egg was from a donor who did not intend to parent the child, the law would still reflect the intentions of the parties rather than some arbitrary or imposed preference . . . .

In context, then, the high court's considered dicta is directly applicable to the case at hand. The context was not limited to just *Johnson*—style contests between women who gave birth and women who contributed ova, but to any situation where a child would not have been born "'but for the efforts of the intended parents.'"

Finally, in addition to its contravention of statutorily enunciated public policy and the pronouncement of our high court in *Johnson*, the adoption default model ignores the role of our dependency statutes in protecting children. Parents are not screened for the procreation of their own children; they are screened for the adoption of other people's children. It is the role of the dependency laws to protect children from neglect and abuse from their own parents. The adoption default model is essentially an exercise in circular reasoning, because it assumes the idea that it seeks to prove; namely, that a child who is born as the result of artificial reproduction is somebody else's child from the beginning.

In the case before us, there is absolutely no dispute that Luanne caused Jaycee's conception and birth by initiating the surrogacy arrangement whereby an embryo was implanted into a woman who agreed to carry the baby to term on Luanne's behalf. In applying the *artificial insemination* statute to a gestational surrogacy case where the genetic donors are unknown, there is, as we have indicated above, no reason to distinguish between husbands and wives. Both are equally situated from the point of view of consenting to an act which brings a child into being. Accordingly, Luanne should have been declared the lawful mother of Jaycee . . .

John Is the Lawful Father of Jaycee Even If Luanne Did Promise to Assume All Responsibility for Jaycee's Care

{5} {6} The same reasons which impel us to conclude, that Luanne is Jaycee's lawful mother also require that John be declared Jaycee's lawful father. Even if the written surrogacy contract had not yet been signed at the time of conception and implantation, those occurrences were nonetheless the direct result of actions taken pursuant to an oral agreement which envisioned that the fertilization, implantation and ensuing pregnancy would go forward. Thus, it is still accurate to say, as we did the first time this case came before us, that for all practical purposes John caused Jaycee's conception every bit as much as if things had been done the old fashioned way.[57]

{7} When pressed at oral argument to make an offer of proof as to the "best facts" which John might be able to show if this case were tried, John's attorney raised the point that Luanne had (allegedly, we must add) promised to assume all responsibility for the child and would not hold him responsible for the child's upbringing. However, even if this case were returned for a trial on this point (we assume that Luanne would dispute the allegation) it could make no difference as to John's lawful paternity. It is well established that parents cannot, by agreement, limit or abrogate a child's right to support.[58] . . .

---

[57] See *Jaycee B., supra*, 42 Cal.App.4ᵗʰ at p. 730

[58] See *In re Marriage of Ayo 190 Cal.App.3d 422(1987)*. There, a husband adopted his wife's son from a previous marriage, then the couple were divorced. A year after the dissolution, the son's natural father (despite the fact that he had already been adopted) started visiting him. In light of the natural father's

The rule against enforcing agreement obviating a parent's child support responsibilities is also illustrated by *Stephen K. v. Roni L. 105 Cal.App.3d 640 (1980)*, a case which is virtually on point about Luanne's alleged promise.[59]

There is no meaningful difference between the rule articulated in *Stephen K.* and the situation here-indeed, the result applies a *fortiori* to the present case: If the man who engaged in an act which merely opened the possibility of the procreation of a child was held responsible for the consequences in *Stephen K.*, how much more so should a man be held responsible for giving his express consent to a medical procedure that was intended to result in the procreation of a child. Thus it makes no difference that John's wife Luanne did not become pregnant. John still engaged in "procreative conduct." In plainer language, a deliberate procreator is as responsible as a casual inseminator . . .

---

renewed interest, and in settlement of some arrearages in the division of community property and child support by a lump sum payment, the parties entered into a written agreement in which the wife promised, as Luanne as allegedly promised in this case, to hold the husband "harmless" from any claims of any kind regarding her minor child." The agreement was filed as a written stipulation with the court and was even signed by the trial judge after the words, "it is so ordered." More than five years later the wife reneged on the agreement and sought to renew the husband's support obligation. The Appellate Court held that the agreement was invalid, reasoning that the "rights of the contracting parties under the agreements such as this one affecting children must yield to the welfare of the children.

[59]   In *Stephen K.*, a woman was alleged to have falsely told a man that she was taking birth control pills. In "reliance" upon that statement the man had sexual intercourse with her. The woman became pregnant and brought a paternity action. While the man did not attempt to use the woman's false statement as grounds to avoid paternity, he did seek to achieve the same result by cross-complaining against for damages based on her fraud. The trial court dismissed the cross-complaint on demurrer and the appellate court affirmed. The cross-complaint was "nothing more than asking the court to supervise the promises made between two consenting adults as to the circumstances of their private sexual conduct.

CONCLUSION

Even though neither Luanne nor John are biologically related to Jaycee, they are still her lawful parents given their initiating role as the intended parents in her conception and birth. And, while the absence of a biological connection is what makes this case extraordinary, this court is hardly without statutory basis and legal precedent in so deciding. Indeed, in both the most famous child custody case of all time, and in our Supreme Court's *Johnson v. Calvert* decision, the court looked to *intent* to parent as the ultimate basis of its decision. Fortunately, as the *Johnson* court also noted, intent to parent "'correlate{s} significantly'" with a child's best interests . . .

It is significant that even if the *Johnson* majority had adopted the position of justice Kennard advocating best interest as the more flexible and better rule . . . there is no way the trial court's decision could stand. Luanne has cared for Jaycee since infancy; she is the only parent Jaycee has ever known. It would be unthinkable, given the facts of this case and her role as a caregiver for Jaycee, for Luanne not to be declared the lawful mother under a best interest test.

As for the Father, John would not be the first man whose responsibility was based on having played a role in causing a child's procreation, regardless of whether he really wanted to assume it.

Again we must call on the Legislature to sort out the parental rights and responsibilities of those involved in artificial reproduction . . .

That said, we must conclude the business at hand.

(1) The portion of the judgment which declares that Luanne Buzzanca is not the lawful mother of Jaycee is reversed. The matter is remanded with directions to enter a new judgment declaring her the lawful mother. The trial court shall make all appropriate orders to ensure that Luanne Buzzanca shall have legal custody of Jaycee, including entering an order that Jaycee's birth certificate shall be amended to reflect Luanne Buzzanca as the mother.

(2) The judgment is reversed to the extent that it provides that John Buzzanca is not the lawful father of Jaycee. The matter is remanded with directions to enter a new judgment declaring him the lawful father. Consonant with this determination, today's ruling is without prejudice to John in future proceedings as regards child custody and visitation as his relationship with Jaycee may develop. The judgment

shall also reflect that the birth certificate shall be amended to reflect John Buzzanca as the lawful father.

Luanne has had actual physical custody of Jaycee from the beginning. Obviously, it would be frivolous of John to seek custody of Jaycee right now in light of that fact. However, as the lawful father he certainly must be held to have the right, *consistent with Jaycee's best interest,* to visitation. Our decision today leaves Luanne and John in the same position as any other divorced couple with a child who has been exclusively cared for by the mother since infancy.

And while it may be true that John's consent to the fertilization, implantation and pregnancy was done as an accommodation to allow Luanne to surmount a formality, who knows what relationship he may develop with Jaycee in the future? Human relationship are not static; things done merely to help one individual overcome a perceived legal obstacle sometimes become much more meaningful . . .

(3) To the degree that the judgment makes no provision for child support it is reversed. The matter is remanded to make an appropriate permanent child support order. Until that time, the temporary child support order shall remain in effect.

Luanne and Jaycee will recover their costs on appeal.

SAME-SEX COUPLES

In Adoption of *Tammy, 619 N.E.2d 315 (1993)* the court granted the adoption of the child, conceived by artificial insemination of Susan Love, a well known breast cancer surgeon, by her lesbian partner also a surgeon. The court concluded that adoption statute did not preclude joint adoption by unmarried same-sex cohabitants. The court held that both the natural mother and the adoptive mother had post adoptive rights and as a result the child could inherit as the heir of both the natural mother and the adoptive mother. It was in best interest of child to be adopted jointly by her biological mother and by woman with whom mother cohabitated; women had stable and committed relationship, both women participated equally and jointly in parenting child, child viewed both women as her parents, and, in addition to practical benefits, child would receive from legal recognition of her actual parental relationships, adoption would also allow her to maintain filial ties to mother's partner if mother predeceased partner or if mother and partner separated. A similar adoption was approved by the court in *re Jacob, 660 N.E.2d 397(1995)*.

ADOPTION OF TAMMY
Supreme Judicial Court of Massachusetts
619 N.E.2d 315 (1993)

GREANEY, Justice.

In this case, two unmarried women, Susan and Helen, filed a joint petition in the probate and Family Court Department under *G.L. 210§ 1 (1992 ed.)* to adopt as their child Tammy, a minor, who is Susan's biological daughter. Following an evidentiary hearing, a judge of the probate and Family Court entered a memorandum of decision containing findings of fact and conclusions of law. Based on her finding that Helen and Susan "are each functioning, separately and together, as the custodial and psychological parents of {Tammy}," and that "it is the best interest of said {Tammy} that she be adopted by both," the judge entered a decree allowing the adoption. Simultaneously, the judge reserved and reported to the appeals court the evidence and all questions of law, in an effort to "secure {the} decree from any attack in the future on jurisdictional ground." . . . We transferred the case to this court on our own motion. We conclude that the adoption was properly allowed under G.L. c.210 . . .

{1}{2}We summarize the relevant facts as found by the judge. Helen and Susan have lived together in a committed relationship, which they considered to be permanent, for more than ten years. In June 1983, they *jointly* purchased a house in Cambridge. Both women are physicians specializing in surgery. At the time the petition was filed, Helen maintained a private practice in general surgery at Mount Auburn Hospital and Susan, a nationally recognized expert in the field of *breast cancer*, was director of the Faulkner Breast Center and a surgical oncologist at the Dana Farber Cancer Institute. Both women also held positions on the faculty of Harvard Medical School.

For several years prior to the birth of Tammy, Helen and Susan planned to have a child, biologically related to both of them, whom they will jointly parent. Helen first attempted to conceive a child through artificial insemination by Susan's brother. When those efforts failed, Susan successfully conceived a child through artificial insemination by Helen's biological cousin, Francis. The women attended childbirth classes together and Helen was present when Susan gave birth to Tammy on April 30, 1988. Although Tammy's birth certificate reflects Francis as her biological father, she was given a hyphenated surname using Susan and Helen's last names.

Since her birth, Tammy has lived with, and been raised and supported by, Helen and Susan. Tammy views both women as her parents, calling Helen "mama" and Susan "mommy." . . . Both women jointly and equally participate in parenting Tammy, and both have a strong financial commitment to her . . . . Francis does not participate in parenting Tammy and does not support her. His intention was to assist Helen and Susan in having a child, and he does not intend to be involved with Tammy, except as a distance relative. Francis signed an adoption surrender and supports the joint adoption by both women.

Helen and Susan, recognizing that the laws of the commonwealth do not permit them to enter into a legally cognizable marriage, believe that the best interests of Tammy require legal recognition of her identical emotional relationship to both women. Susan expressed her understanding that it may not be in her own long—term interest to permit Helen to adopt Tammy because, in the event that Helen and Susan separate, Helen would have equal rights to primary custody. Susan indicated, however, that she has no reservation about allowing Helen to adopt. Apart from the emotional and current practical ramifications which legal recognition of the reality of her parental relationships will provide Tammy, Susan indicated that the adoption is important for Tammy in terms of potential inheritance from Helen. Helen and her living issues are the beneficiaries of three irrevocable family trusts. Unless Tammy is adopted, Helen's share of the trusts may pass to others. Although Susan and Helen have established a substantial trust fund for Tammy, it is comparatively small in relation to Tammy's potential inheritance under Helen's family trusts.

Over a dozen witnesses, including mental health professionals, teachers, colleagues, neighbors, and blood relatives and priest and nun, testified to the fact that Helen and Susan participate equally in raising Tammy, that Tammy relates to both women as her parents, and that the three form a healthy, happy, and stable family unit . . .

The Department of Social Services (department) conducted a home study in connection with the adoption petition which recommended the adoption, concluding that "the petitioners and their home are suitable for the proper rearing of this child." . . .

{3} {4} Despite the overwhelming support for the joint adoption and the judge's conclusion that joint adoption is clearly in Tammy's best interests, the question remains whether there is anything in the law of the commonwealth that would prevent this adoption. The law of adoption is purely statutory,[60]and the governing statute, G.L. c. 210 (1992 ed.), is to be strictly followed in all its essential particulars.[61] To the extent that any ambiguity or vagueness exists in the statute, judicial construction should enhance, rather than defeat, its purpose . . . The primary purpose of the adoption statute, particularly with regard to children under the age of fourteen, is undoubtedly the advancement of the best interests of the subject child . . . "It is the right of the children that is protected by this statute . . . The first and paramount duty is to consult the welfare of the child". With these considerations in mind, we examine the statute to determine whether adoption in the circumstances of this case is permitted.

1. The initial question is whether the probate court judge had jurisdiction under G.L. c. 210 to enter judgment on a joint petition for adoption brought by two unmarried cohabitants in the petitioners' circumstances. We answer the question in the affirmative.

{5}There is nothing on the face of the statute which precludes the joint adoption of a child by two unmarried cohabitants such as the petitioners. Chapter 210 § 1, provides that "{a} person of full age may petition the probate court in the county where he resides for leave to adopt as his child another person younger than himself, unless such other person, is his or her wife or husband, or brother, sister, uncle or aunt, of the whole or half blood." Other than requiring that a spouse join in the petition, if the petitioner is married and the spouse is competent to join therein, the statute does not expressly prohibit or require joinder by any person. Although the singular "a person" is used, it is a legislatively mandated rule of statutory construction that "{w}ords importing the singular number may extend and be applied

---

[60] See *Davis v. McGraw, 206 Mass. 294 (1910)*

[61] See *Purinton v. Jamrock, 195 Mass. 187 (1907)*

to several persons" unless the resulting construction is "inconsistent with the manifest intent of the law making body or repugnant to the context of the same statute." . . . In the context of adoption, where the legislative intent to promote the best interests of the child is evidenced throughout the governing statute, and the adoption of a child by two unmarried individual accomplishes that goal, construing the term "person" as "persons" clearly enhances, rather than defeats, the purpose of the statute. Furthermore, it is apparent from the first sentence of G.L. c. 210, § 1, that the legislature considered and defined those combinations of persons which would lead to adoptions in violation of public policy. Clearly absent is any prohibition of adoption by two unmarried individuals like the petitioners.

There is no question that Helen and Susan each individually satisfy the identity requirements of G.L. c. 210, § 1. Although the adoption statute, as it first appeared (St. 1851, c. 324) precluded a person from adopting his or her own child by birth, the statute was amended to permit adoption by the child's natural parents. *Curran, petition of, 314 Mass. 91, 49 N.E.2d 432 (1943)* (natural mother of child born out of wedlock proper party to adoption petition). None of the prohibitions to adoption set forth in § 1 is applicable. Furthermore, there is nothing in the statute that prohibits adoption based on gender or sexual orientation . . .

The provision concerning joinder of spouses is a requirement that has been present in the statute since its enactment in 1851.[62] Adoption by a married person has the effect of changing the legal duties of both spouses because the "infant who is adopted becomes the child not of one but of both." *Lee v. Wood, 279 Mass. 293, 295 (1932)*. Both spouses must freely consent to join in the adoption petition. *Phillips v. Chase, 203 Mass. 556, 565 (1909)*. If a person falsely claims to be the legal spouse of another, the probate court may vacate the adoption decree.[63]

The required joinder of spouses which is jurisdictional in nature, see *Mitchell v. Mitchell, 312 Mass. 154 (1943)* . . . does not by its terms apply to joint petitions by unmarried persons who seek to adopt.[64] . . .

---

[62] See St.1851, c. 324, § 4 ("No petition by a person having a lawful wife shall be allowed unless such wife shall join therein, and no woman having a lawful husband shall be competent to present and prosecute such petition").

[63] See *Lee v. Wood, supra, 279 Mass. at 296, 181 N.E. 229.*

[64] See *Adoption of B.L.V.B., 628 A.2d 1271 (Vt.1993)* (requirement of joinder of

While the legislature may not have envisioned adoption by same-sex partners, there is no indication that it attempted to define all possible categories of persons leading to adoptions in the best interests of children. Rather than limit the potential categories of persons entitled to adopt (other than those described in the first sentence of § 1), the legislature used general language to define who may adopt and who may be adopted. The probate court has thus been granted jurisdiction to consider a variety of adoption petitions . . .

. . . By permitting adoption by unmarried persons, the legislature clearly sanctioned adoption into "non-standard" families. Moreover, the legislature could easily have contemplated circumstances leading to adoption by more than one unmarried party, albeit in circumstances different from this case. For example, orphaned children are frequently taken in and raised by relatives, who may be unmarried siblings, aunts or uncles, or cousins of their parents.[65]

FN5. General Laws. C. 210, § 2 (1992 ed.), provides in relevant part: "A decree of adoption shall not be made, except as provided in this chapter, without the written consent of the child to be adopted, if above the age of twelve; of the child's spouse, if any; of the lawful parents who may be previous adoptive parents, or surviving parent; or of the mother only if the child was born out of wedlock and not previously adopted. A person whose consent is hereby required shall not be prevented from being the adoptive parent." Susan's request to adopt her own child and her consent to Helen's adoption of Tammy satisfies the statute. Although not required by the statute, Francis, the biological father, has provided his written consent to the joint adoption.

The written consent of the child's natural parents is not required if the court has terminated the natural parent's legal rights to the child because there has been a showing by clear and convincing evidence that the natural parents are unfit. G.L. c. 210, § 3 (1992 ed.).

A decree of adoption may not be entered unless one of five preconditions set forth in G.L. c. 210, § 2A, is satisfied. These preconditions include a

---

spouses in Vermont adoption statute does not bar adoption by same-sex partner of children's natural mother)

[65] See *Merrill v. Berlin, 316 Mass. 87 (1944)* Court found that it was in the best interests of two orphaned boys to be raised by their deceased mother's aunt and two female cousins, despite the "wholly feminine" nature of the household.

showing that "the petitioner is a blood relative of the child sought to be adopted" or that "{t}he petition for adoption has been approved in writing by the department of social services or by an agency authorized by said department." Because both Susan and Helen are blood relatives of Tammy, and the department has approved the adoption, two of the preconditions have been satisfied in this case.

The judge is directed to consider "all factors relevant to the physical, mental and moral health of the child" and a decree of adoption may be entered only after the judge has determined that the adopting parties are "of sufficient ability to bring up the child and provide suitable support and education for it, and that the child should be adopted." G.L. c. 210, §§ 5B, 6. Additionally, we have stated, with regard to establishing the status of legal parent, that the judge "must look at the relationship {between the parent and the child} as a whole, and consider emotional bonds, economic support, custody of the child, the extent of personal association, the commitment of the {parent's} to attending to the child's needs, the consistency of the {parent's} expressed interest . . . and any other factors which bear on the nature of the alleged parent-child relationship." *C.C. v. A.B., 406 Mass. 679 (1990).*

In this case all requirements in §§ 2 and 2A are met, and there is no question that the judge's findings demonstrate that the directives set forth in §§ 5B and 6, and in case law, have been satisfied. Adoption will not result in any tangible change in Tammy's daily life; it will, however, serve to provide her with a significant legal relationship which may be important in her future. At the most practical level, adoption will entitle Tammy to inherit from Helen's family trusts and from Helen and her family under the *law of intestate succession* (G.L. c. 210, § 6), to receive support from Helen, who will be legally obligated to provide such support (G.L. c. 209C, § 9; G.L. c. 273, § 1 {1992 ed.}), to be eligible for coverage under Helen's health insurance policies, and to be eligible for social security benefits in the event of Helen's disability or death (42 U.S.C. § 402{d} {1988}).

Of equal, if not greater significance, adoption will enable Tammy to preserve her unique filial ties to Helen in the event that Helen and Susan separate, or Susan predeceases Helen. As the case law and commentary on the subject illustrate, when the functional parents of children born in circumstances similar to Tammy separate or one dies, the children often remain in legal limbo for years while their future is disputed in the courts. *Polikoff*, this child does have two mothers: Redefining Parenthood to Meet the Needs of Children in Lesbian-Mother and Other Nontraditional Families, *78 Geo.J.L. 459, 508-522 (1990);* Comment, Second Parent Adoption for Lesbian-Parented Families: Legal Recognition of the Other Mother, *19 U.C.Davis L.Rev. 729(1986).* In some cases, children have been denied the affection of a functional parent who has been with them since birth, even when it is apparent that this outcome is contrary to the children's best interests. Adoption serves to establish legal rights and responsibilities so that, in the event that problems arise in the future, issues of custody and visitation may be promptly resolved by reference to the best interests of the child within the recognized framework of the law . . . . There is no jurisdictional bar in the statute to the judge's consideration of this joint petition. The conclusion that the adoption is in the best interests of Tammy is also well warranted.

Although Susan has designated Helen guardian of Tammy in her will, Helen's custody of Tammy could conceivably be contested in the event of Susan's death, particularly by Francis, members of his family or members of Susan's family. Absent adoption, Helen would not have a dispositive legal right to retain custody of Tammy because she would be a "legal stranger" to the child.

Cases from other jurisdictions demonstrate the difficulties resulting from the lack of an established legal relationship between a child and its second functional parent . . . . [66]

2. The judge also posed the question whether, pursuant to G.L. c. 210, § 6 (1992 ed.), Susan's legal relationship to Tammy must be terminated if Tammy is adopted. Section 6 provides that, on entry of an adoption decree, "all rights, duties and other legal consequences of the natural relation of child and parent shall . . . except as regards marriage, incest or cohabitation, terminate between the child so adopted and his natural parents and kindred." Although G.L c. 210, § 2, clearly permits

---

[66]   In re the *Interest of Z.J.H., Wis.2d 1002 (1991)*(former lesbian partner of child's adoptive mother, who had planned on adoption, cultivated "parent like" relationship with child since his birth, and has been child's primary caretaker, denied both visitation and custody after partners' separation due to lack of legal relationship with child; court refused to consider issues of child's best interests)

a child's natural parent to be an adoptive parent, § 6 does not contain any express exceptions to its termination provision. The Legislature obviously did not intend that a natural parent's legal relationship to its child be terminated when the natural parent is a party to the adoption petition.

Section 6 clearly is directed to the more usual circumstances of adoption, where the child is adopted by persons who are not the child's natural parents (either because the natural parents have elected to relinquish the child for adoption or their parental rights have been involuntarily terminated). The purpose of the termination provision is to protect the security of the child's newly created family unit by eliminating involvement with the child's natural parents. Although it is not uncommon for a natural parent to join in the adoption petition of a spouse who is not the child's natural parent, see, e.g., *Adoption of a Minor (No 1), 367 Mass. 907(1975),* the statute has never been construed to require the termination of the natural parent's legal relationship to the child in these circumstances. Nor has § 6 been construed to apply when the natural mother petitions alone to adopt her child born out of wedlock.[67] Reading the adoption statute as a whole, we conclude that the termination provision contained in § 6 was intended to apply only when the natural parents (or parent) are not parties to the adoption petition . . .

3. We conclude that the probate court has jurisdiction to enter a decree on a joint adoption petition brought by the two petitioners when the judge has found that joint adoption is in the subject child's best interests. We further conclude that, when a natural parent is a party to a joint adoption petition, the parent's legal relationship to the child does not terminate on entry of the adoption decree.
4. So much of the decree as allows the adoption of Tammy by both petitioners is affirmed. So much of the decree as provides in the alternative for the adoption of Tammy by Helen and the retention of rights of custody and visitation by Susan is vacated.

So ordered.
Dissenting Opinion omitted.

---

[67] See *Curran, petitioner, 314 Mass. 91 (1943)*

NOTES AND QUESTIONS

1. Note: that the courts in both cases {*Buzzanca and Adoption of Tammy*} based their decisions on the *best interests of the child*; are the policies the same as govern inheritance?

2. Note: that *G.L.c. 210, § 6* provides that on entry of an adoption decree, all rights, duties and other legal consequences of the natural relation of child and parent shall terminate between the child and his natural parent. Why is Susan able to retain parental rights despite adoption by Helen? Why would the court assume or conclude that section 6 is directed to the more usual circumstances where the child is adopted by persons who are not the child's natural parents?

3. Do you think as concluded by the court, that it is the legislature's intent to allow the natural parent to keep parental rights in certain circumstances, while the same rights are taken away from the natural parents in other circumstances of adoption? Is it proper to conclude the court, may have misinterpreted legislative intent?

4. Is it proper to argue that the court's ruling on the adoption of Tammy violates equal protection of the constitution, by allowing the natural parent in a cohabitation to keep parental rights while denying such rights to heterosexual couples in other circumstances of adoption?

5. Do you think the court's decision in the adoption of Tammy is consistent with statutory language? If not is the ruling justified by a decision to achieve what is in the best interests of the child?

6. What about the argument that the child's best interests can be accommodated without doing violence to the statute, by accepting the alternative to joint adoption suggested by the probate court judge; that is, permitting Helen to adopt Tammy while allowing Susan to retain her parental rights and obligations. Is such accommodation probable and consistent with the language of the statute?

7. Is it right to conclude that the court through its decision, allowing Susan to retain her parental rights endorsed or gave legal status to a homosexual relationship which our elected representatives and general public have, as yet, failed to endorse?

8. What do you think about the argument that the court has interpreted the statute as permitting a biological parent of full age to petition for the adoption of his or her own child? Is there anything in the

statute indicating a legislative intent to allow two or more unmarried persons jointly to petition for adoption?

9. Do you think there is anything in the statute based on sexual orientation, which would prohibit a homosexual from singly adopting a child? Should a parent be deprived of parental rights just because he or she is a homosexual?

10. Think about a law prohibiting homosexuals from adopting, can such a law pass constitutional challenges?

11. Note: that in the *Buzzanca* case, one of the considerations of the court is based on the legal doctrine of *estoppel*. Is it proper to conclude that when Luanne and John agreed to have an embryo genetically unrelated to either of them implanted in a surrogate, Luanne, relied on the agreement, that the reliance was reasonable, and that Luanne indeed performed by participating in the procedure of artificial insemination of the surrogate. Do you think Luanne's reliance, the reasonableness of her reliance, and her performance satisfy the requirements of *estoppel*? NOTE: In England, the law of parentage of children born through a surrogacy arrangement is different from in the United States. "Where a child is born as a result of surrogacy arrangements, who are his/her, parents? Legally the child's mother will always be the surrogate; the woman of the commissioning couple is not the mother even if her eggs were used. Where the surrogate is married, her husband is the father unless he can prove that he did not consent to the procedure and the man of the commissioning couple is not the father even if his sperm is used." In order for the genetic mother to become the legal mother, she must legally adopt the child.[68]

The Doctrine of Advancement

In order to take in the intestate distribution of the deceased parent's estate, a child (beneficiary) must allow the administrator of the estate to count as part of the distribution shares the value of any property real or personal that the decedent, while alive, gave the child by way of *advancement*. In

---

[68]   See Principles of Medical Law 602-603 (Ian Kennedy & Andrew Grubb eds., 1998)

England, by common law, any gift the child received during the life of the parent is considered an advancement and a prepayment of the child's intestate share. The purpose of the doctrine is to ensure equality among the heirs and beneficiaries. The idea is that true equality can be accomplished only if gifts received during the lifetime of the parent are taken into consideration in determining the amount of the equal shares. When a parent makes an advancement to the child and the child predeceases the parent, the amount of the advancement is deducted from the shares of the child's descendants if other children of the parent survive.[69] Assume the decedent leaves no spouse but three children: A, B, and C and an estate worth $90,000. A received an advancement of $10,000 during the life time of the decedent; in order to calculate the shares in the estate, the $10,000 in advancement is added to the $90,000 for a total of $100,000 to be divided among A, B, and C. To prevent a windfall to A and to allow for equal share among the three, the doctrine of *advancement* will take effect. A has already received $10,000 in advancement thus; he receives only $20,000 from the estate. His siblings B and C each take $30,000 share in the estate. If on the other hand A had been given property worth $80,000 as an advancement, A would not be required to give back a portion of the advancement because it is clear the decedent wanted A to have at least $80,000. However, decedent's $90,000 would be divided equally among A's two siblings B and C.

---

[69]   See Dukeminier: Wills, Trusts, and Estates 7th edition (2005) p. 114

Chapter Five

SLAYER RULE

Bars to Inheritance

Another issue that arises in law is whether one who kills and is responsible for the death of the decedent, be allowed to inherit from his estate. In many jurisdictions in the United States, the slayer is prohibited by statute from taking by descent from the estate of the one he has killed. Suppose *Adebayo*, being of sound mind, makes a will bequeathing the bulk of his estate to his grandson, *Olabisi*. *Olabisi* then murders *Adebayo*. Should *Olabisi* be allowed to enforce the will? The courts answer no. Because wills never contain an express provision disinheriting the testator's slayer, this answer has traditionally been thought to mean that the courts are sacrificing testator's donative intentions for the interest in deterring murder. A person who thinks there is a danger that someone he names in his will as a beneficiary will be his killer is unlikely to name that person in his will. The rule against allowing the slayer to take, serves the function of providing an implied term to govern remote contingencies. It is undoubted that only a few testators if asked whether they would want their killer to inherit from their estate would say yes but, should their desire be honored by the law? And should the slayer rule apply to any accidental, as well as to deliberate, homicides? Should it apply under intestacy?

ESTATE OF MAHONEY
Supreme Court of Vermont
126 Vt.31, 220 A.2d 475 (1966)

SMITH, Justice.

The decedent, Howard Mahoney, died intestate on May 6, 1961, of gunshot wounds. His wife, Charlotte Mahoney, the appellant here, was tried for the murder of Howard Mahoney in the Addison County Court and was convicted by the jury of the crime of manslaughter in March, 1962. She is presently serving a sentence of not less than 12 nor more than 15 years at the women reformatory in Rutland.

Howard Mahoney left no issue, and was survived by his wife and his father and mother. His father Mark Mahoney was appointed administrator of his estate which at the present time amounts to $3,885.89. After due notice and hearing, the probate court for the district of Franklin entered a judgment order decreeing the residue of the Estate of Howard Mahoney, in equal shares, to the father and mother of the decedent. An appeal from the judgment order and decree has been taken here by the appellant's widow. The question submitted is whether a widow convicted of manslaughter in connection with the death of her husband may inherit from his estate.

The general rules of descent provide that if a decedent is married and leaves no issue, his surviving spouse shall be entitled to the whole of decedent's estate if it does not exceed $8,000. *14 V.S.A. § 551(2).* Only if the decedent leaves no surviving spouse or issue does his descend in equal shares to the surviving father and mother. *14 V.S.A. § 551 (3).* There is no statutory provision in Vermont regulating the descent and distribution of property from the decedent to the slayer. The question presented is one of first impression in this jurisdiction.

In a number of jurisdictions, statutes have been enacted which in certain instances, at least, prevent a person who has killed another from taking by descent or distribution from the person he has killed.[70] . . .

Courts in those states that have no statute preventing a slayer from taking by descent or distribution from the estate of his victim, have followed three separate and different lines of decision.

---

[70] See *23 Am.Jur.2d Descent and Distribution, § 98, p. 841*

(1) The legal title passed to the slayer and may be retained by him in spite of his crime. The reasoning for so deciding is that devolution of the property of a decedent is controlled entirely by the statutes of descent and distribution; further, the denial of the inheritance to the slayer because of his crime would be imposing an additional punishment for his crime not provided by statute, and would violate the constitutional provision against corruption of blood. *Carpenter's Estate, 170 Pa. 203, (1875); Wall v. Pfanschmidt, 265 Ill. 180, (1914); Bird v. Plunkett et al. 139 Conn. 491 (1953).*

(2) The legal title will not pass to the slayer because of the equitable principle that no one should be permitted to profit by his own fraud, or take advantage and profit as a result of his own wrong or crime. *Riggs v. Palmer, 115 N.Y. 506 (1989); Price v. Hitaffer, 164 Md. 505 (1933); Slocum v. Metropolitan Life Ins., 245 Mass. 565 (1923).* Decisions so holding have been criticized as judicially engrafting an exception on the statute of descent and distribution and being 'unwarranted judicial legislation.' *Wall v. Pfanschmidt, supra.*

(3) The legal title passes to the slayer but equity holds him to be a constructive trustee for the heirs or next of kin of the decedent. This disposition of the question presented avoids a judicial engrafting on the statutory laws of descent and distribution, for title passes to the slayer. But because of the unconscionable mode by which the property is acquired by the slayer, equity treats him as a constructive trustee and compels him to convey the property to the heirs or next of kin of the deceased.

The reasoning behind the adoption of this doctrine was well expressed by Mr. Justice Cardozo in his lecture on 'The Nature of The Judicial Process.' 'Consistency was preserved, logic received its tribute, by holding that legal title passed, but it was subject to constructive trust. A constructive trust is nothing but 'the formula through which the conscience of equity finds expression.' Property is acquired in such circumstances that the holder of legal title May not in good conscience retain the beneficial interest. Equity to express its disapproval of his conduct, converts him into a trustee.' . . .

The New Hampshire court was confronted with the same problem of the rights to the benefits of an estate by one who has slain the decedent, in the absence of a statute on the subject. *Kelly v. State, 105 N.H. 240* . . . We approve of the doctrine so expressed.

However, the principle that one should not profit by his own wrong must not be extended to every case where a killer acquires property from his victim as a result of the killing. One who has killed while insane is not chargeable as a constructive trustee, or if the slayer had a vested interest in the property, it is property for which he would have been entitled if no slaying had occurred. The principle to be applied is that the slayer should not be permitted to improve his position by the killing, but should not be compelled to surrender property to which he would have been entitled if there had been no killing. The doctrine of constructive trust is involved to prevent the slayer from profiting from his crime, but not as an added criminal penalty. Kelly v. State, supra, p. 70; Restatement of Restitution, § 187(2), comment a.

The appellant here was, as we noted, convicted of manslaughter and not of murder. She calls to our attention that while the Restatement of Restitution, approves the application of the constructive trust doctrine where a devisee or legatee murders the testator, that such rules are not applicable where the slayer was guilty of manslaughter. Restatement of Restitution § 187, comment e.

The cases generally have not followed this limitation of the rule but hold that the line should be drawn between murder and manslaughter, but between voluntary and involuntary manslaughter. *Kelly v. State, supra; Chase v. Jennifer, 219 Md. 564 (1959).*

We think that this is the proper rule to follow. Voluntary manslaughter is an intentional and unlawful killing, with a real design and purpose to kill, even if such killing be the result of sudden passion or great provocation. Involuntary manslaughter is caused by an unlawful act, but not accompanied with any intention to take life. *State v. McDonnell, 32 Vt. 491, 545 (1860).* It is the intent to kill, which when accomplished, leads to the profit of the slayer that brings into place the constructive trust to prevent the unjust enrichment of the slayer by reason of his intentional killing.

In Vermont, an indictment for murder can result in a jury conviction on either voluntary or involuntary manslaughter. *State v. Averill, 85 Vt. 115, 132 (1911).* The legislature has provided the sentences that may be passed upon a person convicted of manslaughter, but provides no definition of that offense, nor any statutory distinction between voluntary and involuntary manslaughter. 13 V.S.A. § 2304.

The cause now before us is here on a direct appeal from the probate court. Findings of fact were made below from which it appears that the judgment of the probate court decreeing the estate of Howard Mahoney to his parents, rather than to his widow, was based upon a finding of the felonious killing of her husband by Mrs. Mahoney. However, the appellees here have asked us to affirm the decree below by imposing a constructive trust on the estate in the hands of the widow.

But the probate court did not decree the estate to the widow, and then make her a constructive trustee of such estate for the benefit of the parents. The judgment below decreed the estate directly to the parents, which was in direct contravention of the statutes of descent and distribution. The probate court was bound to follow the statutes of descent and distribution and its decree was in error and must be reversed.

The probate court was without jurisdiction to impose a constructive trust on the estate in the hands of the appellant, even if it had attempted to do so. Probate courts are courts of special and limited jurisdiction given by statute and do not proceed according to common law. While probate courts possess a portion of equitable powers independent of statute, such power do not extend to the establishment of purely equitable rights and claims . . .

However, the jurisdiction of the court of chancery may be invoked in probate matters in aid of the probate court when the powers of that court are inadequate, and it appears that the probate court cannot reasonably and adequately handle the question. The jurisdiction of the chancery court in so acting on probate matters is special and limited only to aiding the probate court. [71]

The probate court, in making its decree, used the record of the conviction of the appellant for manslaughter for its determination that the appellant had feloniously killed her husband. If the jurisdiction of the court of chancery is invoked by the appellees here it will be for the determination of that court, upon proof, to determine whether the appellant willfully killed her late husband, as it will upon all other equitable considerations that may be offered in evidence, upon charging the appellant with a constructive trust. 'The fact that he is convicted of murder in a criminal case does not dispense with the necessity of proof of the murder in proceedings in equity to charge him as a constructive trustee.' Restatement of Restitution, § 187. Comment d.

The jurisdiction of charging the appellant with a constructive trust on the estate of Howard Mahoney lies in the court of chancery, and not in the probate court.

---

[71] See In re will of Prudenzano, supra; also *Manley v. Brattleboro Trust Co., supra,* *116 Vt. P. 461.*

Decree reversed and cause remanded, with directions that the proceedings herein be stayed for sixty days to give the Administrator of the Estate of Howard Mahoney an opportunity to apply to the Franklin County Court of Chancery for relief. If application is so made, proceedings herein shall be stayed pending the final determination thereof. If application is not so made, the probate court for the District of Franklin shall assign to Charlotte Mahoney, surviving wife, the right and interest in and to the estate of her deceased husband which the Vermont statutes confer.

NOTES

(A). It is appropriate to mention that the source of law is important in deciding how to apply the slayer rule. If the source of law is a statute prohibiting the slayer from taking, the problem usually centers on whether the type of slaying and type of property interest involved are within the statutory language and, if not, whether the statute should be extended by interpretation and analogy. Usually, statutes prohibit the slayer from taking, so the question is whether the statute has extended this far. If the court finds no statute on point or that can be extended by interpretation and analogy, the court will proceed to determine whether a slayer will be allowed to take property of the decedent in interest. The court may decide to follow any of three parts. The first approach is to allow the slayer to take. This is justified on the theory of legislative inaction; this means that by failing to prohibit such inheritance by statute, the legislature is not in apposition to the slayer taking from the estate of the decedent.

The second approach the court may take is a prohibition of inheritance, similar to, but without the authority of a statute. Some courts have adopted this approach today. The last approach is to impose a constructive trust upon the slayer. At the beginning of the twentieth century, courts were reluctant to let the slayer take the property of the victim. Thus, the devise of the constructive trust was utilized. Many courts imposed a constructive trust upon the slaying heir for the benefit of the persons who would otherwise have received the property.

(B). Note: that the type of slaying also is important in determining whether to bar the slayer or not. Criminal law teaches that killing of a human being ranges in degree of culpability from Intentional killing and accidental killing through negligence to various degree of manslaughter (voluntary or involuntary). The more intentional the killing the more culpable the slayer is, and the more likely the court or statute is to deny the slayer inheritance. When a statute demands a certain degree of culpability, a certain degree of murder or manslaughter, or a certain burden of proof, it is difficult for the court to extend the purpose of the statute to a lesser amount. Some statutes, require a criminal burden of proof to be consistent in the finding of fault and thereby, are inconsistent in making the determination of the criminal court conclusive on the civil court. As you can see in the *Mahoney* case, the Supreme Court reversed the probate court for basing its decision on the record of conviction of Charlotte Mahoney for manslaughter for its determination that the appellant had *feloniously* killed her husband. The Supreme Court also noted that the appellant was convicted of *manslaughter* and not of *murder* to further emphasize on the degree of culpability. The court also noted that "it is the intent to kill, which when accomplished, leads to the profit of the slayer that brings into play the constructive trust to prevent the unjust enrichment of the slayer by reason of his intentional killing."[72]

(C) Note: that most statutes and court decisions, distinguish between realty and personality and between testate and intestate estates. Many avoid extending their application to nonprobate estate. The life insurance situation is an example. Any attempt to prevent the insurance company from paying the person named as beneficiary in the policy, when the beneficiary has murdered the insured, would bring to the life insurance domain the rule applied in the casualty insurance area: If an arsonist cannot collect on his or her building, why should a murderer collect life insurance on his or her victim? Normally, the company is required to pay the proceeds however, the question is whether the beneficiary be allowed to take the proceeds and, if not, who should take instead?[73]

Note: that in certain circumstances, the court will find the slayer unfit to take under a will based on statutory provisions for example, where a beneficiary under a will, in order that he might prevent revocation of the provision in his favor and to obtain the speedy enjoyment and possession

---

[72] See *State v. McDonnell, 32 Vt. 491, 545*

[73] See Robert L. Mennel: wills and Trusts, 3rd edition (2007) p. 141.

of the property, willfully murdered the testator. Such beneficiary by reason of the crime committed by him may be deprived any interest in the estate left by his victim, and so not entitled to the property either as donee under the will or as heir or next of kin; and that an action may be maintained to cancel such provisions.

RIGGS V. PALMER
Courts of Appeals of New York
115 N.Y 506, 22 N.E. 188 (1989)

EARL J.

On the 13th day of August 1880, Francis B. Palmer made his last will and testament, in which he gave small legacies to his two daughters, Mrs. Riggs and Mrs. Preston, the plaintiffs in this action, and the remainder of his estate to his grandson, the defendant, Elmer E. Palmer, subject to the support of Susan Palmer, his mother, with a gift over to the two daughters, subject to the support of Mrs. Palmer, in case Elmer should survive him and die under age, unmarried and without any issue. The testator at the date of his will owned a farm and considerable personal property. He was a widower, and thereafter, in March 1882, he was married to Mrs. Bresee, with whom before his marriage he entered into an ante-nuptial contract in which it was agreed that, in lieu of dower and all other claims upon his estate in case she survived him, she should have her support upon his farm during her life, and such support was expressly charged upon the farm. At the date of the will, and, subsequently, to the death of the testator, Elmer lived with him as a member of his family, and at his death was sixteen years old. He knew of the provisions made in his favor in the will, and, that he might prevent his grandfather from revoking such provisions, which he has manifested some intention to do, and to obtain the speedy enjoyment and immediate possession of his property, he willfully murdered him by poisoning him. He now claims the property, and the sole question for our determination is, can he have it? The defendants say that the testator is dead; that his will was made in due form and has been admitted to probate, and that, therefore, it must have effect according to the letter of the law.

It is quite true that statutes regulating the making, proof and effect of wills, and the devolution of property, if literally construed, and if their force and their effect can in no way and under no circumstances be controlled or modified, give this property to the murderer.

The purpose of those statutes was to enable testators to dispose of their estates to the objects of their bounty at death, and to carry into effect their final wishes legally expressed; and in considering and giving effect to them this purpose must be kept in view. It was the intention of the law-makers that the donees in a will should have the property given to them. But it never could have been their intention that the donee who murdered the testator to make the will operative should have any benefit under it. If such a case had been present to their mind, and it had been supposed necessary to make some provision of law to meet it, it cannot be doubted that they would have provided for it. It is a familiar canon of construction that a thing which is within the intention of the makers of a statute is as much within the statute as if it were within the letter; and a thing which is within the letter of the statute is not within the statute, unless it be within the intention of the makers. The writers of laws do not always express their intention perfectly, but either exceed it or fall short of it, so that judges are to collect it from probable or rational conjectures only, and this is called rational interpretation . . .

Such a construction ought to be put upon a statute as will best answer the intention which the makers had in view, . . . In Bacon's Abridgment (Statutes I,5); many cases are mentioned where it was held that matters embraced in the general words of statutes, nevertheless, were not within the statutes, because it could not have been the intention of the law makers that they should be included. They were taken out of the statute by an equitable construction, and it is said in Bacon: 'By an equitable construction, a case not within the letter of the statute is sometimes holden to be within the meaning, because it is within the mischief for which a remedy is provided'. The reason for such construction is that the law-makers could not set down every case in express terms . . .

What could be more unreasonable than to suppose that it was the legislative intention in the general laws passed for the orderly, peaceable and just devolution of property, that they should have operation in favor of one who murdered his ancestor that he might speedily come into the possession of his estate? Such an intention is inconceivable. We need not, therefore, be much troubled by the general language contained in the laws.

Besides, all laws as well as all contracts may be controlled in their operation and effect by general, fundamental maxims of the common law. No one shall be permitted to profit by his own fraud, or to take advantage of his own wrong, or to found any claim upon his own iniquity, or to acquire property by his own crime. These maxims are dictated by public policy, have their foundation in universal law administered in all civilized countries, and have no where been superseded by statutes. They were applied in the case of the New York *Mutual Life Insurance Company v. Armstrong 117 U.S. 591.*[74] . . .

These maxims, without any statute giving them force or operation, frequently control the effect and nullify the language of wills. A will procured by fraud and deception, like any other instrument, may be decreed void and set aside, and so a particular portion of a will may be excluded from probate or held inoperative if induced by the fraud or undue influence of the person in whose favor it is. (*Allen v. M'Pherson, 1 H.L. Cas. 191; Harrison's Appeal, 48 Conn. 202.*) So a will may contain provisions which are immoral, irreligious or against public policy, and they will be held void.

Here there was no certainty that this murderer would survive the testator, or that the testator would not change his will, and there was no certainty that he would get this property if nature was allowed to take its course. He, therefore, murdered the testator expressly to vest himself with an estate. Under such circumstances, what law, human or divine, will allow him to take the estate and enjoy the fruits of his crime? The will spoke and became operative at the death of the testator. He caused that death, and thus by his crime made it speak and have operation. Shall it speak and operate in his favor? If he had met the testator and taken his property by force, he would have had no title to it. Shall he acquire title by murdering him? If he had gone to the testator's house and by force compelled him, or by fraud or undue influenced had induced him to will him his property, the law would not allow him to hold it. But can he give effect and operation to a will by murder, and yet take the property? To answer these questions in the affirmative, it

---

[74] There it was held that the person who procured a policy upon the life of another, payable at his death, and then murdered the assured to make the policy payable, could not recover thereon. Mr. Justice Field, writing the opinion, said: 'Independently of any proof of the motives of Hunter in obtaining the policy, and even assuming that they were just and proper, he forfeited all rights under it when, to secure its immediate payment, he murdered the assured, it would be a reproach to the jurisprudence of this country if one could recover insurance money payable on the death of a party whose life he had feloniously taken. As well might he recover insurance money upon a building he had willfully fired'.

seems to me, would be a reproach to the jurisprudence of our state, and an offence against public policy.

Under the civil law evolved from the general principles of natural law and justice by many generations of jurisconsults, philosophers and statesmen, one cannot take property by inheritance or will from an ancestor or benefactor whom he has murdered . . .

For the same reasons the defendant Palmer cannot take any of the property as heir. Just before the murder he was not an heir, and it was not certain that he ever would be. He might have died before his grandfather, or might have been disinherited by him. He made himself an heir by the murder, and he seeks to take property as the fruit of his crime. What has before been said as to him as legatee applies to him with equal force as an heir. He cannot vest himself with title by crime.

My view of this case does not inflict upon Elmer any greater or other punishment for his crime than the law specifies. It takes from him no property, but simply holds that he shall not acquire property by his crime, and thus be rewarded for its commission.

Our attention is called to *Owen v. Owen (100 N.C. 240),* as a case quite like this. There a wife had been convicted of being an accessory before the fact to the murder of her husband, and it was held that she was, nevertheless, entitled to dower. I am unwilling to assent to the doctrine of that case. The statutes provide dower for a wife who has the misfortune to survive her husband and thus lose his support and protection. It is clear beyond their purpose to make provision for a wife who by her own crime makes herself a widow and willfully and intentionally deprives herself of the support and protection of her husband. As she might have died before him, and never have been his widow, she cannot by her crime vest herself with an estate. The principle that lies at the bottom of the maxim, *volenti non fit injuria,* should be applied to such a case, and a widow should not, for the purpose of acquiring, as such, property rights, be permitted to allege a widowhood which she has wickedly and intentionally created.

The facts found entitled the plaintiffs to the relief they seek. The error of the referee was in his conclusion of law. Instead of granting a new trial, therefore, I think the proper judgment upon the facts found should be ordered here. The facts have been passed upon twice with the same result, first upon the trial of Palmer for murder, and then by the referee in this action. We are, therefore, of opinion that the end of justice does not require that they should again come in question.

The judgment of the General Term and that entered upon the report of the referee should, therefore, be reversed and judgment should be entered as follows: That Elmer E. Palmer and the administrator be enjoined from using any of the personalty or real estate left by the testator for Elmer's benefit; that the devise and bequest in the will to Elmer be declared ineffective to pass the title to him; that by reason of the crime of murder committed upon the grandfather he is deprived of any interest in the estate left by him; that the plaintiffs are the true owners of the real and personal estate left by the testator, subject to the charge in favor of Elmer's mother and the widow of the testator, under the ante-nuptial agreement, and that the plaintiffs have costs in all the courts against Elmer.

Dissenting Opinion Omitted.

QUESTIONS:
(1) Considering the ruling in *Riggs v. Palmer,* do you think it is appropriate for the courts to be bound by the rigid rules of law established by the legislature which by its enactments, prescribed exactly when and how wills may be made, altered, and revoked?

(2) Note: that the court in *Riggs* used its equitable jurisdiction to declare Elmer's interests in his grandfather's estates void. What should happen in a situation where the legislature has left no room for equitable jurisdiction in such matters, may the court go ahead and use its equitable powers or should it adhere to the language of the statute?

(3) Think about an argument that, complete freedom of testamentary disposition of ones property has not been and is not the universal rule; do you agree that such notion conform with the statutes of many of our states? If so, how and why?

(4) Assume that freedom, which is permitted to be exercised in the testamentary disposition of one's estate by law of the state, is subject to its being exercised in conformity with the regulations of the statutes, should the courts conform with such statutes when it has no prohibition against the disposition of property, where the beneficiary murdered the testator? That is, should the court allow the murderer to take when the statute does not prevent him from taking based on his felonious act? To answer think about why equitable jurisdiction and statutory interpretation is important.

(5) Do you agree with an argument that in the absence of legislations prohibiting the murderer from inheriting, the courts are not empowered to impose remedial justice?

DISCLAIMER

It is not uncommon for a beneficiary or a devisee to decline to take a bequest by will or via intestacy, this is known as a *disclaimer*. In most cases a disclaimer is triggered to avoid tax burdens. At common law, when a person dies intestate (without a will), titles to real and personal property of the decedent reverts to his heirs by operation of law. The principle is that, someone must take what the decedent left at death and be responsible for all necessary obligations. The common law rule is not in much operation today however, if the heirs refuses to take the devise, the common law treats the heirs renunciation as if title had passed to the heir and then to the next intestate successor. Also if a person dies leaving a will (testate) the beneficiary can refuse to accept the devise and title will not pass to him. In the United States almost all states have legislation allowing the devisee to disclaim the devise; the disclaimant is treated as having predeceased the testator and the testator's property does not pass to him.[75]

---

[75]   See Dukeminier: Wills, Trusts, and Estates, 7th edition (2005) p. 132-133
See On Disclaimer, *Drye v. United States, 528 U.S. 49 (1999).*

Chapter Six

DEVISE CAPACITY

MENTAL CAPACITY

In the United States, the testator must be at least 18yrs old to be able to make a will. There are many factors which may prevent the testator from being able to form the intention to make a will; *Incapacity, fraud* and *undue influence* are among the factors the court may consider to determine whether or not it is proper to admit a will to probate. Other factors such as *duress* or *menace* also determine the validity of a will; these factors are equitable overrides and the courts of equity will invalidate a will that is otherwise valid if one of these factors is present. To make a will, the testator must be capable of *knowing* and *understanding* (a) the nature and extent of his or her property (b) the natural objects of his or her bounty, and (c) the disposition that he or she is making of that property, and must also be capable (d) relating these elements to one another and forming an orderly desire regarding the disposition of the property.[76] The testator must be able to establish that he or she is of a sound mind and under no mental disability or delusion that may prevent him from satisfying the four requirements indicated above.

Mental incapacity sufficient enough to invalidate a will may be of two forms: (1) insanity of the magnitude that establishes mental incompetence or (2) some specific form of insanity under which the testator is suffering from

---

[76] See, Restatement (third) of Property: Wills and Other Donative Transfers § 8.1 (2003)

some hallucination or delusion. To establish delusion, it must be shown by evidence that the will itself was a product of such delusion, that the delusion indeed influenced the creation of the will and that but for the delusion, the testator would not have devised his property the way he did.

ESTATE of WRIGHT
Supreme Court of California, 1936
7 Cal. 2d 345, 60 P.2d 434

SEAWELL J.

The petition for admission to probate of the will of Lorenzo B. Wright, deceased, having been denied probate on the ground of testamentary incapacity, the executrix named in said will herewith appeals to this court. The grounds urged for reversal are that the evidence is insufficient to sustain the judgment and order. The complaint also alleged the exercise of undue influence, but the probate court decided that issue against contestants. The appeal is presented on a bill of exceptions as per stipulation by the parties and contains the evidence which bears upon the testator's mental capacity. Respondent has not filed a reply brief.

The testator, Lorenzo B. Wright, died at Venice, California, May 2, 1933, at the age of sixty-nine years. Maud Wright Angell, the contestant, is his daughter and the nearest of kin. He left no other children . . . Testator's wife died in 1921.

The decedent left an estate consisting of two improved parcels of land situated in Venice, California, and an interest in an estate situated in Salt Lake City, his former home, and some inconsequential personal property of unknown value. The petition for probate alleges that the total value of his estate does not exceed the total sum of $10,000. His will was formally executed one year and four months prior to his death. By its terms, he devised to Charlotte Josephine Hindmarch, fifty years of age and whom he describes as his friend, his house located at 722 Nowita Place and all his personal "belongings, monies, collateral, notes or anything of value"; he devised to his daughter, the contestant herein, the house located on lot nine, at 724 Nowita Place, and to his granddaughter, Marjorie Jean Angell, his interest in an estate in Salt Lake City. He gave to his grandson, his son-in-law and several other persons, relatives or friends, one dollar each.

We have in this proceeding the unusual spectacle of the drawer of the will, a notary public and realtor, and the two subscribing witnesses testifying that they were of the opinion that the testator was of unsound mind. The testimony of these three witnesses, like the testimony given by all the others, is far too weak and unsubstantial to support the judgment. To a great extent the grounds upon which the witnesses base their opinions are mere trivialities. If it could be said that the testimony of the three persons who participated in the creation of the will and who by their solemn acts gave the stamp of approval and verity to its due execution, and afterwards attempted to repudiate all they had done, had any convincing force or any substantial factual basis, their testimony would nevertheless be subject to the scrutiny and suspicion which courts rightfully exercise in considering the testimony of persons who out of their own mouths admit their guilt of self-stultification. It has been said that such testimony is "simply worthless". Courts, whenever called upon to express themselves on this subject, have not been sparing in the use of forceful language. In *Wrestler v. Custer, 46 Pa. 502,* the court said: "The legal presumption is always in favor of sanity, especially after attestation by subscribing witnesses, for, as was said by Parsons, C.J. in *Buckminster v. Perry, 4 Mass. 593, 594,* it is the duty of the subscribing witnesses to be satisfied of the testator's sanity before they subscribed the instrument. No honest man will subscribe as a witness to a will, or any other instrument executed by an insane man, an imbecile, an idiot, or a person of manifestly incompetent for any reason to perform, with legal effect, the act in question. A duty attaches to the witness to satisfy himself of the competency of the party before he lends his name to attest the act. Like a magistrate who takes an acknowledgment of a deed, he is to be reasonably assured of the facts he undertakes to verify, else he makes himself instrumental in a fraud upon the public."

Our own court in the *Estate of Motz, 136 Cal. 558 {69 Pac. 294},* made the observation which must be in the mind of every person who gives any thought to the subject. We said: "When a witness has solemnly subscribed his name to a will as an attesting witness, knowing the nature of his act, and that deceased would rely upon his name as a part of the execution of the will, undertakes by his evidence to overthrow or cast suspicion upon it, his evidence should be closely scrutinized."

In as much as we are reversing the judgment, we deem it proper to give a brief summary of the testimony of each one of the witnesses upon whom respondent relies to sustain the judgment. Appellant rest her appeal squarely and solely upon the testimony offered by contestant, and none other is brought up.

It appears without contradiction that Lorenzo B. Wright, testator, met Mrs. Grace Thomas, a notary public and realtor with whom he transacted business and whom he had known for many years, in the post office and asked her what her charge would be for drawing his will. He told her he was coming to her office to have her prepare his will. About three weeks thereafter he came alone to her office, bringing with him memoranda sheets upon which he had written the names of the persons whom he wished to enjoy his property and the specific shares thereof after his death. She prepared the will accordingly. She was not acquainted with any of the persons whose names appeared on the memoranda prepared by him. She testified that she believed at the time he executed the will that he was of unsound mind. Pressed for the grounds of her opinion she said it was the "funniest will she had ever seen" in that it gave $1 to each of a number of different persons she did not know; that she had thought him queer for a long time; that he did not have in mind the legal description of the property but that she had it listed for sale and rent. The above contains the entire substance of her testimony.

James Thomas, a witness to the will, was next called by the contestant. It does not appear what relation he bears, if any, to Mrs. Grace Thomas, the scrivener, or who solicited him to become a witness. He stated that he "believed" the testator was not of sound mind; that in his opinion testator had not been of sound mind for some years prior to the execution of the will. He seemed unable to give a single reason supporting his opinion.

G.W. Madden. The other subscribing witness, when pressed for the reason of his opinion that the testator "was not of sound mind" at the time he signed the will, was also unable to say more than that he considered him of unsound mind for some time prior to the making of the will.

Mrs. Brem had known testator for sixteen years and said it was her belief that he was of unsound mind on the day the will was executed. Pressed for the reason of her opinion, she said he had had a serious operation some years prior; he once told her he had lost $50,000 in some bank failure and she was sure from the way he lived alone in his little shack, with all the dirt and junk he had, that he was not right; he once gave her a fish (he spent much time in fishing) which he said he had caught and she found it had been soaked in kerosene and when he asked her how she liked it he laughed and said he had put the kerosene on it before he brought it to her; once he came to her house and insisted on buying her household furniture and when told it was not for sale and that she had not offered it for sale he insisted on buying it anyway. Mr. Brem testified substantially as his wife had testified, but added the statement that "Mr. Wright often chased the children out of his yard and turned the hose on them and that children in the neighborhood were afraid of Mr. Wright." He did not explain why they often returned to his yard if they feared him.

Mrs. Daisy Smith a cousin not named in the will, testified that she believed him to be unsound in mind. Her reasons were that he drank and was drunk much of the time since his wife died; that some years ago he suffered an injury to his head and several stitches were required to close the wound; that the injury seemed to change him; that he had a serious operation in 1921; on one or more occasions he ran out of the house only partly dressed and they had to follow him and had difficulty in getting him back to bed; that he picked up silverware and other articles from the garbage and hid these things around the house; that he picked up paper flowers from the garbage cans, and waste, and pinned them on rose bushes in his yard and took the witness to look at his roses; that he went away with a blanket wrapped around him and was gone several days and made no explanation as to where he went; that he took from his daughter's house a radio which the witness said he had given to his daughter without making any explanation as to why he did so; that she knew he had been quite sick a number of times and that he did not have much care or attention; that he suffered a great deal.

Marjorie Jean Angell, a granddaughter, placed her belief that the testator was unsound of mind on the ground that he acted funny and queer; that he told a number of persons that he had sent Christmas presents and a turkey to them when he had not done so; She related the removal of the radio from her mother's home which they claimed he had given to them; at times he would pass her on the street without speaking and at other times he would speak and seem friendly; one time he told her she had on too much rouge and powder of paint, when she did not have any amount on; that her mother often invited him to their home for dinner. He would say he would come but he did not appear. He collected old articles from the rubbish and garbage wagon when he drove the garbage wagon and had them about the house and he had a lot of old stuff hidden in the house.

Cloyd Angell, the grandson thought testator of unsound mind. His reasons were: He had seen him fishing on the wharf in Venice and he did not tell his friends and acquaintances on the pier that witness was his grandson; neither did the witness tell his friends that testator was his grandfather. He had often seen him drunk on the pier. Some eight or ten years before his death his grandfather seemed fond of him and he used to ride with him on the garbage wagon, but his attitude changed in later years, for no reason of which he was aware, and he did not have much to do with him; he had a lot of junk and old empty liquor bottles around the house.

Hariett E. McClelland said she had known testator for a number of years. She believed him to be of unsound mind. She testified that she had been closely associated with him and that she had often taken him riding in her automobile and he had stayed at her home on many occasions when ill and that when he ran away and his friends or relatives did not know where he was he was at her home; when at her home he drank a good deal; in 1929 and 1930 he was quite ill at her home; he told her about a number of houses that he had at Salt Lake City, his former home and where she had known testator, but she knew that he did not own them; he collected paper flowers from the garbage cans and pinned them on the bushes in his yard and laughingly said to her that he would fool the people as they would think that the flowers were blooming ; that one time he told the witness in the presence of her mother that she was his natural daughter. The mother became exceedingly angry at him and it does not appear that he ever repeated the statement. The witness related an ailment which the testator had while living at her house during which he would be prone, hold his breath and appear to be dead; that when she returned from her quest for help she would find him up and walking about; that he said he did this to scare his neighbors and make them think he was dead.

Minnie Connor, a half-sister of testator, was bequeathed one dollar. She testified that he was in a bad accident at Salt Lake City thirty years before and he had been queer since. In 1919 he had an operation and nine years before death he injured his hand and was sick at her home for some time and was delirious a part of the time and ran out of the house only half clothed; she related the radio incident, the injury to his head, and said once while at her home on her invitation to dine he left before the meal and did not return. On another occasion he asked her which bus to take to go to the pier although he was accustomed to ride on a bus to the pier. The witness also testified that the testator's mother had been insane more than a year before her death. His mother was never adjudged insane but was recognized as being not right. She did not state his mother's age, nor is there the slightest evidence tending to show congenital insanity in the family.

Alma Angell, the son-in-law, against whom an unlawful detainer suit was successfully prosecuted by testator, he and his wife being ejected from the premises of testator, testified that testator and himself had been good friends, pals, up to ten years prior to his death, at which time testator's attitude very radically changed and he did not seem to like either him or his son Cloyd. His testimony followed closely the testimony of the witnesses already set out. In addition he stated that after the Salt Lake City injury the decedent malingered by resulting to the use of a wheel chair "to frame up a showing to prove damages in a suit which was pending as a result of the accident". He was of the opinion that testator had not been right since the Venice accident which occurred some ten years before his demise.

Maud Wright Angell, daughter of testator and contestant herein, testified . . . that testator was of unsound mind . . . premised on his changed attitude toward her and her family which she says took place some ten years prior to his death, occasioned by the injury to his head. She said that he drank a good deal. After he was taken to the hospital and just before he died he sent for her and he was "very usual and normal."

The foregoing sets forth the full strength of contestant's case. Tested by the decisions of this court the judgment is wholly without evidentiary support. There is no evidence that testator suffered from settled insanity, hallucination or delusions. Testamentary capacity cannot be destroyed by showing a few isolated acts, foibles, idiosyncrasies, moral or mental irregularities or departures from the normal unless they directly bear upon and have influenced the testamentary act. No medical testimony as to the extent of any injury the testator has received or its effect upon him either physically or mentally was introduced in the case. The burden was on contestant throughout the case. Taking all the evidence adduced by contestant as true, it falls far below the requirements of the law as constituting satisfactory rebuttal of the inference of testamentary capacity. No proof whatever was offered to rebut the testator's ability to transact or conduct his business or to care for himself except in a few cases of illness brought about by natural causes or excesses or by accident. He went alone to the scrivener's with a list of beneficiaries prepared by himself, giving his daughter one piece of improved real property and Charlotte Josephine Hindmarch, whom he designated as his friend, the other. To his granddaughter he bequeathed his undivided interest in an estate known as the Brazier Estate, and he named seven others to whom he made nominal bequests. There is no evidence that he did not appreciate his relations and obligations to others, or that he was not mindful of the property which he possessed. The opinions or beliefs of those testified that he was not of sound mind rest upon testimony of the most trivial character and do not establish testamentary incapacity at the time he executed his will.

It does not appear that his daughter or members of his family were concerned as to his comfort or well-being, as the testimony of some of the witnesses shows that he lived a portion of his time in a condition of squalor and that he was not cared for when ill by others. The attention given to his comfort by Charlotte Josephine Hindmarch does not appear, as the appeal is based solely upon the evidence adduced by contestant in support of her claim that he lacked testamentary capacity . . .

"Mental derangement sufficient to invalidate a will must be insanity in one of two forms: (1) insanity of such broad character as to establish mental incompetency generally, or (2) some specific and narrower form of insanity under which the testator is the victim of some hallucination or delusion. Even in the latter class of cases, it is not sufficient merely to establish that a testator was the victim of some hallucination or delusion. The evidence must establish that the will itself was the creature or product of such hallucination or delusion; that the hallucination or delusion bore directly upon and influenced the creation and terms of the testamentary instrument. The evidence must establish, in addition to the fact of the existence of the hallucination or delusion, the fact that by reason of these hallucinations or delusions the testatrix devised or bequeathed her property in a way which, except for the existence of such delusions, she would not have done. In short, the abnormality of mind must have had a direct influence upon the testamentary act . . .

For the foregoing reasons the judgment and order are reversed.

NOTES:
1. It is a settled principle of law that testamentary capacity cannot be destroyed, by showing a few isolated acts, foibles, idiosyncrasies, moral or mental irregularities or departures from the normal unless they directly bear upon and have influenced the testamentary act.
2. Contrary to popular belief, not anyone can contest a will. The settled rule is that only persons "with interest" in the estate have *standing* to contest the will. For example, a child has standing to contest the will left by his father for if he is successful in overturning the judgment, he will have a share in the estate but he must have grounds for contest. A *laughing heir* (remote relative) who seems to have no connection with the deceased may nevertheless contest a will that

exclude him if he were mentioned in a previous will however, he must prove it. In general, all heirs who would inherit by intestacy, but not heirs of the heirs, have standing to contest the will.

3. Note: that a spouse's taking his or her share by common law *dower and curtesy* or by *"forced share"* does not constitute a contest of the will. The *forced share* is a statutory right regardless of the provisions of the will.

4. A divorced spouse has no standing to contest the will even though she was mentioned in a previous will. Divorce ends the bequest and places a bar on the inheritance. Likewise, a stepchild has no right to inherit, but if a stepchild was mentioned in an earlier will, he or she would have the right to contest.

5. Creditors of the estate do not have the right to contest the will, nor do creditors of a beneficiary or heir. It is possible in many states, however, for a contestant to offer his rights to contest a will by "assignment" to someone else. That is, an heir who has the right to contest a will could transfer his right to another person either by sale, gift, or exchange, like any other property right.

6. You cannot contest a will simply because you are against the way the provision was made or because you don't like it, or because 'the will' gives you less than you think you could have received, or you think the devise is unfair. You must have legal grounds, which if supported by the evidence, would cause the will to be invalidated by the probate court. For more on legal grounds for contests, refer to the beginning of this chapter.

7. Note: that for a lawyer to draft a will for an incompetent person is a breach of legal ethics. The lawyer, however, may rely on her own judgment regarding the client's capacity she does not have to make an investigation of it.[77]

8. Note: The fact that a person has been declared incompetent and but under a conservator does not necessarily mean the person has no capacity to execute a will thereafter, capacity to make a will is governed by a different legal test and requires less mental ability than to manage one's investment, to make a contract or gift.

---

[77] See, *Logotheti v. Gordon, 607 N.E.2d 1015 (Mass,1993)*

9. Legal capacity to make a will requires a greater mental competency than is required for marriage; a person may have insufficient capacity to make a will on the same day as the person has sufficient capacity to marry. {Thus one suffering from cerebral arteriosclerosis may be able to marry but not make a will. Marriage alone will give the surviving spouse a share of the *senile* spouse's estate, even though he has no capacity to devise it to her.

INSANE DELUSION

If *Olufemi* believes his wife is secretly dating an alien form outer space and as a result decides to disinherit her in his will, his wife may contest the will and the portion of the will disinheriting her is set aside and thus, fail for lack of testamentary capacity; it is a product of *insane delusion* and will not stand in the face of the law. One may have sufficient capacity to make a will but still suffering from an *insane delusion*. If the entire provision in the will was caused by insane delusion, the entire will fails however, if insane delusions are proven but they do not affect the devises, then the entire will stands.

Simply put, a delusion is a false conception of reality. To establish insane delusion as basis for contest, the evidence must show that the will itself was the creature or product of such delusion, that the delusion bore upon and influenced the creation and terms of the will and that the testator devised his property in a way which, except for the existence of such delusion, he would not have done so. The general rule is that, a delusion is insane even if there is some factual basis for it if a rational person in the testator's situation could not have drawn the conclusion reached by the testator.

IN RE STRITTMATER
Court of Errors and Appeals of New Jersey, 1947
140 N.J. Eq. 94, 53 A.2d 205

Appeal from prerogative court.

Proceeding in the matter of the estate of Louisa F. Srittmater, from a decree of the Essex County Orphans' Court admitting to probate the will of the deceased, the contestants appealed to the Prerogative Court, claiming that deceased was insane. From a decree of the Prerogative Court setting aside the probate, the proponents appeal . . .

The opinion of Vice Ordinary Bigelow, follows:

This is an appeal from a decree of the Essex County Orphans' Court admitting to probate the will of Louisa F. Strittmater. Appellants challenge the decree on the ground that testatrix was insane.

The only medical witness was Dr. Sarah D. Smalley, a general practitioner who was Mrs. Strittmater's physician all her adult life. In her opinion, decedent suffered from paranoia of the Bleuler type of split personality. The factual evidence justifies the conclusion. But I regret not having had the benefit of an analysis of the data by a specialist in diseases of the brain.

The deceased never married. Born in 1896, she lived with her parents until their death about 1928, and seems to have had a normal childhood. She was devoted to both her parents and they to her. Her admiration and love of her parents persisted after their death to 1934, at least. Yet four years later she wrote: 'My father was a corrupt, vicious, and unintelligent savage, a typical specimen of the majority of his sex. Blast his wormstinking carcass and his whole damn breed.' And in 1943, she inscribed on a photograph of her mother 'That Moronic she-devil that was my mother.'

'Numerous memoranda and comments written by decedent on the margins of books constitute the chief evidence of her mental condition. Most of them are dated in 1935, when she was 40years old. But there are enough in later years to indicate no change in her condition. The master who heard the case in the court below, found that the proofs demonstrated 'incontrovertably her morbid aversion to men' and 'feminism to a neurotic extreme.' This characterization seems to me not strong enough. She regarded men as a class with an insane hatred. She looked forward to the day when women would bear children without the aid of men, and all males would be put to death at birth. Decedent's inward life, disclosed by what she wrote, found an occasional outlet such as the incident of the smashing of the clock, the killing of the pet kitten, vile language, etc. On the other hand, and I suppose this the split personality, Miss Strittmater, in her dealings with her lawyer, Mr. Semel, over a period of several years, and with her bank, to cite only two examples, was entirely reasonable and normal.

'Decedent, in 1925, became a member of the New Jersey branch of the National Women's Party. From 1939 to 1941, and perhaps later, she worked as a volunteer one day a week in the New York office, filing papers, etc. During this period, she spoke of leaving her estate to the party. On October 31, 1944 she executed her last will, carrying this intention into effect. A month later, December 6, she died. Her only relatives were some cousins of whom she saw very little during the last few years of her life.

The question is whether Miss Strittmater's will is the product of her insanity. Her disease seems to have become well developed by 1936. In August of that year she wrote, "It remains for feministic organizations like the National Women's Party, to make exposure of women's 'protectors' and 'lovers' for what their vicious and contemptible selves are.' She had been a member of the Women's Party for eleven years at that time, but the evidence does not show that she had taken great interest in it. I think it was her paranoic condition, especially her insane delusions about the male, that led her to leave her estate to the National Women's Party. The result is that the probate should be set aside.'

PER CURIAM.

The decree under review will be affirmed for the reasons stated in the opinion of Vice Ordinary Bigelow.

UNDUE INFLUENCE

Undue influence is the improper use of power or trust in a way that deprives a person of free will and substitutes another's objective. Consent to a contract, transaction, relationship, or conduct is voidable if the consent is obtained through undue influence. Likewise, a testamentary disposition, is voidable in the eye of the law and may be set aside if obtained by *undue influence*. For example, when a beneficiary actively procures the execution of a will, a presumption of undue influence may be raised, based on the confidential relationship between the influencer (beneficiary) and the testator. To qualify as undue influence, there must be *coercion* (force). It is only when the will of the testator is coerced into doing that which he or she does not intend to do, that it is *undue influence*. If John who desperately wants his brother's brown Mercedes forces his brother to name him as the beneficiary of the Mercedes in his will and evidence show his brother intended to name his own son Luke as the beneficiary of the Mercedes, but decided instead to name John as the beneficiary due to the pressure and force exerted by John, Luke may contest the portion of the will devising the Mercedes to John as a creation of undue influence.

115

To establish *undue influence* it must be proved {1} that the testator was *susceptible* to undue influence, {2} that the influencer had the *disposition or motive* to exercise undue influence, {3} that the influencer had the *opportunity* to exercise undue influence, and {4} that the disposition is the *product* of the undue influence.

LIPPER v. WESLOW
Texas Court of Civil Appeals, 1963
369 S.W.2d 698

McDONALD, Chief Justice.

This is a contest of the will of Mrs. Sophie Block, on the ground of undue influence. Plaintiffs, Julian Weslow, Jr., Julia Weslow Fortson and Alice Weslow Sale, are the three grandchildren of Mrs. Block by a deceased son; defendants are Mrs. Block's 2 surviving children, G. Frank Lipper and Irene Lipper Dover (half brother and half sister of plaintiff's deceased father). (The will left the estate of testatrix to her two children, defendants herein; and left nothing to her grandchildren by the deceased son, plaintiffs herein). Trial was to a jury, which found that Mrs. Block's will, signed by her on January 30, 1956, was procured by undue influence on the part of the proponent, Frank Lipper. The trial court entered judgment on the verdict, setting aside the will.

Defendants appeal, contending there is no evidence, or insufficient evidence, to support the finding that the will was procured by undue influence.

Testatrix was married 3 times. Of her first marriage she had one son, Julian Weslow, (who died in 1949), who was father of plaintiffs herein. After the death of her first husband testatrix married a Mr. Lipper. Defendants are the 2 children of their marriage. After Mr. Lipper's death, testatrix married Max Block. There were no children born of this marriage. Max Block died several months after the death of testatrix.

On 30 January, 1956, Sophie Block executed the will in controversy. Such will was prepared by defendant, Frank Lipper, an attorney, one of the beneficiaries of the will, and independent executor of the will. The will was witnessed by 2 former business associates of Mr. Block. Pertinent provisions of the will are summarized as follows:

'That I Mrs. Sophie Block, do make, publish and declare this my last will and testament, hereby revoking all other wills by me heretofore made.'

1,2,3 And 4

(Provide for payment of debts for burial in Beth Israel Cemetery; and for minor bequests to a servant, and to an old folks' home.)

5

(Devises the bulk of testatrix's estate to her 2 children, Mrs. Irene Lipper Dover and Frank Lipper (defendant herein), share and share alike.)

6

(States that $7000 previously *advanced* to Mrs. Irene Lipper Dover, and $9300. Previously advanced to Frank Lipper be taken into consideration in the final settlement of the estate; and cancels such amounts "that I gave or advanced to my deceased son, Julian.")

7

Appoints G. Frank Lipper Independent Executor of the estate without bond.

8

Provides that if any legatee contests testatrix's will or the will of her husband, Max Block, that they forfeit all benefits under the will.

9

"My son, Julian A. Weslow, died on August 6, 1949, and I want to explain why I have not provided anything under this will for my daughter in-law, Bernice Weslow, widow of my deceased son, Julian, and her children, Julian A. Weslow Jr., Alice Weslow Sale, and Julia Weslow Fortson, and I want to go into sufficient detail in explaining my relationship in past years with my said son's widow and his children, before mentioned, and it is my desire to record such relationship so that there will be no question as to my feelings in the matter or any thought or suggestion that my children, Irene Lipper Dover and G. Frank Lipper, or my husband,

Max, may have influenced me in any manner in the execution of this will. During the time that my said son, Julian was living, the attitude of his wife, Bernice, was at times, pleasant and friendly, but the majority of the years when my said son, Julian was living, her attitude towards me and my husband, Max, was unfriendly and frequently months would pass when she was not in my home and I did not hear from her. When my said son, Julian, was living he was treated the same as I treated my other children; and, my husband, Max, and I gave to each of our children a home and various sums of money from time to time to help in taking care of medical expenses, as well as outright gifts. Since my said son Julian's death, his widow, Bernice, and all of her children have shown a most unfriendly and distant attitude towards me, my husband Max, and my 2 children G. Frank Lipper and Irene Lipper Dover, which attitude I cannot reconcile as I have shown them many kindnesses since they have been members of my family, and their continued unfriendly attitude towards me, my husband, Max, and my said children has hurt me deeply in my declining years, for my life would have been much happier if they had shown a disposition to want to be a part of the family and enter into a normal family relationship that usually exists with a daughter-in-law and grandchildren and great grandchildren. I have not seen my grandson, Julian A. Weslow, Jr. in several years, neither have I heard from him. My granddaughter, Alice Weslow Sale, I have not seen in several years ad I have not heard from her, but I heard a report some months ago that she was now living in California and has since married William G. Sale. My granddaughter, Julia Weslow Fortson, wife of Ben Fortson, I have not seen in several years and I was told that she had a child born to her sometime in December 1952, and I have not seen the child or heard from my said granddaughter, Julia, up to this writing, and was informed by a friend that Julia has had another child recently and is now living in Louisiana, having moved from Houston; and needless to say, my said daughter-in-law, Bernice, widow of my deceased son, Julian, I have not seen in several years as she has taken little or no interest in me or my husband, Max, since the death of my son, Julian, with the exception that Christmas a year ago, I remember correctly, she sent some flowers, which I acknowledged, and I believe she has sent some greeting cards on some occasions prior to that time. My said daughter-in-law, Bernice Weslow, has expressed to me on several occasions, an intense hatred for my son, G. Frank Lipper, and my daughter, Irene Lipper Dover, which I cannot understand, as my said children have always shown her and her children every consideration when possible, and have expressed a desire to be friendly with her, and them, my said children, G. Frank Lipper, and Irene Lipper Dover, have at all times been attentive to me and my husband, Max, especially during the past few years when we have not been well. I will be 82 years old in June of this year and my husband, Max, will be 80 years of age in October of this year, and we have both been in failing health for the past few years and rarely leave our home, and appreciate any attention that is given us, and my husband, Max, and I cannot understand the unfriendly and distant attitude of Bernice Weslow, widow of my said son, Julian, and his children, before mentioned.'

10

Concerns personal belongings already disposed of.
In testimony whereof, I have hereunto signed my name
(S) Sophie Block
(Here follows attestation clause and signature of the 2 witnesses.)

The record reflects that the will in question was executed 22 days before testatrix died at the age of 81 years. By its terms, it disinherits the children of testatrix's son, who died in 1949. Defendant, Frank Lipper is a lawyer, and is admittedly the scrivener of the will. There is evidence that defendant Lipper bore malice against his dead half brother. He lived next door to testatrix, and had a key to her house. The will was not read to testatrix prior to the time she signed same, and she had no discussion with anyone at the time she executed it. There is evidence that the recitations in the will that Bernice Weslow and her children were unfriendly, and never came about testatrix, were untrue . . . There is also evidence that the Weslows sent testatrix greeting cards and flowers from 1946 through 1954, more times than stated in the will.

Plaintiff offered no direct evidence pertaining to the making and execution of the will on January 30, 1956, and admittedly rely wholly upon circumstantial evidence of undue influence to support the verdict.

All of the evidence is that testatrix was of sound mind at the time of the execution of the will; that she was a person of strong will; that she was in good physical health for her age; and that she was in fact physically active to the day of her death. Mrs. Weslow's husband died in 1949; and after 1952 the Weslows came about testatrix less often than before.

The witness Lyda Friberg, who worked at the home of testatrix from 1949 to 1952, testified that in 1952 she had a conversation with Bernice Weslow in which Mrs. Weslow told her if her children didn't get their inheritance she would sue through every court in the union; that she told testatrix about this conversation, and that testatrix told her 'she would have those wills fixed up so there would be no court business', and that she wasn't going to leave them (the Weslows), a dime,'

The foregoing was prior to the execution of the will on January 30, 1956.

Subsequent to the execution of the will, testatrix had a conversation with her sister, Mrs. Levy. Mrs. Levy testified:

Q. Who did she say she was leaving her property to?
A. She was leaving it to her son and her daughter.
Q. What else did she say about the rest of her kin, if anything?
A. Well she said that Julian's children had been very ugly to her; that they never showed her any attention whatever; they married and she didn't know they were married; they had children and they didn't let her know. After Julian passed away, she never saw any of the family at all. They never came to see her.
Q. Did she make any statement?
A. Yes she did. When she passed away, she didn't want to leave them anything; that they did nothing for her when she was living.

Shortly before she passed away, testatrix told Mrs. Augusta Roos that she was going to leave her property to her two children, and further:

Q. Did she give any reason for it?
A. Yes. She said that Bernice had never been very nice to her and the children never were over.

Again, subsequent to the making of her will, testatrix talked with Effie Landry, her maid. Mrs. Landry testified:

Q. Did Mrs. Block on any occasion ever tell you anything about what was contained in her will?
A. Yes.
Q. What did she tell you about that?
A. She said she wasn't leaving the Weslow children anything.

The only question presented is whether there is any evidence of *undue influence*. The test of undue influence is whether such control was exercised over the mind of the testatrix as to overcome her free agency and free will and to substitute the will of another so as to cause the testatrix to do what she would not otherwise have done but for such control.[78]

The evidence here establishes that testatrix was 81 years of age at the time of the execution of her will; that her son, defendant Lipper, who is a lawyer, wrote the will for her upon her instruction; that defendant Lipper bore malice against his deceased half brother (father of plaintiffs); that defendant Lipper lived next door to his mother and had a key to her home; that the will as written gave defendant Lipper a larger share of testatrix's estate than he would otherwise have received; that while testatrix had no discussion with anyone at the time she executed the will, she told the witness Friberg, prior to executing the will, that she was not going to leave anything to the Weslows; and subsequent to the execution of the will she told the witnesses Mrs. Levy, Mrs. Roos, and Mrs. Landry that she had not left the Weslows anything, and the reason why. The will likewise states the reasons for testatrix's action. The testatrix, although 81 years of age, was of sound mind and strong will; and in excellent physical health. There is evidence that the recitations in testatrix's will about the number of times the Weslows sent cards and flowers were incorrect, to the extent that cards and flowers were in-fact sent oftener than such will recites.

The contestants established a confidential relationship, the opportunity, and perhaps a motive for *undue influence* by defendant Lipper. Proof of this type simply sets the stage. Contestants must go forward and prove in some fashion that the will as written resulted from the defendant Lipper substituting his mind and will for that of the testatrix. Here the will and the circumstances might raise suspicion, but it does not supply proof of the vital facts of undue influence the substitution of a plan of testamentary disposition by another as the will of the testatrix. *Boyer v. Pool, supra.*

All of the evidence reflected that testatrix, although 81 years of age, was of sound mind; of strong will; and in excellent physical condition. Moreover, subsequent to the execution of the will she told 3 disinterested witnesses

---

[78] *Scott v. Townsend, 106 Tex. 322, 166 S.W. 1138; Curry v. Curry, 153 Tex. 421, 270 S.W. 2d 208; Boyer v. Pool, 154 Tex. 586, 280 S.W. 2d 564.*

what she had done with her property in her will, and the reason thereof. A person of sound mind has the legal right to dispose of his property as he wishes, with the burden to those attacking the disposition to prove that it was the product of undue influence. *Long v. Long, 133 Tex. 96; Curry v. Curry, 153 Tex. 421.*

Testatrix's will did make an unnatural disposition of her property in the sense that it preferred her 2 children over the grandchildren by a deceased son. However, the record contains an explanation from testatrix herself as to why she chose to do such. She had a right to do as she did, whether we think she was justified or not.

Plaintiffs contend that the record supports an inference that testatrix failed to receive the cards sent to her, or in the alternative she failed to know she received same, due to conduct of defendant Lipper. Here again, defendant Lipper had the opportunity to prevent testatrix from receiving cards or flowers from the Weslows, but we think there is no evidence of probative force to support the conclusion that he in fact did that. Moreover, the will itself reflected that some cards and flowers were in fact received by the testatrix, the dispute in this particular area, going to the number of times such were sent, rather than to the fact that any were sent . . .

We conclude there is no evidence of probative force to support the verdict of the jury. The cause is reversed and rendered for defendants.

NOTES AND QUESTIONS

Remember Mrs. Block told about three witnesses how she would dispose of her property and why she chose to disinherit the Weslows; would it have made a much better difference if she had left a recorded statement in her own voice along with the written statement? Could there have been any room for contest if she had done so?

Note: that section 8 of Mrs. Block's will has a ***no-contest-clause*** which provides that "if any legatee contests testatrix's will or the will of her husband, Max Block, that they forfeit all benefits under the will. Why is it that the court did not consider the *no-contest-clause* in its ruling for the defendant Lipper? Do you think the *no-contest-clause* could have had any effect if the Weslows had proved that Mrs. Block's will was indeed a product of undue influence exerted by Mr. Lipper?

Note: that a *no-contest-clause* which may be found in the body of a will is designed to discourage will contests; in most cases the court would enforce a no contest clause sometimes as a tool for preventing frivolous suits. However, enforcement of a no contest clause may prevent a lawsuit proving forgery, fraud, or undue influence and destroy the safeguard built around the testamentary disposition of property. Under the majority rule, a no contest clause is enforced unless there is a probable cause not to do so. For example, where the contestant established that the will is a product of fraud, forgery, or undue influence, the court may set the no contest clause aside. In a minority of jurisdictions, courts enforce no contest clauses unless the contestant alleges forgery or subsequent revocation by a later will or codicil, or the beneficiary is contesting a provision benefiting the drafter of the will or any witness.[79]

DEVISES TO ATTORNEYS

Note: that Mrs. Block's will give the bulk of her estate to her son Frank Lipper, who happened to be an attorney and also the drafter of her will. In many jurisdictions, the presumption of undue influence arises when an attorney drafter receives a devise from the estate however, the presumption may be rebutted if the attorney can establish he is a relative of the testatrix. The attorney must show by clear and convincing evidence that the devise is not a product of his influence on the testator.

CAUTION: For attorneys, it is always better to encourage the testator to seek an *independent counsel* to avoid all presumption of undue influence. When this is not the case, the attorney should make sure that the will is properly witnessed by independent parties with no connections to the attorney and who may properly testify that the dispositions represents the intent of the testator. In using *independent counsel*, the attorney must make sure the client has a full benefit of such a counsel and if possible the independent counsel should be a person with no connection to the attorney. Attorneys are properly trained, and the presumption is that the specialized training, places them in a position of power and influence over their clients. For more on this, please see *Will of Moses, 227 So. 2d 829.*

---

[79]   See Dukeminier: Wills, Trusts, and Estates, 7th edition (2005) P. 167

BEQUESTS BY FRAUD

Assuming a beneficiary makes changes to your will which you never authorized and as a result, gets what you never intended to give, after your death, the portion of the will changed is void and may be subject to contest by interested parties as a product of *fraud*, this is known as (*fraud in the execution*). Fraud can also be a willfully false material statement of fact made by the heir or will beneficiary with the intention of deceiving the decedent, which in-fact deceived the decedent, and cause the decedent to write or change (or refrain from writing or changing) a will in reliance upon such statement; this is (*fraud in the inducement*). In other words, Fraud in the inducement occurs when a person misrepresents facts, so as to cause the testator to execute a will, to include particular devises in the wrong-doer's favor, or to refrain from executing or revoking a will. Fraud in the execution is when a person misrepresents the character or contents of the instrument signed by the testator to create a diversion from the testator's intent.

In determining whether the will is obtained by fraud, two questions are raised (1) whether the bequest would have been made "but for" this fraud. (2) whether the fraud was the sole motive for the gift. Partial invalidity is also possible due to undue influence or a delusion as discussed earlier. Generally, the entire will fails for improper execution (will formalities), lack of intent or a generalized mental (or age) incapacity.

PUCKETT v. KRIDA
Court of Appeals of Tennessee
S.W. 2d, 1994,WL 475863

LEWIS, Judge.

This appeal is from the judgment of the trial court setting aside both a deed and will, executed by Nancy Porch Hooper, deceased, after finding that the will and deed were procured by undue influence, fraud, deceit, and/or misrepresentation of the respondent/appellant, Laverne Krida and respondent, Mattie Ruth Reeves.

Nancy Porch Hooper, deceased, lived in Humphreys County, Tennessee prior to her death. She had one brother, Tom Meredith, who also lived in Humphreys County, and a sister, Lucille Puckett of Michigan. The deceased also had several nieces and nephews who lived outside Tennessee. Appellee Jean Law was one of those nieces.

In 1987, Ms. Hooper suffered a stroke. After suffering the stroke, she executed separate powers of attorney to her sister, Lucille Puckett, and her niece, Jean Law. In June 1989, Ms. Hooper suffered a second stroke and because of her limited ability to care for herself, Jean Law began to act under her power of attorney.

In the summer of 1990, Ms. Hooper was hospitalized as an Alzheimer's patient. Ms. Hooper was concerned that she might be placed in a nursing home. In October 1990, appellee Jean Law employed defendants, Laverne Krida and Mattie Ruth Reeves, to provide (24) hour care for Ms. Hooper. At the time defendants were employed, Ms. Hooper had improved physically, but was still experiencing hallucinations.

There is evidence that prior to Ms. Krida and Ms. Reeves employment, the appellees experienced a good relationship with Ms. Hooper. However, after defendants were employed, Ms. Hooper's relationship with the appellees began to change.

Following an evidentiary hearing, the trial court made extensive findings of fact, which are in pertinent part as follows:

But when you get around the fraud and undue influence, the case, as I indicated the other day, has tones that tend to give rise to a normal outrage in the sense of the community . . . You have an elderly lady who is of an advanced age, has had mental problems, hallucinations, sickness; and who apparently has fondness for some of her family members, especially her sister, Lucille; and her niece, Jean Law; and who has apparently been trying to take care of her and doing things for her. And all at once everybody who has testified on the family's side has indicated Porch Hooper didn't want to go to a nursing home. I think that is normal, natural, and most people feel that way, it was well known . . . So then she hired Mrs. Reeves and Mrs. Krida and the record is clear and undisputed that Mrs. Krida and Mrs. Reeves took the best of care of this elderly lady. They fed her. They clothed her. They gave her medication, kept her house clean, kept her happy, and did things for her such as the garden and taking her places. And so apparently, they took real good care of her. And now then here is the unusual thing that would raise at least a question mark in almost anybody's mind These two strangers were hired in October of 1990, Now Mrs. Krida indicated that she had known Mrs. Hooper back some previous years because of Mrs. Hooper's husband going to the doctor. But make no mistake about it, the proof was clear that she was not a close friend of Mrs. Hooper's . . . They were hired in October. Well, by February there was a telephone call to Mr. Bradley wanting to change the power of attorney . . . On the 8ᵗʰ day of March power of attorney is executed to Mrs. Krida. We go down on the 26ᵗʰ, I believe it was, and we changed out all of the bank accounts. The bank employees indicate they were of the opinion she don't know what she was doing, she didn't understand what she was doing. And they couldn't explain it to her. They couldn't get her to tell them what she wanted, but they finally said, "Do you want us to do what Mrs. Krida said? And she said "Yeah, do what she says." And the bank employee's version of why they accepted that was because Mrs. Krida had power of attorney and they didn't feel they had any choice anyway. Well then by the 15ᵗʰ of April she makes a will leaving everything to these two ladies . . . 25ᵗʰ of July they made a deed, deeding everything, the home place to Reeves and Krida. Now if you just present that scenario . . . Well, isn't it strange? I think it raises, as I said, a question in anybody's mind, that timing and sequence of events, and oddly enough it fits a pattern that a review of cases will reveal exists in many cases where elderly people involved in cases such as this where charges of undue influence have been tried . . . It is also significant to note that they were not hired to manage her financial affairs or make her arrangements for surgeries or manage her money or any of those kinds of things, but they took all of those things on . . . They sold her truck for $2,500 . . . And they sold it to guess who? A relative of one of the caretakers, and for $2,500 . . . Why would caretakers who are charged with the responsibility of looking after her and seeing after her financial affairs, sell an asset or let her sell an asset for what might be well below value? I don't know. Could it be because it was sold to one of their relatives? I don't know . . .

Now clearly in this case there is evidence of a *confidential relationship*. Once the power of attorney was executed the confidential relationship is there.

Now apparently from the testimony, the things that Mrs. Hooper was doing, she was doing because she became upset. Why was she upset? Well, several reasons. She thought Jean Law was squandering her money. She thought Jean Law was spending Mrs. Hooper's money to come back and forth down here on an airplane to look after her. And the truth was that Mrs. Law was keeping meticulous account of her funds. Mrs. Law was spending Mrs. Law's money to travel back and forth. She was only spending Mrs. Hooper's money on Mrs. Hooper. She was having the Social Security check direct deposited into the bank. She was putting the dividend money off of the insurance to Mrs. Hooper's use, putting that in the bank, accounting for everything . . .

. . . When you start examining the records, once Mrs. Krida took over, right away you see her writing unusual checks. There was the $700 check which she explained was because she wasn't paying herself every week and it was for a longer period of time, it was for two weeks. And later on there was a period of time where she wrote both herself and Mrs. Reeves a two thousand and some odd dollar check each . . . When Mrs. Law kept the records she paid them each and every week and paid them precisely what they were entitled to for that week . . . You can look at the records and know what was going on. Not when Mrs. Krida got a hold of the records then you couldn't tell what was going on . . .

Now I find and I hold that there are only two possibilities with regards to all of these things that Mrs. Porch Hooper was led to believe, that they were trying to put her in a nursing home, squandering her money, that they were going to move in with her, come and live with her and all that . . . So there is two possibilities, either they were the source of these misinformation never once did they say, "Mrs. Law is not squandering your money." And never once did they call Mrs. Law and say "Mrs. Hooper thinks you are wasting her money. You need to come down here and explain to her and talk to her." They didn't check with the family members about putting her in the hospital, you know, to see what they wanted to do about it. They just took it upon themselves . . . They were either the source of the misinformation or they intentionally let her think that, knowing it was false. Either way is fraud and undue influence. And then they persuade her to deed and will everything she had to them to take care of her for the rest of her life, and they had already been paid to do that . . .

So my ruling and holding is, gentlemen, obviously, from a review of the evidence that there is *Fraud and Undue Influence* in this case. The power of attorney establishes a confidential relationship. The law presumes undue influence.

The appellant has presented the following three issues:

1. Whether the trial court erred in holding that Ms. Krida and Ms. Reeves failed to carry their burden of proving the lack of undue influence in connection with the will and deed executed by Ms. Hooper.

127

2. Whether the trial court erred in finding that the will and the deed executed by Ms. Hooper were the product of undue influence, fraud, deceit and/or misrepresentation.
3. Whether the trial court erred in admitting and relying upon hearsay statements purportedly made by Judge Danny Bradley.

We discuss these issues together.

In a will contest, the proponent of the will has the initial burden of proving due execution of the will and its *prima facie validity*. The burden of proof then shifts to the contestant to prove facts necessary to void the will. *Taliaferro v. Green, 622 S.W. 2d 829(Tenn. 1981)*. The law does not presume fraud or undue influence, and generally the contestant who alleges fraud or undue influence must prove them. The execution of a will brought about as a result of fraud or undue influence is void. To invalidate a will, the undue influence must destroy the free agency of the testator to the extent that the will is in reality that of another. *Crain v. Brown, 823 S.W. 2d 187(Tenn.App.1991)* . . .

The two grounds of undue influence and fraud are closely related, but in the case of fraud the free agency of the testator remains, but he is misled into doing that which otherwise he would not have done . . . To set aside a will on the basis of fraud, "the fraud must be of active, tortious, deceitful kind and not of the constructive or resultant nature.

It is recognized . . . that undue influence may be grounded on false and fraudulent representations made to the testator and insofar as the present case is concerned, the distinction between the two grounds of attack is of no practical importance . . . It is essential in order to avoid a will for undue influence of this nature that the statements be false; that the testator be unable, through weakness of mind and body, or concealment of the facts, to determine the falsity of the statements and resist the influence; and that he rely and act on them rather than on other motives and inducements."

False representations will constitute a ground for voiding a will, even in the absence of proof that they were used to bring pressure to bear upon the testator; but it must appear that the person making such representations knew them to be false, that they were made with the intention of deceiving the testator and for the purpose of obtaining a bequest or at least, of affecting a testamentary disposition, and that he wad deceived by such representations and induced to act in reliance thereon by preparing a will different from what he would have made but for the misrepresentation and deception.

Fraud sufficient to invalidate a will may be predicated upon a false accusation that one in a position to be the natural recipient of the testator's bounty had been guilty of an act causing great displeasure to the testator {or} had stirred up trouble in the family . . .

Concealment or suppression of facts may constitute fraud sufficient to invalidate a will, in a case where there was a duty to disclose such facts to the testator, as where a confidential relation existed between the testator and the person accused of perpetrating the fraud. But even concealment or misrepresentation by a beneficiary for the purpose of deceiving the testator does not invalidate a bequest if it appears that it might have been made for some other reason.

Generally, it is difficult to invalidate a will on the basis of undue influence and/or fraud because direct evidence rarely exists. *Mitchell v. Smith, 779 S.W.2d 384 (Tenn. App.1989)*. "Without direct evidence, a contestant must establish the existence of more than one suspicious circumstance . . . Proof of confidential relationship alone will not support a finding of undue influence."

Once the existence of a confidential relationship and suspicious circumstances are proven, undue influence or fraud is presumed. A confidential relationship will be found to exist when there is proof that one of the parties was in a "position to exercise dominion, control, or influence over the other." *Owen v. Stanley, 739 S.W.2d 782,787 (Tenn.App.1987)* . . .

Once the presumption of undue influence or fraud arises, the presumption may be rebutted by proof of the fairness of the transaction established by a preponderance of the evidence. *Crain v. Brown, 823 S.W.2d at 194.*

Where . . . the contestant shows the existence of suspicious circumstances such as a confidential relationship in combination with the beneficiary's involvement in procuring the will, or in combination with impairment of the testator's mental capacity, there arises a presumption of fraud or undue influence which the proponent of the will must overcome by a preponderance of the evidence . . .

In the instant case, the evidence shows that at the time the defendants were employed, the deceased loved her family and was very close to them. She was frugal and conservative, but entrusted the management of her financial affairs to her niece, Jean Law. The evidence is that Mrs. Law carefully managed these finances and promised to keep the deceased out of a nursing home, making every effort to do so. She never reimbursed herself for any of her expenses.

Subsequent to the defendants' employment, the deceased began to believe that Jean Law wanted to put her in a nursing home and that Ms. Law has misappropriated funds. The evidence shows that neither of these beliefs were true. The evidence further shows that these false beliefs originated with the defendants who systematically separated the deceased from her family and friends and isolated her from all those individuals with whom she had previously dealt, personally and professionally. All of these was done in order to perpetuate the fraud . . .

"Since frauds are generally secret {they} have to be tracked by the footprints, marks, and signs made by the perpetrators and discovered by the light of the attending facts and circumstances." *Henry R. Gibson, Gibson's suits in Chancery, § 448 (William H. Inman, ed., 7th ed. 1988).*

By limiting information available to the deceased and by concealing their acts from the critical examination of those whom the deceased had previously known and trusted, the defendants isolated the deceased and controlled access to her. The defendants terminated the deceased's former legal and financial relationships and arranged new ones. They made her neighbors feel unwelcome and threatened her family with legal action. They replaced her long-time tenant with a family member of one of the defendants. Furthermore, the defendants made detrimental decisions regarding the sale of the deceased's real property, to avoid contact with a realtor who had previously handled the deceased's affairs.

The dealings with the deceased's money by the defendants was irregular and unusual. Defendant's offered no suitable explanation at trial to account for any of the cash funds that the deceased received while defendant Krida managed the financial affairs.

The evidence in this record fully supports the findings and judgment of the trial court.

We find no error under issues one and two and have determined that even if there was error in the trial court's admission of hearsay statements reportedly made by Judge Danny Bradley, that these were harmless, in view of the other overwhelming evidence in this record.

We have considered each of the arguments of appellants and find them to be without merit.

The Judgment of the trial court is affirmed in all respects, and the cause is remanded to the trial court for the implementation of its judgment and any further necessary proceedings. Costs on appeal are taxed to the respondent/appellant, Laverne Krida.

DURESS

Assuming **A** son of **B** held a gun at **B** and threatened to kill him unless he makes a will bequeathing all his belongings to **A**, should such a will be admitted to probate? The answer is no because the will is a product of duress and was obtained by such means that does not demonstrate **B**'s intent. When undue influence becomes extensively coercive it becomes duress. According to the Restatement (Third) of Property: Wills and Other Donative Transfers §8.3(c) (2003), "A donative transfer is procured by duress if the wrongdoer threatened to perform or did perform a wrongful act that coerced the donor into making a donative transfer that the donor would not otherwise have made."

Through the use of force, the wrongdoer intentionally substitutes the donor's will for his own, and since the will no longer demonstrates donor's intent, it must not be allowed to stand and thus, void as a product of force. However, the contestant must be able to show that force was indeed used and that 'but for' the duress, the donor would not have transferred his property the way he did.

LATHAM v. FATHER DIVINE
Court of Appeals of New York, 1949
299 N.Y. 22, 85 N.E.2d 168, 11 A.L.R.2d 802

DESMOND J.

The amended complaint herein has, in response to a motion under rule 106 of the Rules of Civil Practice, been dismissed for insufficiency. Its principal allegations are these: Plaintiffs are first cousins, but not distributes, of Mary Sheldon Lyon, who died in October, 1946, leaving a will, executed in 1943, which gave almost her whole estate to defendant Father Divine, leader of a religious cult, and to two corporate defendants in some ways connected with that cult, and to an individual defendant (Patience Budd) said to be one of Father Divine's active followers; that said will have been, after a contest instituted by distributees, probated under a compromise agreement with the distributees, by the terms of which agreement, to which plaintiffs were not parties, the defendants just above referred to will receive a large sum from the estate; that after the making of said will, decedent on several occasions expressed 'a desire and a determination to revoke the said will, and to execute a new will by which the plaintiffs would receive a substantial portion of the estate', that shortly prior to the death of the deceased she had certain attorneys draft a new will in which the plaintiffs were named as legatees for a very substantial amount, totaling approximately $350,000'; that by reason of the said false representations, the said undue influence and the said physical force' certain of the defendants 'prevented the deceased from executing the said will'; that, shortly before decedent's death, decedent again expressed her determination to execute the proposed new will which favored plaintiffs, and the defendants 'thereupon conspired to kill, and did kill, the deceased by means of a surgical operation performed by a doctor engaged by the defendants without the consent or knowledge of any of the relatives of the deceased.'

Nothing is better settled than that, on such a motion as this, all the averments of the attacked pleading are taken as true. For present purposes, then, we have a case where one is possessed of a large property and having already made a will leaving it to certain persons, expressed an intent to make a new testament to contain legacies to other persons, attempted to carry out that intention by having a new will drawn which contained a large legacy to those others, but was, by means of misrepresentation, undue influence, force, and indeed, murder, prevented, by the beneficiaries named in the existing will, from signing the new one. Plaintiffs claim that those facts, if proven, would entitle them to a judicial declaration, which their prayer for judgment demands, that defendants, taking under the already probated will, hold what they have so taken as constructive trustees for plaintiffs, who decedent wished to, tried to, and was kept from, benefiting.

We find in New York no decision directly answering the question as to whether or not the allegations above summarized state a case for relief in equity. But reliable texts, and cases elsewhere answer it in the affirmative. Leading writers (3 Scott on Trusts, pp. 2371-2376; 3 Bogert on Trusts and Trustees, part 1, §§ 473-474, 498, 499; 1 Perry on Trusts and Trustees {7[th] ed.}, pp. 265, 371) in one form or another, state the law of the subject to be about as it is expressed in comment I under section 184 of the *Restatement of the Law of Restitution:* '*Preventing revocation of Will and Making New Will.* Where a devisee or legatee under a will already executed prevents the testator by fraud, duress or undue influence from revoking the will and executing a new will in favor of another or from making a *codicil*, so that the testator dies leaving the original will in force, the devisee or legatee holds the property thus acquired upon a *constructive trust* for the intended devisee or legatee.'

A frequently cited case is *Ransdel v. Moore (153 Ind. 393)* where with listing of many authorities, the rule is given thus (pp. 407-408): "When an heir or devisee in a will prevents the testator from providing for one for whom he would have provided but for the interference of the heir or devisee, such heir or devisee will be deemed a trustee, by operation of law, of the property, real or personal, received by him from the testator's estate, to the amount or extent that the defrauded party would have received had not the intention of the deceased been interfered with. This rule applies also when an heir prevents the making of a will or deed in favor of another, and thereby inherits the property that would otherwise have been given such other person."

While there is no New York case decreeing a constructive trust on the exact facts alleged here, there are several decisions in this court which, we think, suggest such a result, and none which forbids it. *Matter of O'Hara (95 N.Y. 403), Trustees of Amherst College v. Ritch (151 N.Y. 282), Edson v. Bartow (154 N.Y. 199), Ahrens v. Jones (169 N.Y. 555)* Which need not be closely analyzed here as to their facts, all announce, in one form or another, the rule that, where a legatee has taken property under a will, after agreeing, outside the will, to devote that property to a purpose intended and declared by the testator, equity will enforce a constructive trust to effectuate that purpose, lest there be a fraud on the testator. (In *Williams v. Fitch, 18 N.Y. 546,* a similar result was achieved in a suit for money had and received.) In each of those four cases first above cited in this paragraph, the particular fraud consisted of the legatee's failure or refusal to carry out the testator's designs, after tacitly or expressly promising so to do. But we do not think that a breach of such an engagement is the only kind of fraud which will impel equity to action. A constructive trust will be erected whenever necessary to satisfy the demands of justice. Since a constructive trust is merely "the formula through which the conscience of equity finds expression" (*Beatty v. Guggenheim Exploration Co., 225 N.Y. 380,386* . . . Its applicability is limited only by the inventiveness of men who find new ways to enrich themselves unjustly by grasping what should not belong to them. Nothing short of true and complete justice satisfies equity, and always assuming these allegations to be true, there seems no way of achieving total justice except by the procedure used here.

The Appellate Division held that *Hutchins v. Hutchins (7 Hill 104)* decided by the Supreme Court, our predecessor, in 1845, was a bar to the maintenance of this suit. *Hutchins v. Hutchins (supra)* was a suit at law, dismissed for insufficiency in the days when law suits and equity causes had to be brought in different tribunals; the law court could give nothing but a judgment for damages . . .

This complaint does not say that decedent, or defendants, promised plaintiffs anything, or that defendants made any promise to decedent. The story is, simply, that defendants, by force and fraud, kept the testatrix from making a will in favor of plaintiffs. We cannot say, as matter of law, that no constructive trust can arise therefrom.

The ultimate determinations in *Matter of O'Hara and Edson v. Bartow (supra)* that the estate went to testators' distributees do not help defendants here, since, after the theory of constructive trust had been indorsed by this court in those cases, the distributees won out in the end, but only because the secret trust intended by the two testators were, in each case, of kinds forbidden by statutes.

We do not agree with appellants that *Riggs v. Palmer (115 N.Y. 506)* completely controls our decision here. That was the famous case where a grandson, overeager to get the remainder interest set up for him in his grandfather's will, murdered his grandsire. After the will had been probated, two daughters of the testator who, under the will, would take if the grandson should predecease testator, sued and got judgment decreeing a constructive trust in their favor. It may be, as respondents assert, that the application of *Riggs v. Palmer* (supra) here would benefit not plaintiffs, but this testator's distributees . . . But *Riggs v. Palmer* (supra) is generally helpful to appellants, since it forbade the grandson profiting by his own wrong in connection with a will; and despite an already probated will and the Decedent Estate Law, *Riggs v. Palmer* used the devise or formula of constructive trust to right the attempted wrong, and prevent unjust enrichment . . .

This suit cannot be defeated by any argument that to give plaintiffs judgment would be to annul those provisions of the Statute of Wills requiring due execution by the testator. Such a contention, if valid, would have required the dismissal in a number of the suit herein cited. The answer is in *Ahrens v. Jones (169 N.Y. 555, 561 supra):* "The trust does not act directly upon the will by modifying the gift, for the law requires wills to be wholly in writing, but it acts upon the gift itself as it reaches the possession of the legatee, or as soon as he is entitled to receive it. The theory is that the will has full effect by passing an absolute legacy to the legatee, and that then equity, in order to defeat fraud, raises a trust in favor of those intended to be benefited by the testator, and compels the legatee, as a *trustee ex maleficio*, to turn over the gift to them.

The judgment of the Appellate Division, insofar as it dismissed the complaint herein, should be reversed, and the order of Special Term affirmed, with costs in this court and in the Appellate Division.

NOTE

Duress is an extreme form of undue influence. To be duress however, the action must be an unlawful one. When a husband induced his wife to give him property by threatening to divorce her, she could not avoid the deed for duress because he had not threatened to do an unlawful act. But if he held a gun to her head threatening to kill her if she fails to comply, an unlawful act may be found so as to avoid the deed.[80]

Note: that the burden of proving undue influence lies with the contestant, but there can be presumption of undue influence, if a person in a confidential relationship with the testator, participated in preparing the will. For example in *Puckett v. Krida* the court set aside the will executed by Nancy Porch Hooper, after finding that the will was procured by undue influence, fraud, deceit, and misrepresentation. One of the reason the court gave for its ruling was the fact that, the *power of attorney* acquired by the defendant shows a confidential relationship between decedent and defendant to establish a presumption of undue influence.

Note: Suspicious circumstances may be enough to establish a presumption of undue influence. Remember in *Puckett v. Krida*, the court noted that the circumstances surrounding the disposition of Mrs. Hooper's belongings and the timing of events such as: changing the bank accounts, the transfer of the deed, the sale of decedent's truck, the isolation of decedent from her family etc establish undue influence.

---

[80] See *Rubenstein v. Sela, 672 P.2d 492 (Ariz. App. 1983)*.

Chapter Seven

VALID WILL & FORMALITIES

The only thing that speaks for you when you are no more is your will, it is the voice that shows your intentions and from it, we may determine how you want your belongings distributed among your loved ones. While wills are essential (most especially for a large estate), not all wills are valid. For a will to qualify for probate, it must satisfy the demands of the law and meet the standard required for wills or else, the will is useless and is nothing but a piece of paper. One who leaves behind an invalid will, is not different from one who died intestate (without a will), since the will may not be probated, the *default rule* takes effect and all real and personal belongings of the decedent is distributed, according to intestacy law of the jurisdiction involved. Since it is presumed there is no will, the proper thing to do is to set aside decedent's intentions and allow the law to take his position by ensuring proper distribution of the estate.

In the United States, there are different requirements depending on the jurisdiction. In most states, a will, to be *valid*, must satisfy very strict requirements of signing and witnessing, and in some cases, notarizing as well. In some states, a simple statement entirely in the handwriting of the deceased signed and dated by him or her will do and can be considered a valid enforceable will. However, it must be made with the intention that it be a will. Such wills are termed '*Holographic Wills*' (written entirely by hand).

There are many essential provisions that should be in a will, all will whether handwritten (holographic) or not, must meet these requirements, and wills that are not handwritten must be signed with certain formalities to establish validity. In this chapter, we shall discuss what is needed to make your will valid and satisfy requirements of the law.

WRITING

One of the essential requirements is that the will must be in *writing*, except for special cases as we have in *holographic wills* (or in a life-and-death situations) where an oral or *nuncupative* will may be accepted; A jurisdiction such as New York, require that three people must hear the oral will and must reduce the oral will to writing soon after. However, ordinary wills must be in writing. If a will fails to meet this requirement, the will is invalid and void; no matter how close it comes to meeting this requirement, the will cannot be valid but if the requirement of *writing* is satisfied along with all other essentials, the will is accepted and may be nullified only on grounds of other factors such as: incapacity, duress, undue influence and the like which normally invalidates even a valid will. That the will must be in *writing* is the basic rule dating back to 1677 Statute of Frauds. The requirement excludes non-written wills, but failed to answer the questions of what is a writing and in what language must it be written. However, the writing need not be in English. A will may be written in any language, even in a language the testator did not understand, so long he understood the contents and *intended* that the document be his will and there is someone who can translate it. The written document must be affixed to a permanent surface. Letters have been held to constitute a valid will and there have been instances where courts have admitted handwriting on a nurse's petticoat and on a desk as valid wills.

SIGNED & SUBSCRIBED

Another requirement is that the will be subscribed and signed at the end by the testator. With the exception of a *nuncupative* or one that is orally made during a life-and-death situation, this is a strict requirement for every type of will in every state. Signature, which can be any act combined with intent is still required from the testator however, the signature need not be legible, a misspelled word can still pass as a signature if done and affixed with intent; it must be established that the testator intended the mark to *authenticate* the document as his will. Any mark such as a fingerprint, a dot, or an 'X' is sufficient if intended to authenticate the material. A disabled and physically challenged, may have another person sign the document for her however, it must be done in the testator's presence, at her direction, signed in her name and she must understand the contents of her will. The principle behind this idea is to allow those that are illiterate or physically challenged the opportunity to make a will. The signature may be in testator's full name or an abbreviated version as long as there is no intent to deceive.

The signature in most cases is only required once and must be placed at the end of the will, but to avoid future contests, the attorney should make the testator sign and initial each page to ensure no additions and changes are made after the will is signed. However, this is not a legal requirement but a precautionary measure to protect against future contests of the will. For example, an addition *under* the signature of the testator may invalidate a will since it creates a presumption of fraud committed after the will is signed.

WITNESSED

Another requirement is that the will be *witnessed*. In some jurisdictions, at least two witnesses are required to be in the presence of the testator when he signs the will. However, the witnesses are not required to know the contents of the will but they must be persons of sound mind and able to testify that they witnessed the will. A witness must have no interest in the bounty of the will and should not be a person named as a beneficiary under the will nor the spouse of a beneficiary named under the will, the beneficiary may not be allowed to take his or her devise should that be the case. This rule however, does not apply to other relatives of the beneficiary but the spouse. However, a beneficiary who later married a witness after the fact is not barred from taking. A will that has more than the required number of witnesses is still valid but if it has less than the prescribed number it is invalid. The same rule that applies to the signature of the testator, applies to the witnesses; they do not have to sign their full name but any abbreviation must show intent to authenticate the instrument.

The Statute of Frauds required wills of land to be subscribed by the witnesses in the presence of the testator as well as by the testator. Most modern statutes impose the same requirement for all wills. Normally, the witness are required to sign after the testator, however, if they sign first, the will may still be valid as long as, the signatures are part of a continuous transaction. Most statutes do not indicate a precise place for the witnesses' attestation.

NOTE: In addition to the three requirements, the testator must sign in the presence of the witnesses and the witnesses must also attest to the will in the presence of the testator. The witnesses and the testator must be in the same room when the will is signed and if needed in the presence of testator's attorney. In some jurisdiction, the testator who for example, signed his will a day before in the absence of the witnesses, is allowed to acknowledge his signature in the presence of the witnesses, they must see him acknowledge it as his true signature but the witnesses must sign in the presence of the testator for the will to be valid. All must be present in the same room for the signing ceremony or else, the will may be questioned.

Do You Need an Attorney?

The answer is not really, but it is always in the best interests of a testator to have a lawyer draft his or her will. Failure to seek the help of a professional may have a devastating effect, for example, somebody with a very large estate; it is not uncommon for an estate to be subject to tax problems after the will is probated. An attorney or probate expert knows the law and what to do in case the widow left behind is entitled to marital deductions and all other estate tax deductions that the beneficiary may be entitled to. If a will is not properly done, the estate may be subject to fees caused by sloppy drafting and to avoid contest problems among beneficiaries, having an attorney do it right may be the best thing however, this does not immune the will from contests. **Note**: that you can still make your own will, however, for your will to be valid it must satisfy the requirements for a formal will.

Keeping Your Will

When the signing ceremony is over, the will is usually given to the testator who decides where to keep it. It is always better to keep the will in a safe place where your family can find it when they need it for probate. Some testator, leave it with the attorney and in some states the will may be deposited in the probate court for safekeeping. It is better to have your attorney make two exact copies of the will, one for you and one for the attorney to be kept for record purposes so that incase the original is lost, the attorney can present a copy on file.

NOTE: An attorney should not always depend on the formalities requirements of the statute in the client's home state. It is not uncommon for the client's will to be offered for probate in another state. In most cases, the law of the domicile of the client at death determines how the will is probated insofar as it disposes of personal property. As for real property, the law of the state where the property is located governs and determines the validity of the disposition. In case the will exercise a power of appointment governed by the law of another states, the law of the state of appointment determines the validity of the disposition.

HOLOGRAPHIC WILLS

Sometimes one may choose to write his or her will entirely by hand in the testator's handwriting. *Holographic wills* are entirely handwritten by the testator and from the face of such wills, the testator's handwriting is easily identifiable and may help to prevent future contest as to whether or not the testator actually wrote the will. Such wills are considered to have less risk of forgery therefore no witnesses are needed for them.

In states that allow such wills, while the testator may choose a handwritten will, there are still requirements that must be met. In many states, there is the requirement that *holographic* will {1} be dated; {2} be entirely in the testator's own handwriting; and {3} establish testamentary intent of the testator to make a will.

The Uniform Probate Code does not require that *holographic* wills be dated but in some states an undated will may be invalid if during contest, the date is found to be *material* to the will. In States that require *holographic* wills to be dated, it is also necessary that the date be complete with month, day, and year clearly stated. All material portion of the will must be in testator's handwriting including the signature.

While *holographic* wills are not required to be witnessed, the testator's testamentary intent to make a will must be established or else the will is invalid. By using the word 'will' on the face of the will may help to establish testamentary intent and remove doubts as to whether the testator intend the writing to be his or her will.

WILLS FORMALITIES & CONTESTS

Requirement of proper witness:

STEVENS V. CASDORPH
West Virginia Supreme Court of Appeals
203 W. Va. 450, 508 S.E. 2d 610

PER CURIAM.

The plaintiffs below and appellants herein Janet Sue Lanham Stevens, Peggy Lanham Salisbury, Betty Jean Bayes, and Patricia Miller Moyers (hereinafter collectively referred to as "Stevenses") appeal a summary judgment ruling for the defendants by the Circuit Court of Kanawha County. The Stevenses instituted this action against Patricia Eileen Casdorph and Paul Douglas Casdorph, individually and as executor of the estate of Homer Haskell Miller, defendants below and appellees herein (hereinafter referred to as "Casdorphs"), for the purpose of challenging the will of Homer Haskell Miller. The Circuit Court granted the Casdorphs' cross-motion for summary judgment. On appeal, the Court is asked to reverse the trial court's ruling. Following a review of the parties' arguments, the record, and the pertinent authorities, we reverse the decision of the circuit court of Kanawha County.

On May 28, 1996, the Casdorphs took Mr. Homer Haskell Miller to Shawnee Bank in Dunbar, West Virginia, so that he could execute his will. Once at the bank, Mr. Miller asked Debra Pauley, a bank employee and public notary, to witness the execution of his will. After Mr. Miller signed the will, Ms. Pauley took the will to two other bank employees, Judith Waldron and Ms. Reba McGinn, for the purpose of having each of them sign the will as witnesses. Both Ms. Waldron and Ms. McGinn signed the will. However, Ms. Waldron and Ms. McGinn testified during their depositions that they did not actually see Mr. Miller place a signature on the will. Further, it is undisputed that Mr. Miller did not accompany Ms. Pauley to the separate work areas of Ms. Waldron and Ms. McGinn.

Mr. Miller died on July 28, 1996. The last will and testament of Mr. Miller, which named Mr. Paul Casdorph as executor, left the bulk of his estate to the Casdorphs. The Stevenses, nieces of Mr. Miller, filed the instant action to set aside the will. The Stevenses asserted in their complaint that

Mr. Miller's will was not executed according to the requirements set forth in W. Va. Code § 41-1-3 (1995). After some discovery, all parties moved for summary judgment. The circuit court denied the Stevenses motion for summary judgment, but granted the Casdorphs cross motion for summary judgment. From this ruling, the Stevenses appeal to this court.

Paul Casdorph was a nephew of Mr. Miller. Mr. Miller's probated estate exceeded $400,000.00. The will devised $80,000.00 to Frank Paul Smith a nephew of Mr. Miller. The remainder of the estate was left to the Casdorphs.

As heirs, the Stevenses would be entitled to recover from Mr. Miller's estate under the intestate laws if his will is set aside as invalidly executed.

The Stevenses' contention is simple. They argue that all evidence indicates that Mr. Miller's will was not properly executed. Therefore, the will should be voided. The procedural requirements at issue are contained in *W. Va. Code § 41-1-3(1997)*. The statute reads:

> *No will shall be valid unless it be in writing and signed by the testator, or by some other person in his presence and by his direction, in such manner as to make it manifest that the name is intended as a signature; and moreover, unless it be wholly in the handwriting of the testator, the signature shall be made or the will acknowledged by him in the presence of at least two competent witnesses, present at the same time; and such witnesses shall subscribe the will in the presence of the testator, and of each other, but no form of attestation shall be necessary.*
> (Emphasis added.)

The relevant requirements of the above statute calls for a testator to sign his/her will or acknowledge such will in the presence of at least two witnesses at the same time, and such witnesses must sign the will in the presence of the testator and each other. In the instant proceeding the Stevenses assert, and the evidence supports, that Ms. McGinn and Ms. Waldron did not actually witness Mr. Miller signing his will. Mr. Miller made no acknowledgment of his signature on the will to either Ms. McGinn or Ms. Waldron. Likewise Mr. Miller did not observe Ms. McGinn and Ms. Waldron sign his will as witnesses. Additionally, neither Ms. McGinn nor Ms. Waldron acknowledged to Mr. Miller that their signatures were on the will. It is also undisputed that Ms. McGinn and Ms. Waldron did not actually witness each other sign the will, nor did they acknowledge to each other that they had signed Mr. Miller's will. Despite the evidentiary lack of compliance with *W.Va.Code § 41-1-3*, the Casdorphs' argue that there was substantial compliance with the statute's requirements, insofar as everyone involved with the will knew what was occurring. The trial court found that there was substantial compliance with the statute because everyone knew why Mr. Miller was at the bank. The trial court further concluded there was no evidence of fraud, coercion or undue influence. Based upon foregoing, the trial court concluded that the will should not be voided even though the technical aspect of *W.Va. Code § 41-1-3* were not followed.

Our analysis begins by noting that "the law favors testacy over intestacy." Syl. Pt. 8 *In re Teubert's Estate, 171 W.Va. 226, 298 S.E.2d 456(1982)*. However, we clearly held in syllabus point 1 of *Black v. Maxwell, 131 W.Va. 247, 46 S.E. 804 (1948)*, that "testamentary intent and a written instrument, executed in the manner provided by *W.Va. Code § 41-1-3*, existing concurrently, are essential to the creation of a valid will." *Black* establishes that mere intent by a testator to execute a written will is insufficient. The actual execution of a written will must also comply with the dictates of *W.Va. Code § 41-1-3*. The Casdorphs seek to have this court establish an exception to the technical requirements of the statute. In *Wade v. Wade, 119 W.Va. 596, 195 S.E. 339 (1938)*, this court permitted a narrow exception to the stringent requirements of the *W.Va. Code § 41-1-3*. This narrow exception is embodied in syllabus point 1 of *Wade:*

> *Where a testator acknowledges a will and his signature thereto in the presence of two competent witnesses, one of whom then subscribes his name, the other or first witness, having already subscribed the will in the presence of the testator but out of the presence of the second witness, may acknowledge his signature in the presence of the testator and the second witness, and such acknowledgment, if there is no indicia of fraud or misunderstanding in the proceeding, will be deemed a signing by the first witness within the requirement of Code, 41-1-3, that the witness must subscribe their names in the presence of the testator and of each other . . .*

Wade stands for the proposition that if a witness acknowledges his/her signature on a will in the physical presence of the other subscribing witness and the testator, then the will is properly witness within the terms of *W.Va. Code § 41-1-3*. In this case, none of the parties signed or acknowledged their signatures in the presence of each other. This case meets neither the narrow exception of *Wade* nor the specific provisions of *W.Va. Code § 41-1-3*.

In view of the foregoing, we grant the relief sought in this appeal and reverse the circuit court's order granting the Casdorphs' cross-motion for summary judgment.

Reversed.

WORKMAN, Justice, dissenting:

The majority once more takes a very technocratic approach to the law, slavishly worshiping form over substance. In so doing, they not only create a harsh and inequitable result wholly contrary to the indisputable intent of Mr. Homer Haskell Miller, but also a rule of law that is against the spirit and intent of our whole body of law relating to the making of wills.

There is absolutely no claim of incapacity or fraud or undue influence, nor any allegation by any party that Mr. Miller did not consciously, intentionally, and with full legal capacity convey his property as specified in his will. The challenge to the will is based solely upon the allegation that Mr. Miller did not comply with the requirement of *W.Va. Code § 41-1-3* that the signature shall be made or that the will acknowledged by the testator in the presence of at least two competent witnesses, present at the same time. The lower court, in its very thorough findings of fact, indicated that Mr. Miller had been transported to the bank by his nephew Mr. Casdorph and the nephew's wife. Mr. Miller, disabled and confined to a wheelchair, was a shareholder in the Shawnee bank in Dunbar, West Virginia, with whom all those present were personally familiar. When Mr. Miller executed his will in the bank lobby, the typed will was placed on Ms. Pauley's desk, and Mr. Miller instructed Ms. Pauley that he wished to have his will signed, witnessed, and acknowledged. After Mr. Miller's signature had been placed upon the will with Ms. Pauley watching, Ms. Pauley walked the will over to the tellers' area in the same small lobby of the bank. Ms. Pauley explained that Mr. Miller wanted Ms. Waldron to sign the will as a witness. The same process was used to obtain the signature of Ms. McGinn. Sitting in his wheelchair, Mr. Miller did not move from Ms. Pauley's desk during the process of obtaining the witness signatures. The lower court concluded that the will was valid and that Ms. Waldron and Ms. McGinn signed and acknowledged the will "in the presence" of Mr. Miller . . .

In *Wade v. Wade, 119 W.Va. 596(1938),* we addressed the validity of a will challenged for such technicalities and observed that "a narrow, rigid construction of the statute should not be allowed to stand in the way of right and justice, or be permitted to defeat a testator's disposition of his property." *119 W.Va. at 599, 195 S.E. at 340-341.* We upheld the validity of the challenged will in *Wade* noting that "each case must rest on its own facts and circumstances to which the court must look to determine whether there was a subscribing by the witnesses in the presence of the testator; that substantial compliance with the statute is all that is required . . . A contrary result, we emphasized, "would be based on illiberal and inflexible construction of the statute, giving preeminence to letter and not to spirit, and resulting in the thwarting of the intentions of testators even under circumstances where no possibility of fraud or impropriety exists." *195 S.E. at 341.*

The majority's conclusion is precisely what was envisioned and forewarned in 1938 by the drafters of the *Wade* opinion: illiberal and inflexible construction, giving preeminence to the letter of the law and ignoring the spirit of the entire body of testamentary law, resulting in the thwarting of Mr. Miller's unequivocal wishes . . .

To hold the will invalid on a strictly technical flaw would "be to observe the letter of the statute as interpreted strictly, and fail to give heed to the statute's obvious purpose. Thus, the statute would be turned against those for whose protection it had been written . . .

The majority embraces the line of least resistance. The easy, most convenient answer is to say that the formal, technical requirements have not been met and that the will is therefore invalid. End of inquiry. Yet that result is patently absurd. The manner of statutory application is inconsistent with the underlying purposes of the statute. Where a statute is enacted to protect and sanctify the execution of a will to prevent substitution or fraud, this court's application of that statute should further such underlying policy, not impede it. When, in our efforts to strictly apply legislative language, we abandon common sense and reason in favor of technicalities, we are the ones committing the injustice.

Justice MYNARD joins the dissent.

QUESTIONS

Note: that the exception rule in *Wade* permits a witness, who subscribed his name in the presence of the testator but not in the presence of the other witness, to declare his signature in the presence of the testator and the other witness; is the exception consistent with most statute's requirement that both witnesses be present in the same room for the subscription? Why does the court in *Wade* permit such narrow exception as precedence in *Stevens v. Casdorph*?

Note: Based on the ruling, the will was declare invalid for improper execution which violates dictates of the Virginia statute, does this mean in actuality that the will did not demonstrate testator's intent, if there is clear evidence that testator's wish was to leave the bulk of his estate to the Casdorphs?

Note: the dissenting opinion that "to hold the will invalid on a strictly technical flaw would "be to observe the letter of the statute as interpreted strictly, and fail to give heed to the statute's obvious purpose." Do you agree with the opinion? What about an argument that a statute is what it is and must be upheld as such and not construed otherwise. Does declaring the will invalid for failure to follow dictates of the statute, a misinterpretation of the statute's obvious purpose in this case?

Note; The argument that everyone present had knowledge of what was occurring when Mr. Miller visited the bank and as a result the will should be valid. Do you think knowledge alone is substantial enough to override dictates of the statute? Should a will be admitted to probate based on knowledge of intent, when there is evidentiary lack of compliance with the code?

Witness must not be beneficiary:

ESTATE of PARSONS
California Court of Appeals, First District, 1980
103 Cal.App.3d 384, 163 Cal.Rptr. 70

GRODIN, J.

This case requires us to determine whether a subscribing witness to a will who is named in the will as a beneficiary becomes "disinterested" within the meaning of Probate Code § 51 by filing a disclaimer of her interest after the testatrix' death. While our own policy preference tempt us to an affirmative answer, we feel constrained by existing law to hold that a disclaimer is ineffective for that purpose.

I

Geneve Parsons executed her will on May 3, 1976. Three persons signed the will as attesting witnesses: Evelyne Nielson, respondent Marie Gower, and Bob Warda, a notary public. Two of the witnesses, Nielson and Gower, were named in the will as beneficiaries. Nielson was given $100; Gower was given certain real property. Mrs. Parsons died on December 13, 1976, and her will was admitted to probate on the petition of her executors, respondents Gower and Lenice Haymond. On September 12, 1977, Nielson filed a disclaimer of her $100 bequest. Appellants then claimed an interest in the estate on the ground that the devise to Gower was invalid. The trial court rejected their argument, which is now the sole contention on appeal.

The disclaimer was filed pursuant to Probate Code § 190.1, which provides in part: *"A beneficiary may disclaim any interest, in whole or in part, by filing a disclaimer as provided in this chapter."* The disclaimer here was filed within the statutory period set forth in *Probate Code § 190.3, subdivision (a),* which provides in part *"{A} disclaimer shall be conclusively presumed to have been filed within a reasonable time if filed as follows {1} in case of interests created by will, within nine months after the death of the person creating the interest . . .*

Appellants base their claim on *Probate Code §51* which provides that a gift to a subscribing witness is void "unless there are two other and disinterested subscribing witnesses to the will. Although Nielson disclaimed her bequest after subscribing the will, appellants submit that "a subsequent disclaimer is ineffective to transform an interested witness into a disinterested one." Appellants assert that because there was only one disinterested witness at the time of the attestation, the devise to Gower is void by operation of law.

Respondents contend that appellants' argument is "purely technical" and "completely disregards the obvious and ascertainable intent" of the testatrix. They urge that the property should go to the person named as devisee rather than to the distant relatives who, as the testatrix stated in her will, "have not been overlooked, but have been intentionally omitted." They stress that there has been no suggestion of any fraud or undue influence in this case, and they characterize Nielson's interest as a "token gift" which she relinquish pursuant to the disclaimer statute. (Probate Code,§ 190 et Seq.) Finally, respondents point to the following language of Probate Code § 190.6: "In every case, the disclaimer shall relate back for all purposes to the date of the creation of the interest." On the basis of that language, respondents conclude that Nielson "effectively became disinterested" by reason of her timely disclaimer. According to respondents, the conditions of Probate Code § 51 have been satisfied, and the devise to Gower should stand.

II

This appears to be a case of first impression in California, and our interpretation of Probate Code § 51 will determine its outcome. We are required to construe the statute "so as to effectuate the purpose of the law." *Select Base Material v. Board of Equal. (1959) 51 Cal.2d 640,645* . . . To ascertain the purpose, we may consider its history . . .

At Common Law a party to an action, or one who had a direct interest in its outcome, was not competent to testify in court because it was thought that an interested witness would be tempted to perjure himself in favor of his interest. Centuries ago, this principle concerning the competence of witnesses in litigation was injected into the substantive law of wills. The Statute of Frauds of 1676 required that devises of land be attested and subscribed "by three or four credible witnesses, or else they shall be utterly void and of none effect." The word "credible" was construed to mean "competent" according to the common law principles then prevailing, and "competent" meant "disinterested" so that persons having an interest under the will could not be "credible witnesses" within the meaning of the statute. The entire will would therefore fail if any one of the requisite number of attesting witnesses was also a beneficiary. (*Holdfast v. Dowsing (K.B. 1746) 2 Str. 1253 {93 Eng. Rep. 1164}.*) In 1752 Parliament enacted a statute which saved the will by providing that the interest of an attesting witness was void. Under such legislation, the competence of the witness is restored by invalidating his gift . . . The majority of American jurisdictions today have similar statutes; and California Probate Code § 51 falls into this category . . .

The common law disabilities to testify on account of interest have long been abolished. Having become a part of the substantive law of wills, Probate Code § 51, on the other hand, survives. Our task is to ascertain and effectuate its present purpose. When a court seeks to interpret legislation, "the various parts of a statutory enactment must be harmonized by considering the particular clause or section in the context of the statutory framework as a whole." *Moyer v. Workmen's Comp. Appeals Bd. (Cal. 1973) 514 P.2d 1224.)* We therefore turn to the Probate Code.

In order to establish a will as genuine, it is not always necessary that each and every one of the subscribing witnesses testify in court. (Probate Code §§ 329,372.) Moreover, Probate Code § 51 does not by its terms preclude any witnesses from testifying; nor does the section void the interest of a subscribing witness when "two other and disinterested" witnesses have also subscribed the will. It is therefore entirely conceivable and perfectly consistent with the statutory scheme that a will might be proved on the sole testimony of a subscribing witness who is named in the will as a beneficiary; and if the will had been attested by "two other and disinterested subscribing witnesses," the interested witness whose sole testimony established the will would also be permitted to take his gift, as provided in the instrument. If Probate Code section 51 serves any purpose under such circumstances, its purpose must necessarily have been accomplished before the will was offered for probate. Otherwise, in its statutory context, the provision would have no effect at all.

The quintessential function of a subscribing witness is performed when the will is executed. We believe that Probate Code § 51 looks in its operation solely to that time. The section operates to ensure that at least two of the subscribing witnesses are disinterested. Although disinterest may be a token of credibility, as at common law, it also connotes an absence of selfish motives. We conclude that the purpose of the statute is to protect the testator from fraud and undue influence at the very moment when he executes his will, by ensuring that at least two persons are present "who would not be financially motivated to join in a scheme to procure the execution of a spurious will by dishonest methods, and who therefore presumably might be led by human impulses of fairness to resist the efforts of others in that direction." (*Gulliver v. Tilson, classification of Gratuitous Transfers (1941) 51 Yale L.J. 1, 11.* No other possible construction which has been brought to our attention squares so closely with the statutory framework.

III

Because we hold that Probate Code section 51 looks solely to the time of execution and attestation of the will, it follows that a subsequent disclaimer will be ineffective to transform an interested witness into a "disinterested" one within the meaning of that section. If the execution of a release or the filing of a disclaimer after the will has been attested could effect such a transformation, the purpose of the statute as we have defined it would be undermined . . .

In this case, when the will was executed and attested, only one of the subscribing witnesses was disinterested. The gift to the other witnesses were therefore void, by operation of law. (*Prob. Code. § 51.*) Neilson's disclaimer was a nullity, because she had no interest to disclaim.

Respondents' concern for the intentions of the testatrix is likewise misplaced. The construction of the will is not at issue here. We are faced instead with the operation of Probate Code section 51, which makes no reference to the intentions of the testatrix. Legislation voiding the interest of an attesting witness "often upsets genuine expressions of the testator's intent." . . .

It has been said that statutes such as this are illsuited to guard against fraud and undue influence. "If the potential malefactor does not know of the rules, he will not be deterred. If he does know of them, which is unlikely, he will realize the impossibility of the financial gain supposed to be the motive of the legatee witness, and so will probably escape the operation of the remedy against himself."

. . . We are mindful that there has been no suggestion of any fraud or other misconduct in the case before us, and it may well be that "the vast majority of testators in modern society do not need the type of 'protection' that is afforded by our statute." (Chaffin, Improving Georgia's Probate Code (1970) 4 Ga. L. Rev. 505, 507.) "The reported decisions give the impression that the remedies are employed more frequently against innocent parties who have accidentally transgressed the requirement than against deliberate wrongdoers, and this further confirms the imaginary character of the difficulty sought to be prevented." (*Gulliver & Tilson, supra, 51 Yale L.J. at p. 12.*) But the legislature has spoken here, and in matters such as this, "the legislature has a wide discretion in determining the conditions to be imposed." . . .

Respondents note that a growing number of states have enacted statutes similar to Uniform Probate Code § 2-505, which dispenses with the rule contained in the California statute . . . Perhaps statutes like California Probate Code § 51 represent a "mediaeval point of view" concerning the proper function of an attesting witness; and perhaps "the question whether he has abused his position should be made one of fact, like any other question having to do with the motives and conduct of parties who take part in the testamentary transaction."[81] We cannot ignore what the statute commands, however, "merely because we do not agree that the statute as written is wise or beneficial legislation" (Estate of Carter (Cal. 1935) 50 P.2d 1057.) Any remedial change must come from the legislature.

The portion of the judgment from which this appeal is taken is therefore reversed.

NOTES:

{1} The Appellate Court indicated that the requirement that witnesses be disinterested, was once part of the Common Law but had been abolished. This means that under current statutes, it is not uncommon for an interested person to be a witness but for such a person to take under the will, two other disinterested persons must witness the document.

{2} The court concluded that Neilson's disclaimer did not matter because, the statute looked to the time when the will was signed, not the time when the estate was divided, therefore, a subsequent disclaimer does not make one a disinterested witness. This means that even though Neilson disclaimed the devise after the will had been attested to, he would have been able to take if neither of the two remaining witnesses is interested.

[3} The Appellate Court felt its hands were tied, because the statute as written, demands that the will be invalidated. The Court, suggested that the legislature modify the statute to be more in line with current jurisprudence.

{4} Under the Uniform Probate Code § 2-505 there is no issue at all with interested witnesses. An interested witness does not forfeit a devise under the will. About one third of the states have adopted the Uniform Probate Code, some of the states have adopted the *purging statute* which purge the interested witness only of the devise

---

[81] Mechem, Why Not a Modern Wills Act? (1948) 33 Iowa L. Rev. 501, 506-507.)

received that go beyond what the witness would have received if the will had not been executed.

The demand of proper signature:

ESTATE of PAVLINKO
Supreme Court of Pennsylvania, 1959
394 Pa. 564, 148 A.2d 528

BELL, Justice.

Vasil Pavlinko died February 8, 1957; his wife, Hellen, died October 15, 1951. A testamentary writing dated March 9, 1949, which purported to be the will of Hellen Pavlinko, was signed by Vasil Pavlinko, her husband. The residuary legatee named therein, a brother of Hellen, offered the writing for probate as the will of Vasil Pavlinko, but probate was refused. The Orphans' Court, after hearing and argument, affirmed the decision of the register of wills.

The facts are unusual and the result very unfortunate. Vasil Pavlinko and Hellen, his wife, retained a lawyer to draw their wills and wished to leave their property to each other. By mistake Hellen signed the will which was prepared for her husband, and Vasil signed the will which was prepared for his wife, each instrument being signed at the end thereof. The lawyer who drew the will and his secretary, Dorothy Zinkham, both signed as witnesses. Miss Zinkham admitted that she was unable to speak the language of Vasil and Hellen, and that no conversation took place between them. The wills were kept by Vasil and Hellen. For some undisclosed reason, Hellen's will was never offered for probate at her death; in this case it was offered merely as an exhibit.

The instrument that was offered for probate was short. It stated:

I Hellen Pavlinko of . . . , do hereby make, publish and declare this to be my last will and testament . . .

In the first paragraph she directed her executor to pay her debt and funeral expenses. In the second paragraph she gave her entire residuary estate to "my husband, Vasil Pavlinko absolutely". She then provided:

Third if my aforesaid husband, Vasil Pavlinko, should predecease me, then and in that event, I give and bequeath:

(a) To my brother in-law, Mike Pavlinko, of McKees Rocks, Pennsylvania, the sum of two hundred ($200) dollars.

(b) To my sister in-law, Maria Gerber, (nee Pavlinko), of Pittsburg, Pennsylvania, the sum of two hundred ($200) dollars.

(c) The rest, residue and remainder of my estate, of whatsoever kind and nature and wheresoever situate, I give, devise and bequeath, absolutely to my brother, Elias Martin, now residing at 520 Aidyl Avenue, Pittsburg Pennsylvania.

"I do hereby nominate, constitute and appoint my husband, Vasil Pavlinko, as Executor of this my Last Will and Testament." It was then mistakenly signed: "Vasil Pavlinko {Seal}"

While no attempt was made to probate, as Vasil's will, the writing which purported to be his will but was signed by Hellen, it could not have been probated as Vasil's will, because it was not signed by him at the end thereof.

The Will's Act of 1947 provides in clear, plain and unmistakable language in § 2: "*Every will shall be in writing and shall be signed by the testator at the end thereof*", 20 P.S. § 180.2, with certain exceptions not here relevant. The court below correctly held that the paper which recited that it was the will of Hellen Pavlinko and intended and purported to give Hellen's estate to her husband, could not be probated as the will of Vasil and was a nullity.

In order to decide in favor of the residuary legatee, almost the entire will would have to be rewritten. The court would have to substitute the words "Vasil Pavlinko" for "Hellen Pavlinko" and the words "my wife" wherever the words "my husband" appear in the will, and the relationship of the contingent residuary legatee would have likewise have to be changed. To consider this paper-as-written-as Vasil's will, it would give his entire residuary estate to "my husband, Vasil Pavlinko, absolutely" and "Third if my husband Vasil Pavlinko should predecease me, then I give and bequeath my residuary estate to my brother, Elias Martin." The language of this writing, which is signed at the end thereof by Vasil Pavlinko, is unambiguous, clear and unmistakable, and it is obvious that it is a meaningless nullity.

While no authority is needed to demonstrate what is so obvious, there is a case which is directly in point and holds that such writing cannot be probated as the will of Vasil Pavlinko. This exact situation arose in *Alter's Appeal, 67 Pa. 341* . . . [82]

---

[82] See, Alter's Appeal, 67 Pa. 341 for the courts opinion through Mr. Justice Agnew (at Page 344).

... Our Act of 1833 as well as the statute of Victoria, are in part borrowed from the Statute of Frauds, two sections of which have been so evaded by judicial construction as to be practically appealed. We do not propose that the Act of 1833 shall meet with the same fate. The Legislature have laid down a rule so plain that it cannot be evaded without a clear violation of its terms. No room is left for judicial construction of interpretation. It says a will must be signed at the end thereof, and that's the end of it ...

Once a court starts to ignore or alter or rewrite or make exceptions to clear, plain and unmistakable provisions of the Wills Act in order to accomplish equity and justice in that particular case, the Wills Act will become a meaningless, although well intentioned, scrap of paper, and the door will be opened wide to countless fraudulent claims which the Act successfully bars.

Decree affirmed. Each party shall pay their respective costs.

DISSENTING OPINION

MUSMANNO, Justice.

Vasil Pavlinko and his wife, Hellen Pavlinko, being unlettered in English and unlearned in the ways of the law, wisely decided to have an attorney draw up their wills, since they were both approaching the age when reflecting persons must give thought to that voyage from which there is no return. They explained to the attorney, whose services they sought, that he should draw two wills which would state that when either of the partners had sailed away, the one remaining ashore would become the owner of the property of the departing voyager. Vasil Pavlinko knew but little English. However, his lawyer, fortunately, was well versed in his client's native language, known as little Russian or Carpathian. The attorney thus discussed the whole matter with his two visitors in their language. He then dictated appropriate wills of his stenographer in English and then, after they had been transcribed, he translated the documents, paragraph by paragraph, to Mr. and Mrs. Pavlinko, who approved of all that he had written. The wills were laid before them and each signed the document purporting to be his or her will. The attorney gave Mrs. Pavlinko the paper she had signed and handed to her husband the paper he had signed. In accordance with customs they had brought with them from the old country. Mrs. Pavlinko turned her paper over to her husband. It did not matter, however, who held the papers since they were complementary of each other. Mrs. Pavlinko left her property to Mr. Pavlinko and Mr. Pavlinko left his property to Mrs. Pavlinko. They also agreed on a common residuary legatee, Elias Martin, the brother of Mrs. Pavlinko . . .

. . . This court, however, says that it can do nothing for the victim of a mistake in this case, a mistake which was caused through no fault of his own, nor of his intended benefactors . . .

We have said more times than there are tombstones in the cemetery where the Pavlinkos lie buried, that the primary rule to be followed in the interpretation of a will is to ascertain the intention of the testator. Can anyone go to the graves of the Pavlinkos and say that we do not know what they meant? They said in English and Carpathian that they wanted their property to go to Elias Martin.

We have also said times without number that the intent of the testator must be gathered from the four corners of the will. Whether it be from the four corners of the will signed by Vasil Pavlinko or whether from the eight corners of the will signed by Vasil and Hellen Pavlinko, all set out before the court below, the net result is always the same, namely that the residue of the property of the last surviving member of the Pavlinko couple was to go to Elias Martin . . .

Even if we accept the majority's conclusion . . . that all provisions in the Pavlinko's will, which refer to himself, must be regarded as nullities . . . it does not follow that the residuary clause must perish. The fact that some of the provisions in the Pavlinko will cannot be executed does not strike down the residuary clause, which is meaningful and stands on its own two feet. We know that one of the very purposes of a residuary clause is to provide a catch-all for undisposed—of or ineffectually disposed property . . . I see no insuperable obstacle to probating the will signed by Vasil Pavlinko. Even though it was originally prepared as the will of his wife, Hellen, he did adopt its testamentary provisions as his own. Some of its provisions are not effective but their ineffectuality in no way bars the legality and validity of the residuary clause which is complete in itself. I would, therefore, probate the paper signed by Vasil Pavlinko.

QUESTIONS

[A} Consider the dissenting opinion that, since the residuary clause is the same for both wills therefore, the will signed by Vasil should be allowed probate. Do you think this is so even though, the statute demands proper signature by the testator who intended to give his or her estate?

{B} Think about an argument that this is one of those situations, where remedial justice is applicable. Do you think the doctrine of judicial interpretation is applicable in cases like this, when the legislature has clearly stated its purpose for requesting that the will be signed by the proper testator?

{C}Do you think that since mistakes are common to mankind, the court should get in the business of remedying mistakes, or try to interpret the law?

Chapter Eight

WILLS REVOCATION

Your will is now complete, you have done everything the law required; the will is in writing, it is properly signed and witnessed according to statutory dictates; You have now transitioned and your will is offered for probate by the executor but, for one reason or the other, the will is denied probate, why? Because by your own act or omission you have unintentionally revoked the will without knowledge; the ways a will can be revoked are fairly well defined in the law. For example, if you tear up your will into small pieces with the *intention* of revoking it, it clear that you have legally revoked it.

As a general rule, you can successfully revoke your will by:

{1} Physical act done to the will such as: (tearing, canceling, or burning the will);
{2} A subsequent writing executed with testamentary formalities revoking the previous will.

Note: A will can also be revoked by getting married after the will is made, unless the will is made in anticipation of marriage.

UNIFORM PROBATE CODE § 2-507

{a} A will or any part thereof is revoked:
{1} by executing a subsequent will that revokes the previous will or part expressly or by inconsistency; or

{2} by performing a revocatory act on the will, if the testator performed the act with the intent and for the purpose of revoking the will or part or if another individual performed the act in the testator's conscious presence and by the testator's direction. For purposes of this paragraph, "revocatory act on the will" includes burning, tearing, canceling, obliterating, or destroying the will or any part of it. A burning, tearing, or canceling is a "revocatory act on the will," whether or not the burn, tear, or cancellation touched any of the words on the will.

{b} If a subsequent will does not expressly revoke a previous will, the execution of the subsequent will wholly revokes the previous will by inconsistency if the testator intended the subsequent will to replace rather than supplement the previous will.

{c} The testator is presumed to have intended a subsequent will to replace rather than supplement a previous will if the subsequent will makes a complete disposition of the testator's estate. If this presumption arises and is not rebutted by clear and convincing evidence, the previous will is revoked; only the subsequent will is operative on the testator's death.

{d} The testator is presumed to have intended a subsequent will to supplement rather than replace a previous will if the subsequent will does not make a complete disposition of the testator's estate. If this presumption arises and is not rebutted by clear and convincing evidence, the subsequent will revokes the previous will only to the extent the subsequent will is inconsistent with the previous will; each will is fully operative on the death of the testator to the extent they are not inconsistent.

Note: The Uniform Probate Code provides two alternate ways of revocation: (a) revocation by writing (i.e. *express and implied*) and (b) revocation by physical act.

REVOCATION BY WRITING

Since most statutes require a testamentary writing to revoke a will, a testator may revoke his will by his own words expressly printed in the body of the will; for example, It is not uncommon to find at the beginning of a will words like, "I *John McDonald,* make this my final will revoking all wills and *codicils* previously made by me." If the will is properly signed and satisfies all will formalities and requirements for a formal will, the writing, will operate as a subsequent will revoking all previous wills and *codicils* thus, giving it the effect of the law. The testator must clearly indicate in writing that, the new will revokes all other wills and the intent to revoke must be clear and convincing on the face of the will. Confusion occasionally arises as to whether a writing that revokes a *codicil* to a will or a direct destruction or revocation of the *codicil* itself revokes the underlying will. The general rule is that revocation of a *codicil* does not revoke the underlying will since a *codicil* is a supplement to a will.

Besides express revocation, a will may also be revoked by implication. Implied revocation arises only when there is no express writing indicating testator's intent to revoke; but an implied revocation is often less ambiguous than an act of revocation. A subsequent testamentary document without an express revocation clause does not wholly revoke a prior will; it is considered a *codicil* or supplement to the prior will unless it is totally inconsistent with it thereby, making it the new will and revoking the prior one.

REVOCATION BY ACT

According to the Uniform Probate Code § 2-507 (2) a will can be revoked by performing a revocatory act on the will. Such physical act may include: burning the will, tearing it, obliterating it or by canceling it. The will so destroyed by a physical act is considered revoked by operation of law, whether or not the burn, tear, or cancellation touched any of the words on the will. It is not necessary that the tearing, burning, mutilating, canceling and the like be a complete physical destruction of the will beyond recognition. In fact, the slightest tearing or burning is enough, so long as it is done with the intent to revoke the will. If a testator chooses someone else to help destroy his will, he must make sure the person does the act in his presence. If the testator is not present at the time of destruction, the revocation is ineffective even though he may have directed the act. To establish complete revocation by an act, *presence* and *intent* of the testator along with the *physical act* are essential ingredients. For example, if *Olufemi* has two wills and decides to revoke one of them. By mistake he tears up the wrong one. Is either will revoked? No. Neither will was revoked by the act of tearing because there was no intent to revoke the will that was torn by mistake and the will intended for revocation was not even torn.

In order to complete the act of revocation, any destruction done to the will must be done with the intent to revoke. If someone else other than the testator is doing the destruction, it must be done in the presence of the testator. The destruction need not be complete but must reflect the testator's wish to destroy and revoke the will. The testator can change his mind and recover the will before the destruction is complete, interference by another person without the testator's authorization will not prevent a revocation if the other elements are present.

REVOCATION BY MARRIAGE

If one gets married after making a will, the rule is that the marriage automatically revokes the will unless the will was made in *anticipation* of the marriage. When this is the case, expressed writing in the will must indicate such. In most jurisdictions, divorce revokes a will. At one time a divorce had no effect at all on a previous will, but now most states provide that a divorce revokes the particular devise made to the ex-spouse. If the testator executes his will and then marries, a large majority of states have statutes giving the spouse her intestate share, unless it appears from the will that the omission was intentional or the spouse is provided for in the will or substitute with the intent that the transfer be in lien of a testamentary provision. Where the spouse omitted from a premarital will does not take an intestate share because mentioned in the will, the spouse may take a *forced share* of the decedent's estate which is given to all spouses whether or not the spouse is intentionally or unintentionally disinherited.

BIRTH OF CHILDREN

A small minority of states follow the common law rule that marriage followed by birth of children revokes a will executed before marriage. This rule is not incorporated in the Uniform Probate Code however, most states have *pretermitted child statute,* giving a child born after execution of the parent's will and not provided for in the will a share in the parent's estate. This may also include children born before the execution of the will. This kind of statute results in the revocation of a will to the extent of the child's share.

HARRISON V. BIRD

Supreme Court of Alabama 1993

621 So. 2d 972

HOUSTON, J.

The proponent of a will appeals from a judgment of the Circuit Court of Montgomery County holding that the estate of Daisy Virginia Speer, deceased, should be administered as an intestate estate and confirming the letters of administration granted by the probate court to Mae S. Bird.

The following pertinent facts are undisputed:

Daisy Virginia Speer executed a will in November 1989, in which she named Katherine Crapps Harrison as the main beneficiary of her estate. The original of the will was retained by Ms. Speer's attorney and a duplicate original was given to Ms. Harrison. On March 4, 1991, Ms. Speer telephoned her attorney and advised him that she wanted to revoke her will. Thereafter, Ms. Speer's attorney or his secretary, in the presence of each other, tore the will into four pieces. The attorney then wrote Ms. Speer a letter, informing her that he had "revoked" her will as she had instructed and that he was enclosing the pieces of the will so that she could verify that he had torn up the original. In the letter, the attorney specifically stated, "As it now stands, you are without a will."

Ms. Speer died on September 3, 1991. Upon her death, the postmarked letter from her attorney was found among her personal effects, but the four pieces of the will were not found. Thereafter, on September 17, 1991, the probate court of Montgomery County granted letters of administration on the estate of Ms. Speer, to Mae S. Bird, a cousin of Ms. Speer. On October 11, 1991, Ms. Harrison filed for probate a document purporting to be the last will and testament of Ms. Speer and naming Ms. Harrison as executrix. On Ms. Bird's petition, the case was removed to the circuit court of Montgomery County. Thereafter, Ms. Bird filed an "Answer to Petition to Probate Will and Answer to Have Administratrix Removed," contesting the will on the grounds that Ms.Speer had revoked her will.

Thereafter, Ms. Bird and Ms. Harrison moved for summary judgment, which the circuit court denied. Upon denying their motions, the circuit court ruled in part (1) that Ms. Speer's will was not lawfully revoked when it was destroyed by her attorney at her direction and with her consent, but not in her presence, *Ala. Code 1975, § 43-8-136(b)*; (2) that there could

161

be no ratification of the destruction of Ms. Speer's will, which was not accomplished pursuant to the strict requirements of § 43-8-136(b); and (3) that, based on the fact that the pieces of the destroyed will were delivered to Ms. Speer's home but were not found after her death, there arose a presumption that Ms. Speer thereafter, revoked the will herself. However, because the trial court found that a genuine issue of material fact existed as to whether Ms. Harrison had rebutted the presumption that Ms. Speer intended to revoke her will even though the duplicate was not destroyed, it held that "this issue must be submitted for trial."

Subsequently, however, based upon the affidavits submitted in support of the motions for summary judgment, the oral testimony, and a finding that the presumption in favor of revocation of Ms. Speer's will had not been rebutted and therefore that the duplicate original will offered for probate by Ms. Harrison was not the last will and testament of Daisy Virginia Speer, the circuit court held that the estate should be administered as an intestate estate and confirmed the letters of administration issued by the probate court to Ms. Bird.

If the evidence establishes that Ms. Speer had possession of the will before her death, but the will is not found among her personal effects after her death, a presumption arises that she destroyed the will. *Barksdale v. Pendergrass, 294 Ala. 526, 319 So. 2d 267 (1975).* Furthermore, if she destroys the copy of the will in her possession, a presumption arises that she has revoked her will and all duplicates, even though a duplicate exists that is not in her possession. *Stiles v. Brown, 380 So. 2d 792 (Ala. 1980);* see, also, *Snider v. Burks, 84 Ala. 53, 4 So. 225 (1987).* However, this presumption of revocation is rebuttable and the burden of rebutting the presumption is on the proponent of the will. See Barksdale, supra.

Based on the foregoing, we conclude that under the facts of this case there existed a presumption that Ms. Speer destroyed her will and thus revoked it. Therefore, the burden shifted to Ms. Harrison to present sufficient evidence to rebut the presumption to present sufficient evidence to convince the trier of fact that that absence of the will from Ms. Speer's personal effects after her death was not due to Ms. Speer's destroying and thus revoking the will. See *Stiles v. Brown, supra.*

From a careful review of the record, we conclude, as did the trial court, that the evidence presented by Ms. Harrison was no sufficient to rebut the presumption that Ms. Speer destroyed her will with the intent to revoke it. We, therefore, affirm the trial court's judgment.

We note Ms. Harrison's argument that under the particular fact of this case, because Ms. Speer's attorney destroyed the will outside of Ms. Speer's presence, "{t}he fact that Ms. Speer may have had possession of the pieces of her will and that such pieces were not found upon her death is not sufficient to invoke the presumption {of revocation} imposed by the trial court." We find that argument to be without merit.

AFFIRMED.

NOTES:

{1} A subsequent will wholly revokes the prior will by inconsistency if the testator intends the subsequent will to replace the prior will rather than act as a *supplement* or a *codicil*.

{2} A subsequent will that does not expressly revoke the previous will but makes a complete disposition of the testator's estate is presumed to replace the previous will and revoke it by inconsistency.

{3} if the subsequent will does not make a complete disposition of the testator's estate, it is not presumed to revoke the prior will but is viewed as a *codicil*. A *codicil* is a supplement to a will. It is not uncommon for a testator after having the attorney draft his will, to later go back and make an addition to the will; this is called a *codicil*. Usually, a *codicil* will not mention everything that has already been written in the testator's will but rather works as a supplement to his will. For example, if *John Scott* after writing his will making disposition of his belongings, acquired new property and decides to have it included in his will, in order not to revoke his will, *John* may have his attorney draft a *codicil* making disposition of the newly acquired property as part of the written will. At *John's* death, the *codicil* is probated along with the will as a supplement.

{4} *LOST WILL:* Except a statute says otherwise, the fact that a will is *lost* or destroyed does not mean it cannot be admitted to probate. If the will is lost, or is destroyed without the consent of the testator or is destroyed with the consent of the testator but not in compliance with the revocation statute, the will is allowed probate however, its contents must be proved. A lost will can be proved by producing a copy kept with the attorney or by clear and convincing evidence.

{5} In a minority of states, statutes prohibit probate of lost or destroyed wills unless the will was available at the testator's death and then destroyed thereafter or fraudulently destroyed during testator's life.

{6} **DEPENDENT RELATIVE DOCTRINE:** if a testator purports to revoke her will upon a mistaken assumption of law or fact, the revocation is invalid if the testator would not have revoked her will had she known the truth. For example, if *Princess Cinderella* makes a new will bequeathing all her belongings to her kingdom thereby revoking a previous will in which she gave all her belongings to her only son, on a mistaken belief that her son had died when his plane crashed in the ocean, but indeed the son survived and turned up after *Princess Cinderella* had passed; Now do you think her estate should go to the kingdom? The answer is No. Because *Princess Cinderella* acted under a mistaken assumption of fact, she would not have revoked her previous will had she known her son was still alive therefore, the revocation is ineffective and her old will bequeathing her belongings to her son survives; her estate must go to her son and not to the kingdom.

If the court finds that the testator would not have destroyed her old will had she known the new will was ineffective, the court applying the doctrine will cancel the revocation and allow probate of the destroyed prior will. The Dependent Relative doctrine is one of presumptive intent, not actual intent.

EXCEPTIONS: *The Dependent Relative Doctrine* applies only (a) where there is an alternative plan of disposition that fails or (b) where the mistake is recited in the terms of the revoking instrument or established by clear and convincing evidence. For the doctrine to apply, the mistake must be on the face of the will.

{7} A minority of state adhere to the view that a revoked will cannot be revived unless reexecuted with testamentary formalities or republished mentioning it in a later duly executed will.

{8} A majority of state adhere to the rule that upon revocation of a second will, the previous will is automatically revived and resurrected if the testator so intends.

REVOCATION BY STATUTE

A will can be revoked also by operation of law. In all but a few states, statutes have it that a *divorce* revokes any provision in the decedent's will for the divorced spouse. In other states, revocation occurs only if divorce is followed by property settlement. Revocation statutes only apply to probate estates and not to nonprobate transfers such as: life insurance policies, pension plans, Payable on death accounts and the like. Such transfer, always have named beneficiaries in the contract provisions and are not subject to probate.

CONTRACT TO MAKE A WILL

It is not uncommon for people to enter into a contract to *make a will* or to *revoke a will*. A contract to make a will is simply an agreement by one party to devise property to another, such a promise is made in consideration of a promise made by the beneficiary. Actions in such cases are governed by contract law and the contract beneficiary is required to sue under contract provisions. If for example, a party dies and leaves a will not in accordance to the contract entered into, the will is probated however, the contract beneficiary is entitled to a remedy according to the contract provisions. Normally, the enforcement of such contracts is through the imposition of a *constructive trust* on the value of the devise which was to come to the contract beneficiary had the contract been properly executed and not breached.

WILL ANALYSIS

WILL OF ELIZABETH ANANIA EDWARDS

The following is the Will of Elizabeth Anania Edwards (Ms. Edwards), wife of the former U.S. Presidential candidate John Edwards. Ms. Edwards died of Cancer in December 2010 and after her death, her Will was released to the public and made readily available online. The Will is offered here for educational purposes and for analysis on the formalities of a valid Will.

STATE OF NORTH CAROLINA   LAST WILL AND TESTAMENT
COUNTY OF ORANGE

Filed 12-22-10
10E589
Signed by Deputy Clark

I, ELIZABETH ANANIA EDWARDS, of Orange County, North Carolina, do. Hereby revoke all Wills and Codicils heretofore made by me and do hereby make, publish and declare this my Last Will and Testament in the form and manner as follows:

ARTICLE I

I direct that all my just debts, my funeral expenses (including the cost of a suitable grave marker), the expense of my last illness, and cost of administering my estate be paid out of the assets of my estate as soon as practicable after my death.

ARTICLE II

I direct that all estate and inheritance taxes and other taxes in the general nature thereof (together with any interest or penalty thereon) which shall become payable upon or by reason of my death with respect to any property passing by or under the terms of this Will or any Codicil to it hereafter executed by me, or with respect to any other property included in my gross estate for the purpose of such taxes (including life insurance proceeds) shall be paid by my Executor out of my residuary estate, without apportionment.

ARTICLE III

I appoint my daughter, CATHARINE ELIZABETH EDWARDS, to be the Executor of this my last Will and Testament, and I direct that no bond be required of her as Executor. If my daughter shall not survive me or for any reason shall not serve as Executor, or, having qualified, shall die resign, I appoint BARBARA B. WEYHER to be the Executor of this my Last Will and Testament, and I direct that no bond be required for her as executor.

If I am the surviving parent of any child of mine who shall be a minor at the time of my death, I appoint my daughter, CATHARINE ELIZABETH EDWARDS, to be the guardian of the person of any of my minor children, and I direct that no bond be required of her as guardian.

ARTICLE IV

All of my furniture, furnishings, household goods, jewelry, china, silverware and personal effects and any automobiles owned by me at the time of my death I give and bequeath to my children who shall be living at the time of my death and to the living issue of any deceased child per stirpes, to be divided among them with such equality and appropriateness as my Executor, in her sole discretion, shall determine.

If any beneficiary of property under this Article shall be a minor, the minor's share may be delivered to the person with whom the minor is residing, or to the minor's legal guardian, or directly to the minor. The receipt of the guardian, or the person with whom the minor resides, or the receipt of the minor shall constitute a full acquittance of my Executor with respect to the property so delivered. The authority is given my Executor notwithstanding any statute or rule of law to the contrary. I direct that any expenses incurred in safeguarding or delivering such property be paid from my estate as an administrative expense thereof.

ARTICLE V

I bequeath and devise and appoint all the residue and remainder of my property and estate every nature and wheresoever situated, hereinafter referred to as my residuary estate, to CATHARINE ELIZABETH EDWARDS, or to the then acting Trustee, in trust, as an addition to the property held by her as Trustee under the terms of a certain Revocable Declaration of Trust, enter into by me, as Grantor and Trustee, dated December 2, 1992, but amended and restated prior to the execution of this Will, to be a part of the trust and to be managed in accordance with the terms and provisions of the Revocable Declaration of Trust as amended and restated.

ARTICLE VI

I hereby grant to my Executor, including any substitute or successor personal representatives, the continuing absolute, discretionary power to deal with any property, real or personal, held in my estate, as freely as I might in the handling of my own affairs. Such power may be exercised independently and without prior or subsequent approval of any court or judicial authority, and no person dealing with my Executor shall be required to inquire into the propriety of any of her actions.

Subject to North Carolina General Statutes, Section 32-26, I hereby grant to my Executor all the powers set forth in North Carolina General Statutes, Section 32-27, and these powers are hereby incorporated by reference and made a part of this instrument, and such powers are intended to be in addition to and not in substitution of the powers conferred by law.

ARTICLE VII

I have three living children, CATHARINE ELIZABETH EDWARDS, EMMA CLAIRE EDWARDS and JOHN ARTTICUS EDWARDS. As used in this Will, the term "issue" shall include adopted and afterborn issue. Where required by context in this Will, the masculine and feminine genders shall be deemed to include the other gender; the singular shall be deemed to include the plural, and the plural the singular.

IN TESTIMONY WHEREOF, I, ELIZABETH ANANIA EDWARDS, sign my name to this instrument, this 1st day of December, 2010, BC and being duly sworn, do hereby declare to the undersigned authority that I sign and execute this instrument as my last Will and Testament, that I sign it willingly, that I execute it as my free and voluntary act for the purposes therein expressed, and that I am eighteen (18) years of age or older, of sound mind, and under no constraint or undue influence.

SIGNED (SEAL)
ELIZABETH ANANIA EDWARDS, Testator

We, the undersigned witnesses, sign our names to this instrument, being first duly sworn, and do hereby declare to the undersigned authority that the Testator signs and executes this instrument as her Last Will and Testament and that she signs it willingly, and that each of us, in the presence and hearing of the Testator, hereby signs this Will as witness to the Testator's signing, and that to the best of our knowledge the Testator is eighteen (18) years of age or older, of sound mind, and under no constraint or undue influence.

Witness (SIGNED)

Witness (SIGNED)

STATE OF NORTH CAROLINA
COUNTY OF ORANGE

Subscribed, sworn to and acknowledged before me by **ELIZABETH ANANIA EDWARDS**, the Testator, and subscribed and sworn to before me by

Jill B. STEPHENS and Michelle D. Anderson

Witness, this 1st day of December, 2010. BC

(Notary Seal)	**SIGNED**
NOTARY STAMP	Notary Public
	Brandon Cole
	My Commission Expires 6/8/14

ANALYSIS

Formalities: In chapter seven of this book, we discussed the formalities of a valid Will that are required by State law: (1) Writing; (2) Signed and subscribed; and (3) Witnessed by two or more people. Note that Ms. Edwards' Will is in writing even though typed, this format is accepted by law and in satisfaction of the writing requirement for a valid Will.

Also, the requirement that the Will be signed is satisfied here, note that Ms. Edwards signed her Will at the bottom of the instrument before the witnesses an indication that, the witnesses actually saw her sign the Will in their presence therefore, this requirement of Testator's signature and attestation is met.

Lastly, the Will was witnessed by two persons as required by law and was subscribed by the notary public therefore, as to the formalities, Ms. Edwards' Will is indeed valid.

Revocation: Note that before Article I of the Will, Ms. Edwards first revoked all her previous Wills and *Codicils* (refer to the section on Codicils); the purpose of this is to avoid the contest of her Will by anyone who may claim she had another Will that was not revoked and therefore valid. Also, this part satisfied the requirement that the Testator revoke previous Wills before making a new one; a Will may be revoked by writing, by act, by implication or other means (refer to page 216-217), in this case, Ms. Edwards revoked her previous Wills and Codicils by a writing included in the body of her Will, using her subsequent Will to revoke previous Wills and Codicils. Note also that her subsequent Will is not a Codicil which by law does not revoke the underlying Will since a Codicil, is considered a supplement to a Will. However, in her case, she revoked previous Wills by writing in a Subsequent Will, giving her Will the effect of the law.

Article I and II: Here Ms Edwards makes provision for administrative costs and taxes that must be paid after her death, it is important for a Testator to make provisions for such costs to avoid unwanted suits and frivolous claims during the execution. Settlement of costs before distribution helps to determine the proper account, total worth of the estate and remainders before final distribution is made. It is also reasonable to consult an estate tax expert to determine the taxes to be paid before final distribution is made.

Executor: As required, in Article III, Ms. Edwards named her daughter CATHARINE ELIZABETH EDWARDS, the Executor of her Will. Even though, this is not a Will Formality, it is considered part of estate administration, that the Testator name the executor of her Will however, in some cases if the Testator failed to name an executor, the court will select one (refer to page 26) mostly from immediate family members of the Testator. It is also essential to name an alternate executor should the named executor fail in her capacity to carry out her duties; this occurs for example, when an executor dies or is incapacitated by a disability or other circumstances. In her case, Ms. Edwards named her daughter the executor and she also named BARBARA B. WEYHER an alternate in case for some reasons CATHARINE EDWARDS failed to carry out her duties as the named executor.

Notice also that Ms. Edwards requested that no bond be demanded of both named executors. In some cases, the court admitting a Will for probate may require the executor to provide a bond as security in case she mismanage the estate or fails to properly distribute estate property as instructed by the Testator in her Will; the purpose is to protect other beneficiaries and to ensure that the executor carry out her duty according to the intent of the Testator. In this case however, Ms. Edwards chose to protect her executor by including a clause demanding that no bond be required; she may have done so to ensure smooth administration of her estate and to express her trust that the named executor shall carry out her duties as intended in her Will. In certain instances, it may happen the executor is unable to provide the bond required by the court and in such situation, probate is delayed or the executor may decide to withdraw from the position in which case, the court may decide to choose an administrator not intended by the Testator.

Also, in the same Article Ms. Edwards made provision for any surviving child that may be a minor at the time of her death she chose her eldest daughter CATHARINE EDWARDS to be the guardian and again requested that no bond be required of her.

Distribution: There can be no probate without estate property, in Article IV Ms. Edwards named her belongings and how she intended their distribution to her survivors. Notice the use of the words "I give and bequeath to my children who shall be living at the time of my death and to the living issue of any deceased child per stirpes." The words *"Bequeath and Give"* demonstrate her intent to absolutely transfer her belongings to all her *living* children and their issues; Ms. Edwards had a son who died before her and was not named in her Will so, it is clear why she named only her children who shall be living at the time of her death however, she included the living issue of any deceased child; this is somehow vague because the *living issue of any deceased child* may be interpreted as the living issue (if any) of a child who survived her but later died after Ms. Edwards or the living issue (if any) of the son she survived who died years before her. Even though, there was no record that her deceased son had any child before his death, it is not uncommon in other cases to have a living issue come up and claim to be a survivor of a deceased son who did not survive the Testator. The vagueness may be substituted by a sentence such as *the living issue of any child who shall be deceased after me* or *living issue of any child who survived me but deceased after me.*

Under same Article, she provided for when the executor should be relieved of her duty as the executor of her estate; notice that the executor of her estate is also the guardian of any minor beneficiary that may survive her; she intended that the executor be acquitted of her duties on receipt of the property, in her capacity as the guardian of any minor child or by the receipt of the minor himself.

Residuary Estate: In Article V, Ms. Edwards mentioned the remainder of her estate. This clause is essential for Wills since it is possible for a Testator to acquire other properties and assets not mentioned in her Will after her death or assets that she did not even know of. For example, Ms. Edwards may still receive royalties from the books she wrote before her death which she did not receive while alive, she may have shares from business deals with friends which may provide dividends years after her death and there may arise payments for money owed her by others before her death or payments from Social Security and such. All these are residuary estate and it is important for a Testator to mention it in her Will.

Take note also that she bequeathed her residuary estate, to CATHARINE ELIZABETH EDWARDS, or to the then acting Trustee, in trust, as an addition to property held in Trust. This is an indication that Ms. Edwards may have created a Trust while alive (refer to the section on Trusts), she intended that her residuary estate be given to CATHARINE EDWARDS or to be included as part of the Trust property to be managed by the Trustee. You may notice that under Article V she did not mention the beneficiary of the Trust, this is so because in most cases Trusts are considered non-probate property and are guided by instrument and terms which already provide for the beneficiary of such Trust therefore, it is without doubt she must have named the beneficiaries of the Trust in the Trust' instrument.

Discretionary Power: Under Article VI, Ms. Edwards included a clause creating a discretionary power for CATHARINE EDWARDS or the alternate executor, to deal with the estate. However, she also provided that the executor must deal with the estate the way she (Ms. Edwards) might in the handling of her own affairs. This is important to ensure that the executor acts with prudence and not mismanage the estate or misuse the discretionary power conferred on her.

Under State law, there are provisions as to the power of the executor in matters dealing with estate administration; In North Carolina, Section 32-27 of the General Statutes grants some powers to the executor. Even though, she did not include the texts of the Statute, Ms. Edwards incorporated the powers by reference as part of the absolute discretionary power granted to her executor. She also gave the executor power to act independently without approval of any court or judicial authority and provided for what seem like a *no-contest-clause* by stating that "no person dealing with my Executor shall be required to inquire into the propriety of any of her actions."

Interpretation of Terms: In the final Article of her Will she gave definition of terms and words used; this is important to avoid confusion during probate. Even though, the court may interpret the meaning of the terms in the case of confusion, it is always helpful if the Testator clearly states her intentions by explaining the meaning of words used; in that case, her intentions are properly met. For example, except it is clearly stated "issue" may mean only biological children of the Testator and not children adopted or delivered by the wife of a Testator after death of the Testator. Also "masculine and feminine genders" may only mean such genders and not include a transgender child for example. Therefore, it is essential that the Testator carefully choose her words and properly explain her intentions or else the court will offer its own interpretation however, such interpretation are designed to satisfy and be as close as possible to the intent of the Testator.

Disinheritance: In most cases the Testator leaves her belonging to any surviving spouse with the belief that the surviving spouse will transfer the estate to the surviving children upon his death. Notice that Ms. Edwards did not make any mention of her spouse former Presidential candidate John Edwards in her Will rather, she gave executory power to their eldest daughter CATHARINE EDWARDS. In most cases, a Testator may choose to disinherit her spouse as a result of a divorce or separation agreement. Before her death, Ms. Edwards and John Edwards were separated and the couple may have entered into a court agreement in which they agreed to divide their belongings according to the terms of the agreement.

Contest: A will may be subject to contest if such Will is the result of undue influence, duress, incapacity and other legal grounds such as the age of the Testator at the time of making the Will. Ms. Edwards clearly declared her Will to be the result of her free will and voluntary act; she also declared to be of sound mind and under no constraint or undue influence. The same was attested to by the witnesses showing the Will to be of her free will therefore, her Will, may not be contested based on such grounds unless there is evidence to the contrary. Notice also that she declared to be of legal age

(18) years or more to satisfy the State required legal age to make a Will. A Testator should make provisions for such proof of free Will and lack of constraint in his Will to avoid unnecessary contests.

Finally, Ms. Edwards' Will satisfied the requirements of a valid Will however, this does not mean it is immune from future contests; a living spouse may contest such Will unless, as stated earlier there is a court ordered agreement between both parties dividing their estate or there is a divorce agreement to the effect.

Chapter Nine

TRUSTS IN A NUTSHELL

Introduction

While wills focuses upon how distributions are made and what part of an estate is distributed to whom, trusts focuses upon duties of the person making the distribution and how the end result (distribution) is achieved. A trust is a medium through which a trustee manages property as a fiduciary for one or more beneficiaries. It is an intentionally created fiduciary relationship with regards to property in which the legal title resides in the trustee, but the benefits of the trusteeship and equitable title resides in another person, the beneficiary. The trust relationship imposes *fiduciary* duties upon the trustee for the benefit of the beneficiaries who hold equitable title and, in the usual trust are entitled to payment from the trust incomes and sometimes from the trust *corpus* too. Since the subject of trust is broad and may be beyond the scope of this book, I have decided to limit the discussion on trusts to some basic introduction to trust creation and the *fiduciary* duties.

Trusts are designed for different needs, a particular trust may be created for a particular purpose but not proper for another purpose. A *spendthrift* trust for example, is a kind of trust with provisions limiting the assignability of the beneficial interest and creditor's attack on the trust; there are also *living* or *testamentary* trusts and a trust could be *revocable* or *irrevocable* trust.

A trust provides managerial intermediation because the trustee manages the property on behalf of the beneficiary and thus, creates a separation between benefits and the burden of ownership. Normally, the burden and benefits of property ownership are in the same person such that the owner would receive the net benefit or deal with the net loss. In order to separate the burden of ownership from the benefits, the property owner could create a trust by delivering legal title to one person the *trustee* and the benefit or equitable title to another the *beneficiary.*

Once legal title is delivered to the trustee, the trustee becomes the manager of the trust and the trustee would have duties imposed upon him by the terms of the trust and by general trust law. Since the trustee holds legal title to the property, he acquires the power unless denied by the trust instrument, to sell trust property and replace it with property thought more desirable for the advancement of the trust.

TRUST CREATION

Uniform Trust Code § 401(2000 amended 2005).

A trust may be created by:

{1} transfer of property to another person as trustee during the settlor's lifetime or by will or other disposition taking effect upon the settlor's death;

{2} declaration by owner of property that the owner holds identifiable property as trustee; or

{3} exercise of a power of appointment in favor of a trustee

Note: that to create a trust, the trust provisions must comply with all statutory provisions required for trust creation, a contractual trust for example, must comply with the requirement of *offer* and *acceptance* as is found in every legal contractual obligation; a creation by will must comply with the requirements of the statute of wills and satisfy the *testamentary intent* element for creation, an exercise of power of appointment must comply with the laws governing powers of appointment and a lifetime transfer by gift must satisfy the elements of *intent* and *delivery.*

Writing Requirement

Just as in wills except for *nuncupative wills*, writing is usually a requirement for trusts of realty however, writing are seldom required for a trust of personality. Section 407 of the Uniform Trust Code allows oral trusts unless a statute demands otherwise. It states that: "a trust need not be evidenced by a trust instrument, but the creation of an oral trust and its terms may be established by clear and convincing evidence."

Requirements for Creation

In order to create a trust, the Uniform Trust Code § 402 imposed 5 requirements it provides that a trust is created only if:

{1} the settlor has capacity to create a trust;
{2} the settlor indicates an intention to create the trust;
{3} the trust has a definite beneficiary or is;
   {A} a charitable trust;
   {B} a trust for the care of an animal, as provided in section 408; or
   {C} a trust for a noncharitable purpose, as provided in section 409;

{4} the trustee has duties to perform; and
{5} the same person is not the sole trustee and sole beneficiary

Capacity

Just as in wills, there is a demand for legal capacity in trust creation. In order to make a transfer, the settlor must be a person of *sound mind* with the legal capacity required for the form of transfer. For example a minor under the legal age required by law or persons with disability cannot form the intention to transfer a gift during lifetime, doing so violates dictates of the Uniform Trust Code disallowing such transfers.

Intent

The transferor must manifest the intention to establish a trust, mere *wish* to create a trust will not do. Outward intention is necessary for the transfer not to fail but stand. The settlor must show that he does not wish but intend to create a trust.

ELEMENTS OF A TRUST

The Transfer

In order to create a trust, there must be a transfer of the trust *corpus* or property from the settlor to the trustee who holds the property in trust and manages it for the benefits of the intended beneficiaries. Without the transfer there is nothing for the trustee to manage therefore, the element of *transfer* is one of the essentials of trust creation. The person who creates the trust is the *settlor,* the trust may be created during the life of the settlor in which case it is an *inter vivos* trust, or it may be created either by a declaration of trust in which the settlor declares that he holds certain property in trust or by a deed of trust in which the settlor transfers the property to a trustee. There is no valid trust until the res is transferred to the trustee and an asset which cannot be transferred cannot be the trust res.

Trust *Res* or Property

Another element is the requirement of a res or *property* to transfer. The Restatement (Third) of Trusts § 40 allows the trustee to hold in trust any interest in any type of property as long as the property is not unlawful or against public policy. For example, while a trustee may hold in trust for X property to which X has legal title, the trustee cannot hold in trust for X a stolen property that X claims to be his. Why? Because X does not possess legal title to the stolen property and thus, has no interest to transfer. The trust property may be any type of property, real or personal, tangible or intangible, so long as it is in existence. Property not in existence cannot be the subject of a trust.

The Settlor

The settlor is the one who creates the trust. He is an essential element of the trust only until he has transferred the property with the intention to create a trust. The settlor imposes fiduciary duties upon the trustee in relation to the property for the benefit of the beneficiary. Once the settlor transfers the property, he no longer holds legal title to it, the legal title is transferred to the trustee and the settlor has no further role, it is now the duty of the trustee to manage the trust corpus according to dictates of the trust provisions. The settlor must be the owner of the property in order to be able to transfer it; he cannot transfer someone else's property. He must have the necessary capacity to transfer the property and must manifest the intention to do so. The settlor can retain some or all the legal title or the beneficial interest, but not all of both since the trust is created by separating the legal title from the beneficial interest.

Trustee

To establish a trust there must be a trustee to help manage trust property. The appointment of a trustee or successor trustee is usually indicated in the trust instrument. In the case where a settlor fails to name a trustee or a successor trustee who is able and willing to serve, the court will appoint one to manage affairs of the trust. Equity will not allow a trust to fail for want of a trustee except in a rare situation where the settlor expressly manifested the intention that the trust should not come into existence unless a particular individual served as trustee. If a settlor dies without naming a trustee, the legal title is vested in his heirs or will beneficiary, but the equitable title remains in the trust beneficiaries.

The trustee may be the settlor or beneficiary or both however, he cannot be the sole trustee and the sole beneficiary. The combination is impermissible under the doctrine of *merger*. Under section 402 (a) (5) of the Uniform Trust Code, the same person cannot be the sole trustee and the sole beneficiary. In such a situation, both equitable and legal title will merge in violation of the code provision.

If the settlor reasonable expects a trustee to perform a duty set up in the trust instrument, the trustee may not delegate such function to a co-trustee. A trustee can resign as dictated in the trust instrument, in such a situation the court will have supervision of the trust, with the consent of all the beneficiaries if they are competent and all co-trustees. A trustee can be removed as provided in the trust instrument for various reasons such as, for breach of fiduciary duty, mismanagement of trust corpus or for violation of the duty of loyalty and the like; a court having jurisdiction may also remove the trustee and the trust instrument may reserve the power to the settlor or give the power to a third party, including beneficiaries, to remove the trustee. If the trustee fails to perform the required duties, the court may decide that removing the trustee is in the best interests of the beneficiaries and that doing so may help protect trust's assets from depreciation and eventual loss. Other than for the breach of its fiduciary duties and other reasonable duties set up in the trust instrument, a settlor may not remove a trustee just because he thinks the trustee is not performing to his expectation when there is proof that the trustee has not breached any of its duties.

Removal of the trustee is a strict measure and seldom done. Breaches of trust duty such as those, in which the beneficiaries may have remedy, will not necessarily be sufficient cause for removal; for removal to occur, the trustee must have breached a legal duty.

Beneficiary

One of the required elements of a trust is the need for a beneficiary or beneficiaries. At common law, there cannot be a valid devise to an indefinite person; there must be a beneficiary or a class of beneficiaries capable of coming into court to claim the benefits of the bequest {this principle applies to private but not to public trusts and charities}. Like the legatees in a will, trust beneficiaries may be a *class*. Any person with capacity to take and hold legal title to the intended trust property has capacity to be a beneficiary of a trust of that property and one without capacity to hold legal title to property may not be a trust beneficiary.

According to the Restatement (Third) of Trusts, there are two kinds of beneficiaries: *Private beneficiary* and *charitable beneficiary*.

Private Trust Beneficiary

Beneficiaries of a private trust must be ascertainable or established to enforce a trust. Under the Uniform Trust Code § 402(b) a beneficiary is definite "if the beneficiary can be ascertained now or in the future subject to any applicable rule against perpetuities." Private trusts are created gratuitously for the benefit of individual beneficiaries. A private trust can be used to make various gratuitous wealth transfers. A private trust may be used in the following ways:

{1} **Revocable Trust**: a revocable trust may be used to avoid the delays, costs, and the legal process of probate. In the trust instrument, the settlor may choose to retain the power to revoke the trust now or in the future. For example, *Smith* declares himself trustee of a property to pay the income to *Smith* for life, then on *Smith's* death to pay the principal to *Smith's* children and *Smith* retained the power to revoke the trust.

{2} **Testamentary Marital Trust**: Under the Federal Estate Tax Law, marital tax deduction is allowed for a life estate given to the spouse. A settlor may create such a trust for the benefit of his spouse and to qualify for the tax credit, the settlor should make the trust irrevocable and must not retain future interest for himself but may retain such interests for his spouse and children.

{3} **Trust for Incompetent Persons**: This takes place when a settlor transfers property to a trustee for the benefit of a disabled or mentally challenged person or the like. For example, *Smith* transfers property in trust to a trustee, to pay income for life to his disabled son *Max*, remainder to *Max's* children and if *Max* dies without children, the remainder for *Smith's* brother in-law.

{4} **Trusts for Children**: A settlor may transfer property to a trustee to pay income to his minor children. Under the Federal Gift Tax Law, a tax free gift of up to $11,000 is allowed to a beneficiary of such trust.

{5} **Discretionary Trust**: The settlor may transfer property to the trustee to hold in trust and pay the income to a beneficiary; such a trust usually gives the trustee *discretionary power* to pay and use the income of the trust as the trustee may see fit for the benefit of the beneficiary. Discretionary trusts are mostly irrevocable and are useful in reducing tax burdens; they are also protected from the reach of creditors.

Charitable Trusts

Under the Uniform Trust Code § 405(a) "a charitable trust may be created for the relief of poverty, the advancement of education or religion, the promotion of health, governmental or municipal purposes or other purposes the achievement of which is beneficial to the community." For a trust to be charitable, it must establish a charitable purpose, indefinite beneficiaries, and a trustee as provided in the trust document. Unlike the private trust, it does not need an ascertainable beneficiary to be valid. A charity may be described as a gift to be applied, consistently with the existing law, for the benefit of an indefinite class of persons. It is immaterial whether the purpose is called charitable in the gift itself, if it is so described as to show that it is charitable.

Charitable trusts are mostly public in nature unlike private trusts; a charitable trust has the status of validity but a mere benevolence trust is invalid if it offends the rule against perpetuities. Gifts which are transferred to show mere benevolence or liberality, or kindness cannot stand as charities for such transfers only show acts of generosity. To constitute a charity, the use must be public in nature and show a public purpose.

Gifts for Education

Any gifts that does not contradict existing law but for the advancement of science or trends to the education, enlightening benefit or amelioration of the condition of mankind or the diffusion of useful knowledge for public good is considered a charity. It is important that the gift be for the benefit of number of persons.

Gifts for the Poor

A trust that is designated for the benefit of a poor segment of the society is considered charitable however, if the trust is established without regard to whether or not the intended beneficiaries are poor or in need, it is not considered a charity, it is but a mere act of generosity and kindness and of no benefit to the public. Note that a trust does not have to be exclusively for the poor to be charitable. A gift or bequest in trust for the poor can be applied for purposes which fit within the designation; the court may help select one or more charitable purposes or beneficiaries if the trust does not indicate one. A trust which benefits the wealthy and the poor is still capable of being charitable even though it does not fall within the poverty classification.

Gifts for Religious Purposes

Trusts which are designated for the advancement of religion are often considered charitable but, gifts which are mere show of liberality without consideration of their effects on the beneficiaries are not charitable; there must be amelioration of the condition of the donees as a result of the gift and the improvement must be of religious nature. Trusts for religious purposes are considered valid unless when the court determines that the religion is absurd as to be irrational.

Gifts for the Government

Trusts for government purposes which are termed charitable may include gifts for the maintenance of government works such as: libraries, bridges, parks, firehouses and more. A trust for the improvement of the structure of government or with a purpose to bring about a change in the law through a legal means is considered charitable. Federal Income Tax Law denies a charitable deduction for contribution to an organization which seeks to influence legislation and rarely will an individual's campaign be deemed charitable, although the individual may be a spokesperson for a governmental policy.

Gifts for the Community

Trusts that are created for the general benefits of the community may be considered charitable. Such gifts must serve a general purpose and be beneficial to the community a trust with generality of purpose is easily enforced by the court. Private profit is generally not considered charitable. A non-profit hospital is a charity while a private hospital established for the purpose of making profits is not. A scholarship for education is a charity so long as it is not entirely limited in terms, expectation, reality or practice. An award established to honor a great number of people in the community over a period of time is considered charitable but if the number of recipients is limited then, the award is questionable and may not be considered a charity.

The Cy-pres Doctrine

Under this doctrine, if the charitable purpose of the settlor cannot be carried out, the court may direct the application of the trust property to a close alternative charitable purpose. Where the continued enforcement of conditions in a charitable transfer is no longer possible economically, because of illegality or opportunity costs, the court rather than declaring the gift void or transferring it to a residuary legatee, will authorize the administration of the charitable trust to apply the assets to a closely related cy pres purpose within the general scope of the donor's intent. The doctrine preserves charitable transfers by seeking the nearest possible practical alternative to a charitable trust which would have failed for lack of charitable purpose.

UNIFORM TRUST CODE § 413(a) states: if a particular charitable purpose becomes unlawful, impracticable, impossible to achieve, or wasteful:

{1} the trust does not fail, in whole or in part;

{2} the trust property does not revert to the settlor or the settlor's successors in interest; and

{3} the court may apply cy pres to modify or terminate the trust by directing that the trust property be applied or distributed, in whole or in part, in a manner consistent with the settlor's charitable purpose.

Chapter Ten

TRUSTS FIDUCIARY DUTY

Every trust instrument dictates the power and obligations of the trustee, who must manage trust's assets and account to the beneficiary according to the provisions of the trust instrument and relevant statute. The trustee has the power for example, to sell trusts assets and invest it to achieve a productive end. Liabilities of the trustee arise when one or more of the duty is breached. Section 816 of the Uniform Trust Code gives trustee various powers, including the power to collect trust property, reject additions to the trust, acquire or sell property, deposit money to the account of the trust, borrow money and mortgage trust property, acquire stocks and exercise associated ownership rights, acquire and maintain real property, grant options to sell or lease trust property, insure trust property, pay taxes, sign and deliver contracts and many more. While trust law gives the trustee all these powers, the trustee is also charged with duties to ensure the protection of the beneficiary and trust's assets.

The fiduciary obligation in trust law comprises of the following duties: (1) *loyalty,* (2) *prudence* and (3) *a host of subsidiary rules.*

In the absence of legislation a trustee has no power by virtue of his office; his only source of power, are those expressly and impliedly conferred upon him by the terms of the trust. The Uniform Trustees' Power Act empowers the trustee to engage in every conceivable transaction that might wrest market advantage or enhance the value of trust assets. However, to keep the beneficiary safe, fiduciary law imposes the obligations of *loyalty* and *prudence*, that monitors and regulate the exercise of the discretion that modern trustees' powers law confer. The *loyalty* doctrine forbids the trustee from self dealing with trust assets and from engaging in conflict of interest transaction detrimental to the trust. The *prudence* doctrine is an objective norm comparable to the reasonable person rule of tort. Subrules of fiduciary include: duty to keep and render accounts; to furnish information; to invest or preserve trust assets and more as earlier mentioned. Unless modified or ousted, trust default law define the fiduciary relationship; trustees' powers legislation authorizes transactions, and fiduciary law regulates the purposes and standards of transacting.

Because of the higher standards imposed by the fiduciary duties, it is not uncommon for the trustee to breach one or more of the fiduciary obligations and usually it is easier to determine how the breach of duty is inconsistent with the obligation imposed.

FIDUCIARY DUTY OF LOYALTY

HARTMAN v. HARTLE
New Jersey Court of Chancery, 1923
95 N.J. Eq. 123, 122 A. 615

FOSTER, V.C.

Mrs. Dorothea Geick died testate on April 8, 1921, leaving five children, one of them being the complainant. She named her two sons-in-law executors, and they qualified. Among other matters the will expressly directed her executors to sell her real estate and to divide the proceeds equally among her children.

On February 9, 1922, the executors sold part of the real estate known as the Farm, at public auction, for $3,900 to one of testatrix' son, Lewis Geick, who actually bought the property for his sister, Josephine Dieker, who is the wife of one of the executors.

On April 11, 1922, Mrs. Dieker sold the property to the defendant Mike Contra (and another, who is not a party to the action) for $5,500, part cash and part on mortgage.

The executors settled their final accounts on April 21, 1922 and at or about that time complainant expressed to the deputy surrogate her dissatisfaction with the price realized from the sale of the farm.

About March 21, 1923, she filed her bill in this cause charging the sale of the farm to have been improperly and fraudulently made by the executors,

186

to Mrs. Dieker, and further charging that Mrs. Dieker and the other heirs of the testatrix had agreed at sale, because of slow bidding and inadequate price, to have the farm bid in for the benefit of all the heirs.

At the hearing each and every one of these allegations were shown to be untrue by the great weight of the testimony; and this proof was so conclusive that it left complainant with but one contention to sustain her case, viz. that under the law the sale of the property by the executors and trustee to Mrs. Dieker, the wife of one of them, without previous authority from the court, was illegal and void, and that it should be set aside and the farm resold, or, if that be found impossible because of the sale made by Mrs. Dieker to Contra, an innocent purchaser, then that complainant should have paid to her one-fifth of the $1,600 profits realized by Mrs. Dieker from the sale of the property.

It is the settled law of this state that a trustee cannot purchase from himself at his own sale, and that his wife is subject to the same disability, unless leave so to do has been previously obtained under an order of the court. *Scott v. Gamble, 9 N.J. Eq. 218, (1852); Bassett v. Shoemaker, 46 N.J. Eq. 538 (1890);Bechtold v. Read, 49 N.J. Eq. 111(1891).* And under the circumstances of the case complainant cannot be charged with laches under the view expressed in *Bechtold v. Read, supra.*

In view of the fact that the property is now owned by innocent purchasers, a resale cannot be ordered, but, as an alternative, Mrs. Dieker and the executors will be held to account for complainant's one-fifth share of the profits made on the resale of the property under the authority of *Marshall v. Carson, 38 N.J. Eq. 250(1884)*, and a decree will be advised to that effect.

NOTES:

   {1} to protect the beneficiary and trust assets, the trustee is held to a stricter standard of rules. Not honesty alone but the most sensitive standard of behavior. As to this there has developed a tradition that is unbending and inveterate. Uncompromising rigidity has been the attitude of courts when petitioned to undermine the rule of loyalty. The level of conduct for fiduciaries has always been kept higher and will not be lowered by the court.

   {2} the trustee cannot deal in his individual capacity with trust property. The trustee's good faith and reasonableness of the transaction are irrelevant. The beneficiary can hold the trustee accountable for any profit made on the transaction or if the trustee has bought trust property can compel him to restore the property.

{3} the only defenses the trustee has to self-dealing are that the settler authorized the self-dealing transaction or that the beneficiaries consented to it after full disclosure. Restatement (Second) Trust § 170(1) Cmt. 1, 216(1) (1959). Even then, the trustee must have acted in good faith and the self-dealing transaction must be objectively fair and reasonable.

{4} **Note exception**: The *Sole Benefit Rule* and its enforcement through the *No-Further Inquiry* principle are no longer absolute. Statutes in most states allow a bank that is a trustee to deposit the trust assets with its own banking department. Likewise statutes in many states allow an institutional trustee to invest trust assets in a common trust fund or in a mutual fund it operates.

{5} Under Uniform Trust Code § 802 (2000) § (c): a transaction by the trustee with a close relative or his lawyer is presumptively voidable, not absolutely forbidden. Under this provision, the trustee may avoid liability if he can show that the transaction was objectively fair and reasonable and not affected by the conflict of interest.

{6} **Trust Pursuit Rule**: If the trustee, in wrongfully disposing of trust property, acquires other property, the beneficiary is entitled to enforce a *constructive trust* on the property so acquired, treating it as part of the trust assets. Restatement (Second) of Trusts § 202 (1959).

Note: the *Trust Pursuit Rule* is also applied where the property ends up in the hands of a third party, unless the third party is a bona-fide purchaser for value without notice of the breach of trust. As you may notice in *Hartman v. Hartle, supra* the court did not pursue the property sold to Contra, why? Because Contra fits the profile of an innocent purchaser for value without notice of the breach of the duty of loyalty by the trustees; rather than going after Contra, the court held Mrs. Dieker and the executors to account.

{7} if a trustee in breach of trust, transfers trust property to a person who takes with notice of the breach of trust, and the transferee has disposed of the property, the trustee may be charged with the value at the time of the decree, since if it had not been for the breach of trust, the property would still have been a part of the trust estate.

{8} the duty of loyalty imposed on the fiduciary prevents him from accepting employment from a third party who is entering into business transaction with the trust. The trustee while administering the trust must refrain from placing himself in a position where his personal interest or that of a third party does or may conflict with interests of the beneficiaries.

FIDUCIARY DUTY OF PRUDENCE

Among the many duties of the trustee, is the duty to properly administer the trust in a way that makes trust's assets productive for the use of the beneficiaries. The duties of loyalty and impartiality are aspects of proper administration of a trust. So also is the duty to account and make reasonable investment. The duty of *prudence* is an objective approach to dealing with the trustee; under this standard, the trustee in administering the trust, must exercise such care and skill as a man of ordinary prudence would exercise in dealing with his own property.[83] Uniform Trust Code § 801 provides that once a person accepts a trusteeship, he or she must "administer the trust in good faith, in accordance with its terms and purposes and the interests of the beneficiaries." The trustee is expected to do what a reasonable person in the place of the trustee would have done to properly administer his own property. The trustee should do all that is necessary for the good of the trust and those who are interested in it. Thus, the trustee would be held accountable for any breach of duty that brings demise to trust assets or reduce its value. The trustee may also be held accountable for any omissions in the management of trust property or failure to maintain such property.

Under the Uniform Trust Code § 804: "A trustee shall administer the trust as a prudent person would, by considering the purposes, terms, distribution requirements, and other circumstances of the trust. In satisfying this standard, the trustee shall exercise reasonable care, skill, and caution." Whenever a trustee fails to abide by or follow the prudent investor rule, the court of equity may hold him accountable for any destruction or loss visited

---

[83]   See, Restatement (Second) of Trusts § 174 (1959)

on the trust. A trustee may not neglect its trust or abdicate its judgment or show a reckless disregard to the interests of the trust beneficiaries. Alleged good faith on the part of a trustee forgetful of his duty is not enough. He could not close his eyes and remain passive or move with unconcern in the face of the obvious loss to be visited upon trust assets by engaging in fruitless business transactions and then try to shelter himself behind the defense of good faith dealing.

ESTATE of COLLINS
California Court of Appeals, Second District, (1977)
72 Cal. App. 3d 663, 139 Cal. Rptr. 644

KAUS, P.J.

Objectors (plaintiffs) are beneficiaries under a testamentary trust established in the will of Ralph Collins, deceased. Carl Lamb and Charles E. Millikan, Jr., (defendants) were, respectively, Collins' business partner and lawyer. They were named in Collins' will as trustees. In 1973 defendants filed a petition for an order approving and settling the first and final account and discharging the trustees. Plaintiffs objected on grounds that defendants had improperly invested $50,000 and requested that defendants be surcharged. After a hearing, the trial court ruled in favor of defendants, and approved the account, terminated the trust, and discharged the trustees. Plaintiff beneficiaries have appealed.

Facts

The primary beneficiaries under the testamentary trust were Collins' wife and children; his mother and father were also named as beneficiaries. General support provisions were included; the will also specifically provided that the trustees pay his daughter $4,000 a year for five years for her undergraduate and graduate education.

Paragraph (d) of the declaration of trust recited the powers of the trustees in the usual, inclusive fashion. Subparagraph (3) authorized the trustees to purchase "every kind of property, real, personal or mixed, and every kind of investment, specifically including, but not by way of limitation, corporate obligations of every kind, and stocks, preferred or common, irrespective of whether said investments are in accordance with the laws then enforced in the State of California pertaining to the investment of trust funds by corporate trustees."

Subparagraph (3) provided: "Unless specifically limited, all discretions conferred upon the trustee shall be absolute, and their exercise conclusive on all persons interested in this trust. The enumeration of certain powers of the trustee shall not limit its general power, the trustee, subject always to the discharge of its fiduciary obligations, being vested with and having all rights, powers and privileges which an absolute owner of the same property would have."

Collins died in 1963 and his will was admitted to probate. In June 1965, the court ordered the estate to be distributed. After various other payments and distributions, defendant trustees received about $80,000 as the trust principal. After other distributions, such as the annual $4,000 payment for the education of Collins' daughter, the trustees had about $50,000 available for investment.

Defendant Millikan's clients included two real property developers, Downing and Ward. In March 1965, Millikan filed an action on behalf of Downing and Ward against a lender who refused to honor a commitment to carry certain construction loans. In June 1965, defendants learned that Downing and Ward wanted to borrow $50,000. Millikan knew that the builders wanted the loan because of their difficulties with the lender who had withdrawn its loan commitment.

The loan would be secured by a second trust deed to 9.38 acres of unimproved real property in San Bernardino near upland. The property was subject to a $90,000 first trust deed; the note which secured the first trust deed was payable in quarterly installment of interest only, and due in full in three years, that is, in July 1968. The $50,000 loan to be made by defendants would be payable in monthly installments of interests only, at 10 percent interest with the full amount due in 30 months, that is, in January 1968.

Defendants knew that the property had been sold two years earlier in 1963 for $107,000. Defendants checked with two real estate brokers in the area, one of whom said that property in that area was selling for $18,000 to $20,000 an acre. They did not have the property appraised, they did not check with the county clerk or recorder in either Los Angeles or San Bernardino County to determine whether there were foreclosures or lawsuits pending against the construction company. In fact, when defendants made the loan in July 1965, there were six notices of default and three lawsuits pending against Downing and Ward.

Defendants obtained and reviewed an unaudited company financial statement. This statement indicated that the Downing and Ward Company had a net worth in excess of $2 million.

Downing and Ward told defendants that they were not in default on any of their loans, that they were not defendants in any pending litigation, and that there had never been any liens filed on any of their projects. Defendants phoned the bank with whom Downing and Ward had a line of credit and learned that the bank had a satisfactory relationship with the builders.

Based on this information, on July 23, 1965, defendants lent Downing and Ward $50,000 on the terms described above. In addition to the second trust deed, Downing and Ward pledged 20 percent of the stock in their company as security. However, defendants neither obtained possession of the stock, placed it in escrow, nor placed a legend on the stock certificates. Defendants also obtained the personal guarantees of Downing and Ward and their wives. However, defendants did not obtain financial statements from the guarantors.

When the loan was made in July 1965, construction in the upland area was, as the trial court said, "enjoying boom times, although the bubble was to burst just a few months later." From July 1965 through September 1966, the builders made the monthly interest payments required by the note. In October 1966, Downing and Ward Construction Corporation was placed in involuntary bankruptcy and thereafter Mr. and Mrs. Ward and Mr. and Mrs. Downing declared personal bankruptcies. Defendants foreclosed their second trust deed in June 1967, and became the owners of the unimproved real property. They spent $10,000 in an unsuccessful effort to salvage the investment by forestalling foreclosure by the holder of the first trust deed. In September 1968, the holder of the first trust deed did foreclose; this extinguished the trustees' interest in the property and the entire investment. In short, about $60,000 of the trust fund was lost . . .

Discussion

The trial court made finding that defendants exercised the judgment and care "which men of prudence, discretion and intelligence exercised in the management of their own affairs," reflects the standard imposed upon trustees by Civil Code section 2261 . . .

Plaintiffs contend, and we agree, that contrary to the trial court's findings and conclusions, defendants failed to follow the "prudent investor" standard, first, by investing two-third of the trust principal in a single investment, second, by investing in real property secured only by a second deed of trust, and third, by making that investment without adequate investigation of either the borrowers or the collateral.

Although California does not limit the trustee's authority to a list of authorized investments, relying instead on the prudent investor rule (see 7 Witkin, summary of Cal. Law (8th ed.) Trusts, § 63, p. 5424), nevertheless, the prudent investor rule encompasses certain guidelines applicable to this case.

First, "the trustee is under a duty to the beneficiary to distribute the risk of loss by a reasonable diversification of investments, unless under the circumstances it is not prudent to do so." (Rest. 2d Trusts, § 228; see also *Estate of Beach 15 Cal.3d 623 (1975)* . . .

Second, ordinarily, "second or other junior mortgages are not proper trust investments," unless taking a second mortgage is a reasonable method of settling a claim or making possible the sale of property. (Rest.2d Trusts, § 227, p. 533) stated more emphatically: "While loans secured by second mortgages on land are sometimes allowed, they are almost always disapproved by courts of equity. The trustee should not place the trust funds in a position where they may be endangered by the foreclosure of a prior lien . . . In rare cases equity will sanction an investment secured by a second mortgage, but only when the security is adequate and unusual circumstances justify the trustee in taking this form of investment." (Bogert, Trusts and Trustees (2d ed.) § 675, p. 274)

Third, in "buying a mortgage for trust investment, the trustee should give careful attention to the valuation of the property, in order to make certain that his margin of security is adequate. He must use every reasonable endeavor to provide protection which will cover the risks of depreciation in the property and changes in price levels. And he must investigate the status of the property and of the mortgage, as well as the financial situation of the mortgagor." (*Bogert, supra, § 674, at p. 267.*) Similarly, the Restatement rule is that "the trustee cannot properly lend on a mortgage upon real property more than a reasonable proportion of the value of the mortgage property." (§ 229.) . . .

We think it apparent that defendants violated every applicable rule. First, they failed totally to diversify the investment in this relatively small trust fund. Second, defendants invested in a junior mortgage on unimproved real property, and left an inadequate margin of security. As noted, the land had most recently sold for $107,000, and was subject to a first trust deed of $90,000. Thus, unless the land was worth more than $140,000, there was no margin of security at all. Defendants did not have the land appraised; the only information they had was the opinion of a real estate broker that property in the area not that particular parcel was going for $18,000 to $20,000 an acre. Thus, any assumption that the property was worth about $185,000 and therefore the $140,000 in loans were well secured would have been little more than a guess.

Third, the backup security obtained by defendants was no security at all. The builders pledged 20 percent of their stock, but defendants never obtained possession of the stock, placed it in escrow or even had it legended. They accepted the personal guarantees of the builders and their wives without investigating the financial status of these persons. They accepted at face value the claimed $2 million value of the company shown in an unaudited statement. Defendant Millikan apparently ignored the fact that one lender had, for whatever reasons, reneged on a loan commitment to the builders.

Defendants contend that the evidence sustains the trial court's finding that they exercised the judgment and care under the circumstances then prevailing expected of men of prudence. They rely on the rule that the determination whether an investment was proper must be made in light of the circumstances existing at the time of the investment. (*E.g., Witkin, supra, §* *63, p. 5425.)* That rule does not help defendants. Nothing that happened after the loan was made can change the fact that defendants invested two-thirds of the principal of the trust in a single second deed of trust on unappraised property, with no knowledge of the borrowers' true financial status, and without any other security . . .

Defendants alternatively contend that the trust instrument conferred "absolute discretion" on them as trustees, and that the prudent investor standard did not apply to their conduct. Rather, the only question is whether the trustee avoided arbitrary action and used his best judgment. (*Coberly v. Superior Court 42 Cal. Rptr. 64 (App. 1965.)*

We leave aside the question whether even a trustee with "absolute discretion" would be permitted to make this kind of investment, consistent with the rule that an absolute discretion does not permit a "trustee to neglect its trust or abdicate its judgment." (*Coberly, supra, 42 Cal. Rptr. At p. 67.)* The instrument in this case conferred no such absolute discretion.

Defendants rely particularly on the rule that the prudent investor standard does not apply where the settler himself specifies that the trustee of his trust are not limited by what the law provides are proper investments.

(E.g., Stanton v. Wells Fargo Bank, etc. Co. 310 P.2d 1010 (Cal.App.1957).) Their reliance on that rule is misplaced.

First, the provision in the trust instrument to purchase every kind of property and make every kind of investment "irrespective of whether said investments are in accordance with the laws then enforced in the state of California pertaining to the investment of trust funds by corporate trustees" does not authorize the trustees to make improper investments.

Neither Civil Code section 2261 nor any other authority which we can locate authorizes different types of investments for "corporate trustees" and for amateur trustees. The difference, rather, is that the corporate trustee is held to a greater standard of care based on his presumed expertise . . . Thus defendants might have been protected by that clause had they deviated in some respects from the general rules for example, had they accepted a well secured second trust deed, or possibly had they accepted a first trust deed without careful investigation. Here, however, defendants did nothing right. Second, the "absolute discretion" in the trust instrument is "specifically limited" by the requirement that the trustee is "subject always to the discharge of its fiduciary obligations . . ."

In conclusion, the evidence does not support the trial court's conclusion that defendants acted properly in investing $50,000 in the property.

Reversed.

QUESTIONS AND NOTES

{1} Evaluate the investment and management decisions of the trustees in the context of the trust portfolio as a whole and as a part, do you think their investment strategy is objectively reasonable and permissible?

{2} consider the fact that the trust instrument in this case, gave the trustees absolute power to invest with trust assets, should such conferment of discretion be allowed to displace the demand that the trustee manage trust assets as a prudent investor? Should such discretionary power be allowed when there is evidence of conflict of interests as we have in the case above?

{3} a trustee shall take reasonable steps to verify facts relevant to the investment and management of trust assets. Do you think the defendants acted reasonably to verify facts relevant to the investment even though, they did not intend to suffer a loss of trust assets?

{4} Note: that the exercise of care, skill, and caution would be no defense if the property acquired or retained by a trustee, or the strategy pursued for a trust, was characterized as impermissible.

{5} Note: A trustee who has special skills or expertise or is named trustee in reliance upon the trustee's representation that the trustee has special skills or expertise, has a duty to use those special skills or expertise to manage trust assets.

{6} Under the Employment Retirement Income Security Act (ERISA), the trustee shall discharge his duties with respect to a plan solely in the interest of the participants and the beneficiaries and for the exclusive purpose of providing benefits to participants and their beneficiaries; 29 U.S.C. § 404 (a) (1) (D) (i) (2004)

{7} **DIVERSIFICATION**: A trustee shall diversify the investment of the trust unless the trustee reasonably determines that, because of special circumstances, the purposes of the trust are better served without diversifying. *Uniform Prudent Investor Act § 3(1994)*

{8} Note: that whether a fiduciary has acted prudently is a question of fact to be determine by the trial court. In most cases, courts have determined that a fiduciary's retention of a high concentration of one asset in a trust or estate was imprudent. The test is whether under all circumstances and facts of the particular case, the trustee violated the prudent person standard in maintaining a concentration of a particular stock in the estate's portfolio of investment.

EXCEPTION: It may be unreasonable and imprudent to diversify when the tax or other costs of reorganizing the portfolio outweigh the benefits of diversification. Diversification of assets might not be reasonable if the trust is but one component of a larger scheme such that the beneficiary's financial interests are diversified overall. However, the trustee may invest trust assets in a single entity that is itself diversified, like a mutual fund, but the trustee must exercise care in choosing the single entity.

{9} **DELEGATION**: A trustee must not delegate his responsibilities to a co-trustee; a trustee who delegates his duty *improperly* to a co-trustee is subject to liability.; however, the trustee is not liable for loses not caused by a breach of his fiduciary duty.

{10} Note: Uniform Prudent Investor Act § 9 (a) a trustee may delegate investment and management functions that a *prudent* trustee of comparable skills could promptly delegate under the circumstances . . .

IMPARTIALITY

In the case of two or more beneficiaries, the trustee must beware and act *impartially* in investing, managing, and distributing trust assets. He must give regard and pay attention to each beneficiary equally and remove all concerns for preferential treatments; UTC § 803 commands a trustee to act for the benefit of the trust as a whole and not favor the interests of one beneficiary over another.

Under the Restatement (Second) of Trusts § 232 (1959): Settled law requires the trustee to act impartially "with due regard" for the "respective interests" of both the life tenant and the remainderman. The impartial trustee must view the overall picture as it is presented from all facts, and not close its eyes to any relevant facts which might impose excessive burden on one beneficiary in preference to the other.

The trustee acts with risk and may be in breach of its fiduciary obligation, when the trustee follows the suggestions of some, but not all, beneficiaries however, the requesting beneficiaries may be estopped from finding the trustee at fault for a breach of trust arising from the requested transaction.

According to the Restatement (Second) of Trusts § 232 comment (b) the trustee is under a duty to the beneficiary who is ultimately entitled to the principal not to retain property which is certain or likely to depreciate in value, although the property yields a large income, unless he makes adequate provision for amortizing the depreciation.

NOTE: A trustee can be relieved of his duty even if "the charges of his misconduct" are "not made out." The issue is whether ill feeling might interfere with administration of the trust.

FIDUCIARY SUBRULES

{A} Duty to Receive and Protect: According to the Uniform Trust Code § 809 (2000) a trustee has the obligation to take possession of the trust assets without unnecessary delay. When a testamentary trust is established, the trustee should collect the assets from the executor as

quickly as circumstances permit. The trustee is under a duty to examine the property tendered by the executor to make sure it is what the trustee ought to receive. On receiving the assets, the trustee must then administer and manage the assets the way a prudent man would.

{B} Duty to Earmark Trust Assets: In dealing with the issue of earmarking trust assets, two important duties are to be considered (1) the trustee must separate assets of the trust from all other assets and (2) the trustee must be able to identify trust assets as belonging to a particular trust. Under UTC § 810 the trustee must separate trust property from his own and keep adequate records of the administration of the trust. The trustee is not permitted to commingle trust assets with his own assets as this is considered embezzlement and misappropriation of trust property.

"If a fiduciary mixes the "trust" property with his own property, the court may require the fiduciary to separate the interests or to become the guarantor of the value of the fiduciary portion or the court may subject the entire mass to the fiduciary relationship. Equitable principles are involved in such tracing; therefore many factors are relevant: the degree of culpability in commingling, the ownership of the portion commingled, the good faith of the fiduciary, the relative values of the amounts commingled etc.[84]

Note: **exception;** assets not subject to registration such as bearer bonds fall within an exception to the earmarking rule.

Under the older views, any trustee that fails to earmark trust investment is strictly liable for any loss resulting from the investment. Irrespective of the fact that the loss is not caused by the failure to earmark, the trustee is still held accountable for the actual loss sustained by the trust. This strict rule has been amended by the modern view adopted by the Restatement (Second) of Trusts § 179 comment (d) (1959) which holds the trustee liable only, for such loss as results from the failure to earmark and not liable for such loss as results from general economic conditions.

---

[84] Robert L. Mennell et al: *Wills and Trusts In a Nutshell*, Thompson and West (2007) p. 300

{C} Duty to Account and Inform: Under the Uniform Trusts Code § 813 (2000, amended 2004):

(a) A trustee shall keep the qualified beneficiaries of the trust reasonably informed about the administration of the trust and of the material facts necessary for them to protect their interests. Unless unreasonable under the circumstances, a trustee shall promptly respond to a beneficiary's request for information related to the administration of the trust.

(b) A trustee (1) upon request of a beneficiary, shall promptly furnish to the beneficiary a copy of the trust instrument; (2) within 60 days after accepting a trusteeship shall notified the qualified beneficiaries of the acceptance and of the trustee's name, address, and telephone number; (3) within 60 days after the date the trustee acquires knowledge of the creation of an irrevocable trust, or the date the trustee acquires knowledge that a formerly revocable trust has become irrevocable, whether by the death of the settlor or otherwise, shall notify the qualified beneficiaries of the trust's existence, of the identity of the settlor or settlers, of the right to request a copy of the trust instrument and of the right to a trustee's report as provided in subsection (c) and (4) shall notify the qualified beneficiaries in advance of any change in the method or rate of the trustee's compensation.

(c) A trustee shall send to the distributes or permissible distributes of the trust income or principal, and to other qualified or nonqualified beneficiaries who request it, at least annually and at the termination of the trust, a report of the trust property, liabilities, receipts and disbursement, including the source and amount of the trustee's compensation, a listing of the trust assets and, if feasible, their respective market value. Upon a vacancy in a trusteeship, unless a co-trustee remains in office, a report must be sent to the qualified beneficiaries by the former trustee. A personal representative, {conservator} or {guardian} may send the qualified beneficiaries a report on behalf of a deceased or incapacitated trustee.

(d) A beneficiary may waive the right to a trustee's report or other information otherwise required to be furnished under this section. A beneficiary with respect to future reports and other information may withdraw a waiver previously given.

Note: UTC § 105 (b) (9) the settlor could not waive the beneficiary's right under § 813 (a) to information reasonably related to the beneficiary interest in the trust. Also under UTC § 105 (b) (8) the settlor could not waive the right under UTC § 813 (b) (2)-(3) of a beneficiary who is at least 25 years of age to be notified by the trustee of the existence of the trust.

Note: that it is imposed upon the beneficiaries as a duty to properly study the accounts presented by the trustee to the probate court, and to make their objections at the hearing as to any part of the account subject to contest. However, when a trustee makes improper payments for example, to someone other than the qualified beneficiary, the trustee is charged and thus, liable to make restitution unless the payment was authorized by a court with jurisdiction.

NOTE: *SPENDTHRIFT TRUSTS*: This kind of trust contains a written restriction upon the voluntary or involuntary alienation of the beneficiary's share. Many jurisdictions permit such restraints upon alienation but there has been a tendency to limit the scope of the exemption by statute. A settlor who does not want creditors to reach assets of the trust may choose to have the trust *spendthrift* and *irrevocable*. However, this does not prevent creditors from reaching the settlor's interests in a situation where the settlor is also a beneficiary of the trust. While creditors may not reach the principal or assets of the trust, they will be able to reach any benefits transferred to the beneficiary. Also, statutes now make it possible for the government to reach assets of a trust if the settlor owes back taxes.

SELECTED PUBLICATIONS

{1} Alexander A. Bove: *The Complete Book of Wills, Estates & Trusts, 3rd edition:* Owl Books (2005).

{2} Jesse Dukeminier et al, *Wills, Trusts, and Estates, 7th edition:* Aspen Publishers (2005).

{3} Richard A. Posner, *Economic Analysis of Law, 4th edition:* Little, Brown and Company (1992).

{4} Robert L. Mennel et al, *Wills and Trusts in a Nutshell, 3rd edition:* Thompson West (2007).

SELECTED CASES

Shapira v. Union National Bank, 5-6

Estate of Cross, 44-48

In re Estate of Cooper, 49-56

Matter of Estate of Garbade, 58-61

Hall v. Vallandingham, 65-69

Woodward v. Commissioner of Social Security, 72-86

Buzzanca v. Buzzanca, 89-105

Adoption of Tammy, 106-117

Estate of Mahoney, 123-129

Riggs v. Palmer, 132-137

Estate of Wright, 141-150

In re Strittmater, 154-156

CPSIA information can be obtained
at www.ICGtesting.com
Printed in the USA
LVOW08s0525050117

519825LV00001B/118/P

9 781463 403270